Professional Development

Protecting Children

Working together to keep children safe

Heather Flynn

Barbara Starns

www.heinemann.co.uk
✓ Free online support
✓ Useful weblinks
✓ 24 hour online ordering

01865 888058

Heinemann

Inspiring generations

Heinemann Educational Publishers
Halley Court, Jordan Hill, Oxford OX2 8EJ
Part of Harcourt Education

Heinemann is the registered trademark of Harcourt Education Limited

© Heather Flynn and Barbara Starns, 2004

First published 2004

08 07 06 05 04
10 9 8 7 6 5 4 3 2 1

British Library Cataloguing in Publication Data is available from the British Library on request.

ISBN 0 435 45679 2

Designed by Artistix, Thame, Oxon
Typeset by Saxon Graphics Ltd, Derby
Original illustrations © Harcourt Education Limited, 2004
Printed in the UK by Scotprint

Acknowledgements

With thanks to all friends and family who have supported me in the production of this book: John Flynn, Ailis Mackison-Flynn, Hugh and Catherine Bochel, Sue Freer, Diane McKechnie and my parents, not forgetting Barbara, my co-author and all at Heinemann.

Heather Flynn

With thanks to Jon for his support. To Bridge Bennett, Early Years East Riding, for her help and also Martin Henry, Child Protection coordinator, Edinburgh & Lothians, for his information regarding the Scottish system.

Barbara Starns

The authors and publisher would like to thank Alamy (pages 39, 57, 70 & 153); Sally and Richard Greenhill (page 5); Science Photo Library (pages 24, 84, 129 & 208); Rod Thoedorou (page 115) and Tudor Photography (page 120) for permission to reproduce photographs.

Every effort has been made to contact copyright holders of material reproduced in this book. Any omissions will be rectified in subsequent printings if notice is given to the publishers.

Crown Copyright material on pages 25–6, 92, 95, 98, 106, 131, 148, 199, 214 & 217 is reproduced under Class Licence Number C01W0000141 with the permission of the Controller of HMSO and the Queen's Printer for Scotland.

Contents

Introduction

Protecting Children: Working together to keep children safe is one in a series of books published by Heinemann for the professional development of practising, or future, Early Years Practitioners. The term 'Early Years Practitioners' is used in this book to include health, education and social service practitioners together with carers, child minders and those working in educational settings such as school or nurseries. This book is designed to raise awareness of child protection by introducing the basic skills and knowledge required by Early Years Practitioners to fulfil their roles for child in 'need' and in terms of child protection issues.

The book works from the understanding that the most effective means of safeguarding children is to promote their welfare through a range of universal and specifically directed services, and by doing so prevent difficulties escalating to a level that requires a child protection service. Throughout the book child protection is rooted in a child in 'need' context. Chapter One establishes this context and subsequent chapters address the specific structure of a child protection service. Consideration is given to relevant legal issues, the *Framework for Assessment*, how professionals might recognise harm and the process of making a referral. The book looks at the relationship between child protection and child in 'need' services, provides an explanation of an S47 enquiry route, and gives detailed guidance to participation within child protection conferences and core groups. Finally, discussion of case reviews helps identify common themes that can highlight inter-agency issues for the practitioner.

The book is written in a simple, easy-to-understand format that includes many practice-based exercises and real case studies. A detailed references and further reading list is also provided (see pages 240–2) to guide readers' research into any aspect of child protection that they may need.

We hope that you find this book a useful guide through the sensitive, often heart-breaking, but important area of protecting children.

Chapter 1

Child protection – context and background

This chapter introduces you to child protection. It explains the research that has led to the current context of child protection – one that places child protection amongst all services available to support families and safeguard children's welfare. It includes guidance regarding the threshold for a child protection service and, in particular, the nature of significant harm. Information about the process of child protection and the scope of the service is also provided. As an Early Years Practitioner you may come into contact with children who need protecting and you will be involved in making professional judgements and working in partnership with the child protection agencies. This chapter sets the scene and outlines the structure of the child protection service, before its breakdown into more detailed consideration in the remaining chapters.

What is child protection?

Child protection is an activity to promote the well-being of children and protect them from **significant harm**. At the forefront of this action are parents and carers, who are best placed to ensure their children's safety. If families have difficulty in fulfilling these tasks and are unable to protect their children, then local authorities (in England and Wales) are legally obliged to step in and provide protection for the child on the basis of the Children Act 1989.

The Children Act 1989

The Act itself is discussed in greater detail in Chapter 2, which looks at the legal framework for child protection. However, it is important to highlight the Children Act 1989 as the key legislative document for children and families. This Act not only places a duty on local authorities to safeguard children, but also introduces the concept of **children in 'need'** with the emphasis on support to families and assistance to parents in carrying out their responsibilities.

It is useful to remember that safeguarding children exists on several different levels and activities, all of which contribute to the task of protecting children by helping them to achieve their potential. This is shown in the table which follows:

Parents and carers	Provide close positive relationships and an environment conducive to growth and development.
Education and health services	Provide basic minimum standards
Children in need services	Address specific difficulties at an early stage to prevent escalation into greater problems
Child protection services	Address difficulties when they have reached a severe level.

Child protection today

Since the 1980s there have been significant changes in the way we approach the important task of safeguarding children, and they have shaped the context of child protection today. It is helpful if you have an understanding of the context of child protection so that you can identify the part you may play in the process and prepare yourself for that role.

Local authority functions

The introduction of the Children Act 1989 consolidated childcare legislation and gave two major functions to the local authority (in England and Wales):

Child in need process

The first function of the local authority is to supply support to children in 'need', who would be unlikely to reach their potential without such support, thus enabling the authority to tackle problems early and prevent their reaching a severe scale. While this is referred to as a **child in need process**, it forms a protective action by preventing harm escalating to a more severe level that might require a specific **child protection response**. Children with disabilities are automatically included as children in 'need' and are eligible for services on this basis.

Child protection service

The second major function of the local authority is to safeguard a child when it is believed that he/she has suffered **significant harm** or is likely to suffer significant harm. This means that local authorities have the power to intervene in cases when children are considered to be at risk of harm. It is this function that we more formally refer to as a **child protection service**.

Safeguarding children and supporting families

The Children Act 1989 also clarified the rights of parents embodied in the **concept of parental responsibility**; this concept was developed to replace the notion of 'parental rights' and to move away from the idea of parents owning their children. Parental responsibilities are those rights and duties involved in making decisions about a child's life.

The Children Act 1989 provided clarity about the balance between safeguarding children and supporting families. However, following its introduction reviews of progress indicated that local authorities were focusing their efforts on the role of investigating potential situations of significant harm. As a result, they were neglecting their role to provide support services to families at an early stage when elements of lower-risk harm were identified, in order to address the difficulties and prevent their escalation to a severe level. The investigative actions went some way to addressing the short-term needs for a child's safety and in this respect were effective, but failed to address the wider needs of children and families and improve the long-term prognosis for a positive outcome.

Research programme

As a response, the government commissioned a research programme to look at the way child protection was being carried out. Over 20 studies into child protection took place and key messages were produced that have set the context of child protection in its current form. The key findings from the research programme are outlined below. They are also provided in more detail in the document *Child Protection Messages from Research* (Department of Health 1995).

Findings from research

In families where there is severe harm to a child, protective action by professionals is required. For example, sexual assault or a severe physical injury, such as a broken arm, requires immediate investigation and action to protect.

Equally in cases where there are low levels of harm to a child, intervention is not required, such as, for example, some of the inevitable emotional difficulties that children experience when their parents separate or divorce. Intervention is not required if there is a minor accidental injury that resulted from a momentary lapse of supervision by a parent and is a 'one-off' incident.

However, research found that most cases that come to the attention of professionals exist somewhere between these two extremes.

Because there is a grey area between the two ends of the scale, into which most families who are referred to Social Services fall, there was a need for clarity about the point at which help is provided and the nature of help. Researchers used information about what worked in families and what parenting produced positive outcomes, as a comparison to what might be harmful.

Bullock *et al* (Department of Health 1995) found:

> *That the long-term difficulties for children rarely followed a single harmful event but were usually the result of harm within the wider living environment. For example, a smack to a young child causing a mark is unlikely to cause a long-term effect if the child lives in a loving, caring, warm family for whom this is an unusual event. In comparison to a smack to a child, for whom this is a regular occurrence, and who lives in a negative, critical family home.*

Messages from Research concluded that with the exception of sexual assault and severe physical assault, any potentially abusive incident needed to be seen in context before a decision could be made about the nature and level of harm, i.e. family situation, and relationship with parents.

A favourable family environment

To this end the research identified a favourable family environment in which children thrive – one that is high in warmth and low in criticism. It also identified the family environment that is unfavourable to a child, i.e. one that is low in warmth and high in criticism. The table below illustrates some of the factors that might be present to indicate the type of family environment the child lives in.

High warmth	Low criticism
Physical and verbal affection Encouragement Praise Positive reinforcement	Only appropriate admonishment No insults Not referred to with derogatory language No verbal abuse
Low warmth	**High criticism**
Lack of physical and verbal affection Little or no praise No positive encouragement Lack of loving positive relationships	Constant insults Comments and/or actions that undermine the child's self-esteem Continual responsibility or blame attached to a child

This framework and information will help you to identify those children you work with who may be vulnerable to harm because they live in an environment of low warmth and high criticism. You might seek help for the family before problems become more severe for the child. It also gives an indication of how to go about assessing levels of harm to a child by viewing any incidents as part of the wider family functioning.

A favourable family environment has 'high warmth' and 'low criticism'

The professional response

Given these discoveries about how to approach the assessment of harm, the researchers also made some pertinent observations about how professionals were carrying out the duties of addressing harm with children and families.

Bullock *et al* found (Department of Health 1995):

> "
>
> *Most of the inquiries made by local authorities into allegations of child abuse tended to focus on investigations to prove what had happened. In the majority of cases no other services were offered to help the families*
>
> *In cases that involved inquiries the child involved usually remained in the home or returned home quickly. (Note the need to work in partnership with families given this information.)*
>
> *Child protection inquiries appeared to be separate from other activities of local authority support. The result being that inquiries were undertaken and in cases where harm was not of a significant level or allegations unsubstantiated an assessment was not made of the whole situation and no other services were offered.*
>
> "

Child Protection Messages from Research (Department of Health 1995) highlighted a number of very important issues for child protection. The government responded by refocusing attention on supporting families at an early stage when problems are identified, with the aim of preventing harm from escalating to a child protection response. Within this refocusing task, the role of child protection in terms of investigation and protective action would be focused on those fewer children who needed such a response. It is hoped that refocusing services towards support for families will inevitably reduce the number of children requiring a child protection service. As an Early Years Practitioner you may play an active part, not only in the identification and referral of significant harm, but also in the identification of harm and the provision of support services to prevent children falling into the category of significant harm.

What was the refocused response to research?

Child protection was brought into the wider picture of support to children in need as one of a range of services to safeguard children and help them to achieve their potential by means of the following actions:

◆ When considering the nature, severity of harm and the response that is appropriate, the context of family and the environment should be considered. (The government has issued guidance in the form of the *Framework for the Assessment of Children in Need and their Families* (Department of Health, Department for Education and Employment, & Home Office 2000), to help in this task and this is considered in more detail in Chapter 4).

◆ When there has been a child protection response in the form of an investigation and there is no substantiation to allegations, or it is found that the harm is not of a significant level, consideration will be given to the provision of other services to support the family, if appropriate.

◆ Equally, if the family is receiving support on a voluntary basis and an issue of significant harm arises, the family will be referred for a child protection response.

Key for entry into the child protection arena

Before looking at the stages of the child protection process in detail, it is important to consider here the point at which a child enters the child protection service. The key for entry of a child into the child protection arena is the **concept of significant harm**. Significant harm is the criteria for action, or dispensing with action, to safeguard a child.

> To dispense with parental consent when making a referral to Social Services you will need to be clear that there is a risk of or actual significant harm and to seek parental consent would be increasing harm to the child.

> For Social Services and Police to undertake a S47 inquiry there must be a suspicion that a child is suffering or likely to suffer significant harm.

In order for the court to make any public order to protect a child they must be satisfied there is a risk of or actual significant harm.

A child protection conference must be satisfied a child is at continuing risk of significant harm when it makes the decision to place a child's name on the child protection register.

It is therefore clear that as an Early Years Practitioner you will need to have some understanding of this concept, particularly since it is the difference between a child in need and a child protection response. The child protection service is aimed at the prevention or reduction of significant harm to a child.

Significant harm

Definition

Harm is defined in the Children Act 1989 as:

a) ill-treatment (which includes sexual abuse and non-physical ill treatment such as emotional abuse), and

b) the impairment of health or development (section 3199: health means physical or mental health and development means physical, intellectual, emotional, social or behavioural development).

> *…when assessing whether the impairment of health or development is significant, the court must compare the health or development of the child in question with that which could be expected of a similar child, that is a child with similar attributes and needs.*
>
> Department of Health 1989a: p.25

Such a comparison enables the court to take a view on whether the harm suffered by a child is severe and significant.

Elements of significant harm

Working Together to Safeguard Children provides some guidance on what significant harm might include:

> *Consideration of the severity of ill treatment may include the degree and the extent of physical harm, the duration and frequency of abuse and neglect, and the extent of premeditation, degree of threat and coercion, sadism, and bizarre or unusual elements in child sexual abuse. Each of these elements has been associated with more severe effects on the child, and/or relatively greater difficulty in helping the child overcome the adverse impact of the ill treatment'.*
>
> Department of Health 1999: p.8

Professionals should be aware that significant harm can involve a one-off serious event such as a single assault, but more usually it is a series of significant events that lead to a picture of long-term harm that has a significant impact on a child's physical and emotional development.

No Harm	Harm	Significant Harm
No Action	Requiring Child in Need Service	Requiring Child Protection Services
Physically healthy no injuries	Grab marks to arm of child	Fracture, broken arm to child
Growth and weight of baby within health expectations`	Baby's weight has fallen in a pattern with mother presenting as depressed	Severe non-organic failure to thrive. Significant falls in weight and stunted growth
Basic care needs met. Child has positive relationships and appropriate development	Child has hygiene problems and some basic needs that are not being addressed such as speech delay and poor interaction with peers	Child suffering weight loss, skin changes. Delayed speech and development. Poor emotional presentation. Child suffers frequent severe accidents as a result of poor supervision
Demonstration of praise and encouragement by parents and carers to child. Child has a high level of self-esteem	Child showing signs of low self-esteem, lacking in confidence and demonstrating high levels of anxiety. Parents and carers critical of child's performance and have high expectations of child	Parents showing severe rejection of child. Child is used as a scapegoat with all the family's problems, and child views self as bad person. Child has indications of severe emotional problems.

The above table provides some examples of differences between what might constitute harm that requires a child in need service and significant harm.

However, whilst this is a guide to different levels of harm no situation is ever as simple, and it is clear that harm cannot be considered in isolation but is context related.

CASE STUDY:
IS IT ABUSE?

Consider the two scenarios below.

Scenario 1	A mother slaps her fifteen-year-old child across the face during a row about weekly allowance. The home environment is very good and mother and child have a positive relationship in which they soon make up. Mother is very proud of her child's achievements at school and there is further discussion about the allowance. Mother has been working hard recently but is now able to take things a bit easier. She regrets her actions and is shocked, as this is the first time that she has hit her child.
Scenario 2	A child, three-years-old, is slapped across the face, leaving a hand print mark, because she was screaming. The home is cold and damp. The child's clothes are dirty and inadequate for the cold weather. Mother believes the child plays up purposefully when she is busy. She feels no attachment to her child.

1. Which of these two scenarios do you think present a risk of significant harm?

2. What factors did you use to come to this judgement?

Factors to consider when deciding whether harm is significant

Working Together to Safeguard Children outlines a number of factors to take into consideration when defining whether or not harm is significant. These are shown in the table overleaf.

A key factor in this judgement is the child's wishes and feelings, perceptions of what has happened, in accordance with his/her age and understanding.

While it is the decision of Social Services whether to invoke a child protection response because the level of harm is at a significant level, all professionals should have an understanding of this concept, as they will be part of the child protection process and asked for their views regarding this area during the course of the case.

Factors to consider when deciding whether harm is significant:	
The family context	Is it a high-warmth, low-criticism family?
The child's development within the context of family and wider social and cultural environment	Is the child within developmental milestones? Are there positive relationships and experiences beyond the immediate family home?
Any special needs	Does the child have a medical condition, communication difficulty or disability that may affect his/her development and care with the family?
The nature of harm, in terms of ill treatment or failure to provide adequate care	Is the harm one of assault, one-off event or a number of assaults? Is the harm one of neglect? For example, failure to take the child for required medical treatment.
The impact of the harm on the child's health and development	How has the child suffered from the harm? Has it had a serious effect or is the child showing little signs of anything having happened?
The adequacy of parental care	

ACTIVITY

Consider the scenarios below about the same child Raith. They contain slightly different information.

Scenario A

Raith is six-years-old. At school his teachers are concerned that he is withdrawn, pale and looks undernourished. The school nurse has given assurances to staff that Raith is within the growth targets for his age. Fellow parents and carers have reported that they hear his parents fighting at night and Raith is sometimes sat out on the step at these times looking very sad. Raith's father spends a great deal of his time and money in the local pub; his mother is pregnant for a second time, and the pregnancy is not an easy one. Academically, Raith had been doing very well until recently when his progress began to fall off. Parents have worked well with the school in the past and obviously have a very loving relationship with Raith.

Scenario B

Raith is six-years-old. At school his teachers are concerned that he is withdrawn and pale; he looks undernourished. The school nurse does think his weight has fallen. Fellow parents and carers report that Raith's parents are often heard fighting at home and his mother was observed to have a black eye last week. Raith has few friends at school and his behaviour is

➡

very aggressive. Today, he arrived in school with bruising to the side of his face and down his arm. He stated that he had fallen off a wall but later told another boy that his father had caused it. Raith's parents have been aggressive with teachers in the past and various adults collect Raith. There is usually no contact with family. Neighbours suspect drug misuse at the home and often see numbers of visitors calling there every evening. Raith is often out in the street unsupervised well into the night.

1. When you have considered each of the scenarios, decide which one would warrant a child in need response because of issues of harm and which would require a child protection response because harm had reached a significant level.

2. When making your decision think about the following:
   - nature of harm to Raith
   - impact of harm to Raith
   - development and behaviour of Raith
   - stresses to parents
   - parental capacity
   - environment in which Raith lives.

What is the child protection service?

The stages in the child protection service are shown in the diagram overleaf.

The following chapters in this book provide greater detail, guidance and examples of every stage in the child protection service so that you will feel equipped as an Early Years Practitioner to play your part in child protection should the need arise. However, a brief summary of each stage is given below to introduce you to the main components.

Referral

A **referral** is made when someone contacts Social Service with any issues about a child. It records the main factual details of the family, the nature of the issues being raised and some contact details from the person making the referral. The referral is the trigger for an assessment and action by Social Services. A referral can come from any source, for example, a neighbour, a friend or a professional. In the case of a child in day care, the referral can come from any worker who has concerns and it does not necessarily have to be given via a manager or supervisor. It should be the person who holds the concerns who refers the child.

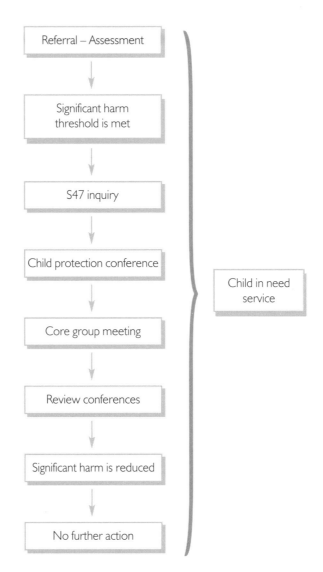

Stages in the child protection service

Assessment

As the research suggested, it is important to gather as much information about the family and concerns to decide what the appropriate intervention may be. This involves Social Services setting in motion, what becomes a continuum of information gathering and analysis within a formal assessment process.

S47 inquiry

If there is a suspicion that a child may be suffering significant harm or at risk of suffering significant harm then the local authority will undertake investigation into the situation, with the police if it is believed a criminal act may have been committed. Such an investigation is known as a **S47 inquiry** because it relates to S47 of the Children Act 1989, which gives the legal remit for such an inquiry. Consideration will also be given as to whether or not immediate legal action is required to make the child safe. This may involve the removal of the child from the home on a temporary basis while longer-term plans are made, dependent on further assessment.

Child protection conference

If there are any outstanding child protection concerns following the S47 inquiry, the local authority will need to decide if immediate action to protect a child is required by application for a legal order. Outstanding child protection issues may mean that a child continues to have contact with an alleged perpetrator or there are issues of unresolved neglect, for example.

A **child protection conference** is convened to consider whether or not a child's name is placed on the **child protection register** and a **child protection plan** is required to address the significant harm. Family and professionals involved with the family and child are invited to attend the meeting. The conference will share and analyse information and agree any actions that people need to take to reduce any harm to the child. If participants feel that the child is at continuing risk of significant harm while work is carried out, then the child's name will be placed on the child protection register. The register is a confidential list, available only to professionals, indicating that the child named is considered at risk of significant harm and there is a plan in place to address the harm.

Core group

If a child's name is placed on the child protection register, the chair of the meeting will identify a **core group**. It will be the task of the core group to detail the plan and meet to review its progress and make changes as necessary to ensure the safety of the child.

Review conference

Conferences meet at regular intervals to review the progress of the plan. The aim of the plan is to reduce levels of significant risk in order to offer the family services on a voluntary basis or cease involvement completely.

The child protection service is a framework of mechanisms that exist to identify significant harm, formulate actions to address harm, carry out the plan and review progress towards the objective of making a child safe as soon as possible, adjusting the plan as required to meet this goal.

What can the child protection service do?

The child protection service is couched in child in need services. Child in need services are those services offered to children and families to provide support and help to promote the child's health and welfare when there are concerns of harm, e.g. nursery provision and parenting advice.

Any child who is receiving support on a child in need basis may also be provided with a child protection service if issues of harm reach a significant level. There will also be cases that will receive a direct child protection response without having received any prior involvement, e.g. incidents of sexual assault.

Also child protection cases in which harm has reduced from a significant level, but there are still areas that require support, will receive services on a child in need basis.

The services are interchangeable. You should be aware of this so that you can be clear on what basis a child you may be involved with is receiving a service from a local authority. There is a need for you to keep yourself informed about the options available when your views are asked for at any multi-agency meetings if there are concerns about a child.

A question that is often asked by professionals is 'what will a child protection service do that a child in need service cannot?' Some points that answer that question are listed below; they will enable you to make the distinction if you are asked which service you believe would be best for a family, either at a child protection conference, or at a child in need meeting.

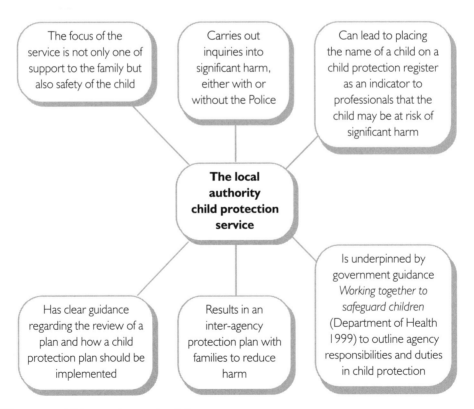

What can a child protection service do?

Inter-agency working

Child protection studies and lessons learnt from child protection tragedies, when a child has been seriously injured or died, highlight the importance of professionals working together to safeguard children. It has become apparent in many situations that professionals each have a piece of information rather like a piece of a puzzle, and it is only when the information is put together that the full picture of concern is identified. For instance, as an Early Years Practitioner you may have concerns about the behaviour of an adult who has been sent by a parent to collect a child. The Probation services may have concerns about the same adult, fearing he is a danger to children but do not know that he has access to a child. It is only when the two pieces of information are put together that we can see the full picture of risk to a child. You are in a position to provide important information about a child who may be subject to child protection registration, as well as identifying harm when it occurs.

Research has also indicated that when there are child protection concerns the wider issues of the family need to be addressed as well as the immediate problem, and as an Early Years Practitioner you will be able to contribute support to such a situation.

The importance of working together to safeguard children has been recognised by the government and *Working Together to Safeguard Children* (Department of Health 1999) provides guidance to agencies about their individual and collective responsibilities in child protection.

For early years, as part of day care provision to children, the document states:

> *Day Care Services – Family centres, early years centres, nurseries (including workplace nurseries, childminders, playgroups and holiday out of school schemes) play an increasingly important part in the lives of large numbers of children. Many services will be offering help to families and children with problems and stresses. This makes them well placed to help prevent problems from developing into abuse and neglect through support to families, and to recognise and act upon potential indicators of abuse and neglect.*

Department of Health 1999: p.23

The guide also specifies that professional bodies that provide a service to children, including Early Years services, should have in place agreed procedures about recognising harm and how to make a referral. Your agency may already have a policy in place, or it may be your task to formulate or contribute to one. Either way, it is an important document to guide yourself and others in your agency on what to do if harm is present for a child.

Area Child Protection Committee

Working Together to Safeguard Children also outlines the roles and responsibilities of the **Area Child Protection Committee** (ACPC). An ACPC exists in all local authority areas. It is a body made up of senior managers of the main agencies of child protection, e.g. Health, Education, Police, Social Services, Probation, and Voluntary Agencies. It is their job to oversee the effective inter-agency working arrangements for child protection in the local area.

The main functions of the ACPC are shown in the diagram below:

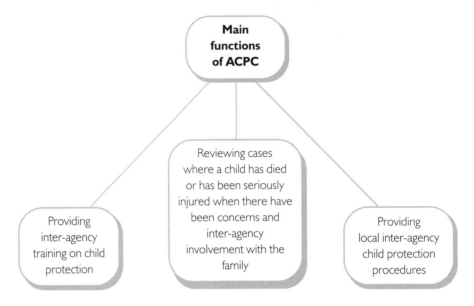

Main functions of the ACPC

Early Years organisations are not always represented on the ACPC, but it may be useful to find your local committee and discuss how Early Years input is provided and if training is available to you. There should also be a copy of the ACPC procedures in your agency or access to a copy. If not, discuss with your line management or your local ACPC. ACPCs are soon to become known as Children's Management Boards – see appendix 1 'Every Child Matters' page 243.

Scope of child protection

Child protection is about keeping children safe from significant harm. This may traditionally conjure up thoughts of a child being harmed by an adult, usually in a family setting, but it does include other settings in which children can be harmed. You will need to be aware of these areas to identify harm appropriately if it presents itself to you in one of these areas, as listed below:

Setting	Example
Children who suffer harm within their families	Injury caused by a parent or main carer or sibling
Children who suffer harm from strangers	Sexual assault by a stranger in the park
Children who suffer harm from their peers	Child who suffers severe bullying at school (note this area is probably less applicable to Early Years settings.) But you may become aware of an older sibling who is suffering harm in this way.
Young people who perpetrate harm to children	Teenager who sexually assaults young children while babysitting
Children who suffer harm outside the family by adults known to them	Child physically injured by a neighbour, family friend
Children who suffer harm in an institutional setting	Child who is assaulted by a carer in a residential home, or by a professional or peer at a nursery or school
Children who are involved in prostitution	This setting probably speaks for itself and is perhaps less applicable to Early Years areas. Although it is possible for an adult to be involved with offering young children for sex to other adults
Children involved in drugs/alcohol misuse	Again professionals need to be aware of concern for children involved with drugs or alcohol

(Department of Health 1999: p.63)

It is important to be aware of the wide remit of child protection and that referrals of child harm can be made about areas outside of the family home.

ACTIVITY

Look at the scenarios below and from the information given decide which area of child protection, identified above, the situation may fit into:

◆ Five-year-old collected from school by older brother. Reports that his older brother punched him in the stomach and hit him about the head.

◆ Three-year-old sexually assaulted by an uncle.

◆ Father who seeks help after losing control with his baby and shaking it to try to stop it crying.

Can you identify which area of child protection this situation may fit into?

Making professional judgements

To achieve some objectivity in making decisions about harm it is necessary to acknowledge some of the forces that come into play when we make judgements about family situations. It is only by recognising the variety of influences on us as professionals that we take steps to ensure we are taking a balanced view. Some of the influences are provided below.

Professional culture

All working bodies develop their own values, rules and cultures, some of which are explicit, for example, written procedures, and some that are implicit that evolve from people with similar minds joining an organisation. When we approach a situation, we do so from a particular professional perspective and should be aware this is the starting point for our decision-making. A person working in an educational environment may approach a situation with education taking priority. A health professional may approach the same situation with a medical model in mind. It is important to remember that all perspectives are valid and while it may lead to disagreement about the needs of a child, recognition should be given to people approaching the same problem from different starting points. All views are important and we should listen to them. The ideal will be an acknowledgement and understanding of these variant perspectives by professionals and a working together with families to achieve a common understanding of the problems and how to address them.

Personal values and experiences

All of us have acquired our own values and views about the world from our experiences of growing up. We carry that personal view with us throughout our personal and professional lives. Often our own experiences will influence the choices we make and the way in which we react with family situations when we work with children. Our personal experiences are unique to us and we need to be aware that there are personal influences on our decision-making about what to do if we think a child is being harmed. This point is perhaps best illustrated in the debate about whether or not children should be smacked as a method of control. There is a view that smacking is not harmful; those who support this view often cite their own examples of being smacked and suggest that it didn't cause them harm. Again there is an opposing view that it is harmful and does not work as a method of control.

Any one of us taking part in this debate will inevitably be drawing on our own experiences to support our argument. It is important that we recognise that our personal experiences and values influence our decision-making and this may lead us to take a view that is not compatible within a professional context. In these cases it is helpful if we pursue best practice and consider another point of view from a colleague or manager to ensure that we are doing our best to be objective.

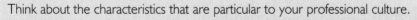

THINK ABOUT IT

Think about the characteristics that are particular to your professional culture.

Think about your personal experiences and values that influence what you do in your professional life.

Stereotypes

In our society many stereotypes exist, often enhanced by their portrayal in the media, for example, portrayal of the housewife as house-proud and child friendly, and portrayal of a drug user as aggressive, poor and unemployed. The problem with stereotypes is that they lead us to make assumptions about a person or a situation that might not be correct. By making such assumptions we may not recognise the reality of situations and this may inhibit us from making the response needed to ensure the welfare of a child. We may feel that a child is not at risk of harm from a drug user because she is a working mother with relative wealth and employment. Equally, we may assume a parent or carer is a drug user because his/her lifestyle fits the picture we are used to seeing in the media.

The solution is to keep an open mind, make an objective assessment and question a situation to ensure that you are operating with the facts and reality, rather than responding to stereotypical assumptions.

Race, ethnicity and culture

Children suffer harm in all cultures, and culture cannot be used to explain or justify significant harm. The child protection process applies to every child in the United Kingdom, whatever the culture.

However, in order to complete an accurate assessment and ensure a sound basis for any intervention with a family, professionals should be aware of different cultures and parenting styles. If there is a lack of knowledge then advice and information should be sought from a reliable source.

Working Together to Safeguard Children highlights the desirability of professionals understanding the wider context of issues that discriminate against black and ethnic minority people. Such understanding can help to inform any assessment of a family and identify the right source of support.

THINK ABOUT IT

Explore and discuss any cultural differences in child rearing with your colleagues. Consider what impact they might have on your practice.

Can you think of any other difficulties that might be specific to your workplace?

What can be done within your work to address the difficulties?

Possible difficulties encountered when working with ethnic minorities

Some of the difficulties that may arise when working with families from ethnic minority backgrounds are illustrated in the diagram that follows.

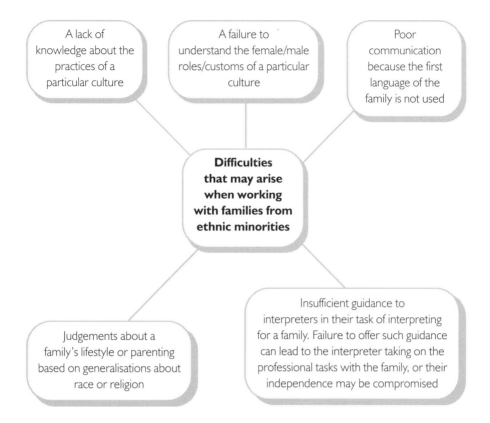

Problems encountered when working with families from ethnic minority backgrounds

Perhaps one of the greatest dangers to our making good balanced judgements when working with families from ethnic minorities seems to be one of lack of information and knowledge about a culture different from our own. It is important that we take time to acquire such knowledge before we are faced with a difficult situation, when we may fall back onto reactions, based on assumption, which only serve to exacerbate any harm to a child.

The public inquiry into the death of a child, Victoria Climbie in 2002, provided a clear example of cultural misunderstanding. Victoria Climbie died while in the care of her great aunt and her aunt's partner. Both were convicted of murder. Victoria, who originated from the Ivory Coast, was brought to the United Kingdom by her aunt, with the permission of her parents who hoped for a better life for Victoria. Victoria died of neglect and physical injures, despite the involvement of Social Services, Education, Police, Health and NSPCC in her life.

The inquiry highlighted many mistakes made by professionals involved in her life. Of importance was the assumption that because her social worker was black she would have greater knowledge of Victoria's culture. This was, sadly, a grave misjudgement.

> *Assumption based on race can be just as corrosive in its effect as blatant racism … racism can affect the way people conduct themselves in other ways. Fear of being accused of racism can stop people acting when otherwise they would. Assumptions that people of the same colour, but from different backgrounds, behave in similar ways can distort judgements.*
>
> Department of Health & Home Office 2003: p.15

Such comments highlight the importance of making it our own responsibility to acquire knowledge and information in order that we may offer a balanced informed approach when working with families from an ethnic minority background.

Focus on the child

To effectively support a child and safeguard its welfare, we need to work in partnership with parents and carers. However, it is also important to be aware of the need to maintain focus on the child's welfare.

Often when working with families we develop a close and often empathetic relationship with parents. This can lead to a lack of recognition that a child is being harmed; this is particularly true in long-term neglect cases, where there is no single incident to trigger a response but a steady significant decline. Parents and carers themselves can also represent their own difficulties to you, perhaps health problems, and so on, and this can shift the focus of work away from the child to the adults in the case. Although work should include the whole family, and support should be given to address all areas of weakness in which improvements can be made to create positive change for the child, the focus of attention should be the child. For example, in the case of Victoria Climbie, the social worker became focused on the housing issue for Victoria's aunt, and this moved her attention away from monitoring the welfare of Victoria during visits to the family home.

Balanced working should involve a partnership with the family to address the context of harm as well as harm but also maintain as the focus the safety and welfare of the child.

THINK ABOUT IT

Can you think of any other influences that may affect your decision-making in child protection situations?

REFLECT ON YOUR PRACTICE

◆ Be aware of your values and experiences that might influence your perception of a situation.

◆ Seek as much information as possible regarding the family and circumstances. This includes consulting the family, in circumstances when it does not place the child at further risk of significant harm, and the child (in accordance with age and understanding).

◆ Continually update your professional knowledge and development, particularly in relation to other cultures and parenting styles.

◆ Seek an external view for an alternative perspective. Consult with colleagues, your manager, and other agencies for a different angle.

Disability

There is a level of increased vulnerability to take into account when assessing the welfare and safety of a disabled child. Research suggests that children with disability are at increased risk of abuse and the presence of multiple disabilities increases the risk further.

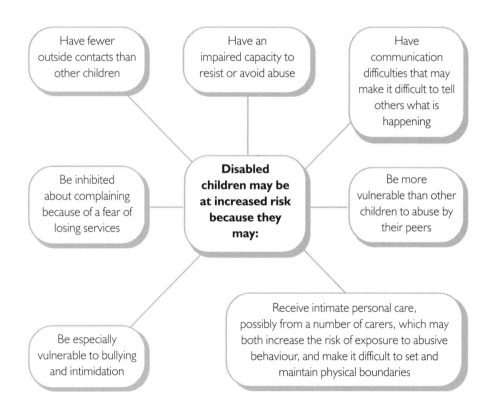

Reasons why disabled children may be at increased risk of abuse

We must, as professionals, be aware of the increased vulnerability of a disabled child in order to recognise harm and the need for support and/or protection when it arises.

Partnership

Given the *Messages From Research* (1995) finding that most children about whom there are concerns of significant harm either remain at home or return home quickly, it is clearly important for the safety of children that professionals work in partnership with families to create positive change.

There will inevitably be instances when local authorities, because of the very nature of the situation, will not be able to engage in a full partnership role with parents and carers, for example, when the parent is the alleged abuser and is refusing to cooperate with agencies. However, given the restrictions of some protective situations for sharing information, professionals will strive to carry out the principles of working in partnership whenever possible.

Working in partnerships with professionals associated with a child can create positive change

WORKING TOGETHER

Working Together to Safeguard Children (Department of Health 1999: p.75) provides guidance in the form of 15 points to consider in relation to partnership with families on a child protection basis:

1. Treat all family members as you would wish to be treated, with dignity and respect.

2. Ensure that family members know that the child's safety and welfare must be given first priority, but that each of them has a right to a courteous, caring and professionally competent service.

3. Take care not to infringe privacy any more than is necessary in order to safeguard the welfare of the child.

4. Be clear with yourself and with family members about your power to intervene, and the purpose of your professional involvement at each stage.

5. Be aware of the effects on family members of the power you have as a professional, and the impact and implications of what you say and do.

6. Respect the confidentiality of family members and your observations about them, unless they give permission for information to be passed onto others or it is essential to do so to protect the child.

7. Listen to the concerns of children and their families, and take care to learn about their understanding, fears and wishes before arriving at your own explanations and plans.

8. Learn about and consider children within their family, and their place within their own families.

9. Consider the strengths and potential of family members, as well as their weaknesses, problems and limitations.

10. Ensure children, families and other carers know their responsibilities and rights, including any right to services, and their right to refuse services, and any consequences of doing so.

11. Use plain, jargon-free language, appropriate to the age and culture of each person. Explain unavoidable technical and professional terms.

12. Be open and honest about your concerns and responsibilities, plans and limitations, without being defensive.

13. Allow children and families' time to take in and understand concerns and processes. A balance needs to be found between appropriate speed and the needs of people who may need extra time in which to communicate.

14. Take care to distinguish between personal feelings, values, prejudices and beliefs, and professional roles and responsibilities. Ensure that you have good supervision to check that you are doing so.

➡

15. If a mistake or misinterpretation has been made, or you are unable to keep to an agreement, provide an explanation. Always acknowledge any distress experienced by adults and children and do all you can to keep it to a minimum.

© Crown copyright

These are useful points to keep in mind for any person involved in working with children. Partnership with parents and carers to work towards the safety and welfare of children can only serve to contribute to a child's well being. However, it should not take precedence over actions to ensure the safety of a child, for example, dispensing with parental consent to make a referral when a child is at risk of significant harm.

Summary

For the Early Years Practitioners the following points are important to note.

◆ The local authority has a duty to provide support services to children and families if the child is in need of help to reach his/her potential.

◆ Early Years Practitioners are in a position to identify possible harm early to discuss with parents and offer support, or refer to another agency, such as Social Services for support.

◆ It is important to work in partnership with parents and carers when there are problems.

◆ Child protection service is part of a wider picture of services for children's needs and is applied along with other services if there is a risk of significant harm.

CHECKPOINT

1. Name four different 'levels' involved in safeguarding children.
2. Give an example of high-warmth parenting.
3. Give an example of high-criticism parenting.
4. Describe a finding from *Messages from Research*.
5. What was the response to *Messages from Research*?
6. Give an example of what the Child Protection Service can do.
7. What is the purpose of the ACPC?
8. What will ACPCs become known as when the government document *Every Child Matters* comes into force?
9. What is significant harm?
10. What factors should you take into account when considering a child protection judgement?

Chapter 2

The legal framework for child protection

It is likely that as an Early Years Practitioner you may come into contact with a child who is subject to a legal order, at which point it will be helpful if you have an understanding of the basis of the legal framework for childcare – predominantly the Children Act 1989. This chapter includes a brief history of the legislation relating to child protection and introduces you to the Children Act 1989, highlighting those areas of the Act that may be relevant to your work, together with other pieces of legislation that may have some bearing on the work you do. This chapter provides greater detail about the responsibilities to children in need and to safeguarding children. It also considers some of the wider legal components that have implications for working with children; namely the Human Rights Act 1998, Data Protection Act 1998 and the Protection of Children Act 1999 (aimed at keeping children safe from dangerous professionals).

You may also find yourself in a supportive role, either directly or indirectly, if an investigation takes place into allegations of harm involving a child you work with. This chapter provides a summary of some of the relevant aspects of *Achieving Best Evidence in Criminal Proceedings* (Home Office 2001); this provides government guidance on the interview of children for criminal evidence. Finally, there is guidance about your role in court, should you ever be required to give evidence as a witness as part of criminal or civil proceedings.

A brief history of child protection

Until the introduction of the Children Act 1989, legislation concerning the protection of children was piecemeal. Here is a summary of some significant dates.

Year	Legislation
1889	The Prevention of Cruelty to and Protection of Children Act came into being in 1889. The Act enabled state intervention into family life, and into issues of employment of children. The National Society for the Prevention of Cruelty to Children (NSPCC) was established in 1889.
1904	The 1889 Act was extended to allow children to give **court evidence**. The 1904 Prevention of Cruelty to Children Act recognised **emotional harm** and established a child's right to medical attention.
1932	The Children & Young Person Act introduced **supervision orders** for children. Supervision orders enabled the supervisor to befriend the child and family to provide advice and guidance for the child's best interests.
1933	The Children & Young Persons Act consolidated childcare legislation.
1948	The death of a child, Denis O Neil, in foster care was followed by the Children Act 1948. The Act led to the introduction of a children's committee and children's officers in local authorities.
1970	In 1970 the Local Authority Social Services Act was introduced. The Act led to the provision of social work departments with specific responsibilities for the welfare of children.
1974	Area Child Protection Committees (ACPCs) were brought into being to improve coordination of agencies in the management of child protection. The Committees were a response to the public inquiry into the death of Maria Colwell. Maria was a child who died in the care of her mother and stepfather whilst under the care of Social Services. The inquiry established that the coordination of information in the case was poor and led to Maria being unprotected.
1989	The Children Act incorporated previous childcare legislation into one document. It introduced the concept of significant harm for a child protection response. It also introduced the duty to provide services to children in need of support to achieve their potential. The Act established the principle that if possible, and compatible with safety, children are best looked after at home with their families, and identified the concept of parental responsibilities to support this aim.
1991	The Department of Health published the first *Working Together document*. This outlined the duties and responsibilities of agencies to work together for the protection of children. In particular, it outlined the duties of the Area Child Protection Committee.

➡

Year	Legislation
1995	*Child Protection Messages From Research* was published (Department of Health 1995). This document outlined the findings of 20 studies into child protection. The research found that professionals concentrated on the investigation of child abuse, often with no clear or satisfactory outcome, to the detriment of services to children in need. The document led to the refocusing of services to a preventative child in need approach to safeguarding children.
1998	Government introduced the Quality Protects agenda with the aim of improving all services to children and families and ultimately produce better outcomes. The strategy incorporated a quality assurance system for child protection with key objectives for the child protection service.
1999	Publication of *Working Together to Safeguard Children* (Department of Health: 1999). This replaced the earlier *Working Together* document published in 1991. The Protection of Children Act 1999 was introduced. The Act aims to prevent those people who pose a risk of significant harm to children from acquiring positions of work with children.
2000	The *Framework for Assessment of Children in need and their families* was published this year (Department of Health: 2000). The *Framework for Assessment* was introduced to provide a consistent method of assessing a child and family to inform the nature of intervention required. The assessment introduced a holistic approach that incorporated three dimensions for consideration – the child, parenting capacity and environmental factors. The *Framework for Assessment* encourages the recognition of a family's strengths, on which to build improvements, as well as weaknesses that may need support. The Children & Young Persons Unit was also established in 2000. The Unit administers the Children's Fund, finance provided for projects to improve services for children and produce positive outcomes.
2001	Death of a child, Victoria Climbie, leads to a public inquiry. Victoria, a child from the Ivory Coast, died in the care of her aunt and her aunt's partner. The death prompted public concern, as her death occurred despite the involvement of Social Services and partner agencies and a number of inquiries into her well-being.

The Children Act 1989

A comprehensive legal framework underpins the child protection system in England and Wales. This framework gives local authorities and the courts the remit to safeguard the well-being of children.

The predominant feature of the legal framework is the Children Act 1989. Prior to the introduction of this Act, children's legislation had been very piecemeal, dispersed between several statutes. The Children Act 1989 encompassed legislation for both public and private parties and provides a definitive legal document for working with children and families.

As a professional working with children, you will need to be aware of the existence of the Act and that there may be a time when you will need to refer to it for guidance.

Throughout your work you may encounter situations that require legal clarification. In these instances you might seek legal advice, but you should also be aware that several guides to the Children Act 1989 exist and these will prove helpful in detailing the specific areas of the law that apply to your situation. (Department of Health 1989a & 1989b)

Principles of the Act

The underlying theme of the Children Act is the view that children are best looked after at home with their families so far as this is compatible with their safety and well-being. Alongside this premise, the Children Act 1989 introduced and reinforced several themes for the childcare arena. These are shown in the table below.

Principles of the Children Act 1989:	
The child's welfare is paramount – the focus of all those involved should be the child	This principle is maintained from previous legislation, and in respect of any case involving a child, it instructs the court to consider all information and circumstances relating to the child, including the child's wishes and feelings. However, it must finally make a decision that is in the child's best interests even if that is against the child's view.
No delay principle	The Act is clear that to delay a decision relating to a child's life may be detrimental to his/her welfare. Therefore, emphasis is placed on the need to avoid delay and the court is required to draw up a timetable for legal proceedings to avoid such an occurrence. Delay can be mitigated if it is time spent reaching an agreement by conciliation. For example, a delay can be justified if parents are using the time to negotiate a contact issue about a child, time that may ultimately result in no order being made because parents can reach agreement without the help of the court.

➡

The court will only make an order if it is necessary	This principle creates a presumption against an order being made unless it is going to be beneficial to the child. There had been concern that in the past, once conditions for an order were satisfied, the court made the order without considering whether this would be better for the child than no order at all. For example, in private proceedings, **custody** and **access orders** became automatic as part of matrimonial hearings, whereas this might not have always been necessary; parents may have been able to reach their own arrangements for access without a legal order in place. In fact, the order may have created an unwelcome barrier between parents and prevented their reaching amicable agreements about what is in the best interests of the child.
Parental responsibility	Perhaps the most innovative concept, and one that has direct impact on professionals working with children, is the idea of parental responsibility.

The meaning of parental responsibility

The Children Act 1989 uses the phrase 'parental responsibility' to sum up the collection of duties, rights and authority that a parent has in respect of his child. (Department of Health 1989b)

In short, parental responsibility sums up the legal role of parenting. Parental responsibility confers to the parent a duty of care to raise a child to 'moral, physical and emotional well-being' (Department of Health 1989b). It has the effect of giving parents the power to make most decisions in a child's life.

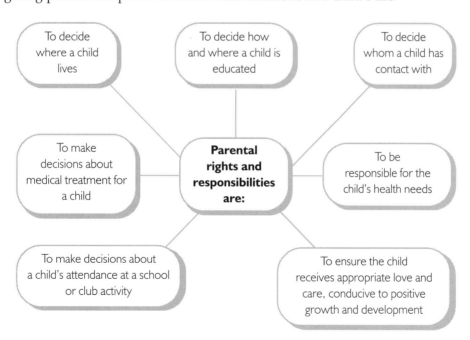

Examples of parental rights and responsibilities

Who has parental responsibility?

There are several ways in which parental responsibility (PR) is acquired:

◆ Mothers always receive parental responsibility for a child.

◆ Fathers automatically acquire PR if they are married to the mother. Alternatively, they can acquire it via a voluntary written agreement with the mother, by application to court or by virtue of a **residence order** deciding where a child lives.

◆ Any adult who is awarded a residence order by court automatically acquires PR.

◆ The local authority can acquire parental responsibility for a child if it is awarded an **interim** or full **care order**.

It is important to note that parental responsibility is not a finite idea. When one person acquires PR it does not necessarily mean that another loses it. Parental responsibility for a child can be spread over a number of different parties.

As a professional working with children you will need to know which adults have parental responsibility for a child. They will be the adults you will contact

Which adults have parental responsibility?

in an emergency, for example, or the person who can give permission for activities outside of your service.

For a child in care it will either be both the local authority and parents who have parental responsibility, or the parents alone will hold responsibility if they have chosen to voluntarily accommodate a child. It will not be the **foster parents** or necessarily extended family members unless they have a residence order.

Parental responsibility is an important concept and is constantly referred to throughout this book in all the activities of child protection.

Legal basis for local authority involvement

The Children Act 1989 bestows two main duties on the local authorities in England and Wales to help ensure children are safeguarded and are well cared for.

Note that the request of these duties is not placed entirely on Social Services but on the local authority to ensure the best use of a wide range of services that might be available, including Early Years.

Section 17 service

The Act places a duty on local authorities to help children 'in need'. You may encounter professionals referring to this duty as a Section 17 service. This gives local authorities the responsibility of working with families, using a whole range of services to ensure that a child reaches his/her potential both in health and development. A child is taken to be 'in need':

◆ if there is a likelihood that he/she will not reach her/his potential without services being offered, or

◆ a child will suffer significantly without the provision of such services, or

◆ the child is disabled.

The services can be offered from any agency (including Sure Start) and might include:

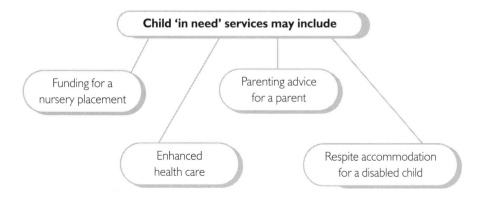

Examples of child in need services

Section 47 inquiries

The Act places a duty on local authorities to investigate any instance when a child might be at risk of significant harm or may be suffering significant harm, and to make inquiries about whether the child is in need of protection. The local authority refers to such investigations as **Section 47 inquiries**. They are the gateway to child protection services if there continues to be outstanding child protection concerns on completion of the inquiries.

The Police will take part in these inquiries if there is a possibility that a criminal offence has been committed. They will join the inquiries at the **strategy discussion** stage (this is outlined in Chapter 5 covering referrals). The Police are guided in their investigation by a guide *Achieving Best Evidence in Criminal Proceedings* (Home Office 2001), a government document on how children should be interviewed as vulnerable witnesses in these inquiries.

The inquiry, therefore, will involve interviewing the child about the allegations. This process contributes to both the Social Services' role to gather information in order to contribute to the assessment to make a child safe, and to the Police role of gathering criminal evidence.

Supporting a child during an investigation

Only trained Social Services and Police personnel can interview a child about harm, but you may find yourself supporting a child who is taking part in an investigation process. A guide to those aspects of *Achieving Best Evidence in Criminal Proceedings* most relevant to you when either taking part in the interview of a child as a supporter, or providing support to a child who is part of an investigation, via your workplace, is provided at the end of this chapter.

Child Protection Conference

If child protection concerns persist following a Section 47 inquiry, then a child protection service will continue, predominantly in the form of a child protection conference. The conference will consider whether or not a child is at **continuing risk of significant harm**, and if child protection registration, together with a child protection plan, is required to help make the child safe. However, there is also a range of **legal orders** available to the local authority to safeguard the child who might be in immediate danger, such as for example, when parents do not cooperate with professionals and there continues to be a real risk of significant harm, perhaps in the form of **physical injury** or **sexual assault**. The local authority can apply for these orders if during child protection registration the situation deteriorates to the extent that it is no longer safe for the child to remain at home.

Emergency protection order

This order provides temporary immediate protection for a child. An **emergency protection order** gives protection for a child in the short term, in circumstances when a child is suffering or is likely to suffer immediate significant harm. For example, one might be used to ensure a new born baby remains in hospital for medical treatment when parents threaten to remove it. It can be made on application by the local authority and will usually be made with the court only hearing evidence of the authority. It is often the case that to let other parties have knowledge of the application (for example, parents and carers) may jeopardise the enforcement of the order. The emergency protection can be in effect for eight days and may in circumstances that warrant it, for example, further assessment, be extended by the court for another seven days.

Prior to application for an emergency protection order the local authority will explore any alternative means of making the child safe without resort to a legal order, for example they may pursue alternative accommodation with a safe carer such as a member of the extended family. It is only when these options have been exhausted that the authority will seek legal action to protect the child from significant harm.

Child assessment order

This is an order that requires a child to be made available for any necessary assessments that are necessary to ensure the child's well-being. The order is valid for seven days, by which time further action needs to have been considered. Circumstances in which the **child assessment order** might be used include a situation in which there are concerns about a child's emotional well-being and parents refuse to make the child available for **psychological assessment**. In this instance an application can be made for a child assessment order to enable health assessments to take place, if parents refuse to cooperate. It is an order that is little used, as an application for a care order can achieve the same result.

Supervision order

This places a child under the supervision of a local authority or Probation while remaining at home. The role of the supervisor is to assist, advise and befriend a child. A **supervision order** is granted for the period of one year. After one year, a local authority can make application to extend the order for a further year if it feels there continues to be a need for such an order. If after one year no application is made for an extension, the order will lapse.

Care order

When the local authority applies for a **care order** for a child, it seeks parental responsibility for a child and for a child to be subject to local authority care. The authority has to make plans for the child's care and this can include remaining at home subject to the order; it might mean **foster** or **residential care**, or permanent alternative care such as **adoption**.

A care order can remain in force until such time as concerns about significant harm to a child diminish, if the child is with parents, or until the child is adopted if a return to the care of parents is not possible. In some instances the order can remain until the child is aged eighteen. A care order can only be **revoked** on application to court, at which point the local authority must demonstrate grounds on which the order is no longer required, i.e. the child's care has significantly improved.

There may be a period of time when a court needs to consider its final order, for instance it may need to obtain further information by means of assessment. During this period the court can take temporary measures by means of an **interim order**, e.g. an interim care order, to safeguard a child while further work is being undertaken.

The Children Act 1989 also offers a range of **private legal orders** that parents and family can make application for in order to protect a child, or to decide contact and where a child lives.

Orders that can be used in private proceedings:	
Contact order	An order requiring the person with whom a child lives, or is to live, to allow the child to visit or stay with the person named in the order
Prohibited steps order	An order that no step, which could be taken by a parent in meeting his parental responsibility for a child, and which is of a kind specified in the order, shall be taken without the consent of the court
Residence order	An order settling the arrangements to be made about whom the child is to live with
Specific issue order	Order giving directions for the purpose of determining a specific question with an aspect of parental responsibility for a child

These orders are collectively known as **Section 8 orders** and can be used in private proceedings to settle issues about the welfare of a child. If there have been any significant concerns about a child subject to such proceedings then the court may seek a report from Social Services.

The court process

There are two main occasions when an Early Years worker may be required to go to court or submit a legal statement. These are as follows:

- if a child has informed the worker of abuse to him/herself or someone else, the worker may be required to make a **witness statement** and appear in court as a witness in criminal proceedings.

- if the local authority has made an application to court for a legal order in respect of a child you work with, a statement regarding the child's behaviour, presentation or progress may be required.

Criminal proceedings

If a child has made a **disclosure** of harm by an adult and during the inquiry you gave a statement to the Police, perhaps because the child has disclosed to you, then you may be asked to give evidence in **criminal proceedings**.

In such a situation you may wish to identify a work colleague or manager to act as your support. It may also be possible for you to receive support from a witness service at court. The service will provide guidance about where you have to go to give evidence and will probably have a private waiting area if you feel the need to wait away from the public.

A criminal hearing about harm to a child takes place in a criminal court with a Judge and Jury present. The court is also open to the public.

If a case does go to court, one cannot of course assume the alleged perpetrator will be convicted. The **burden of proof** in criminal proceedings is higher than that for civil proceedings. The jury must be satisfied beyond **all reasonable doubt** that the accused committed the offence.

It should be noted that even if the adult is not prosecuted, child protection action in the form of a child protection conference or **civil proceedings** can still take place, as the **threshold for action** in these arenas is different and is on the **balance of probabilities**, rather than belief beyond reasonable doubt. If the information suggests that the adult probably carried out the harm, then child protection registration or a legal order to safeguard the child can be put in place.

Civil proceedings

If a local authority has made an application for a supervision or care order, you may be asked by any of the parties involved to supply information to court in the form of a witness statement, and you may be asked to give evidence in court according to your statement. The parties will be the local authority, either of the parents, extended family or carers, or the guardian *ad litem* (the independent social worker to represent the child's interests). If you are asked to provide a statement to court, you should contact the solicitor requesting the information. If you are in the employment of a local authority, you should contact the local authority legal department. If you are provided with legal support as part of your job, then you should get in touch with your employer.

The information you will be asked to supply will be similar to that requested by a child protection conference. An example statement format for submission of information to court is given in Chapter 9 (page 229).

Going to court

If a local authority has made an application for a supervision or care order and you have submitted a statement as part of the process, you may be asked to go to court to give verbal evidence.

Structure of the Magistrates Court

The type of court you attend will depend on the complexity of a case. Most childcare cases are heard at a **Magistrates Court** local to the town where the child lives. The structure of the Magistrates Court is shown in the diagram above.

If a case becomes particularly complex it may be passed upwards to the County Court or **High Court**.

The structure of people present in this type of Court is as follows:

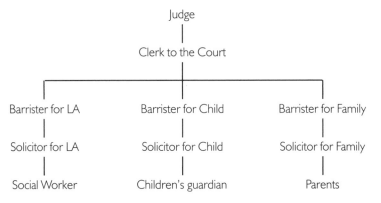

People present in County Court or High Court

Both courts are closed to the public because civil court hearings about children are private. The people listed above will be the only persons you will see when you give evidence. A children's guardian is present in all children's hearings and he/she is a person appointed by court to independently represent the interests of the child in legal proceedings. The child will also have a solicitor to protect his or her interests in court. Often the children's guardian and child's solicitor work together when their views coincide.

The Magistrates Court is a more informal venue than a **County Court**. The cases are heard in small rooms in the court building, often at tables. Three magistrates are present to hear the case.

A County Court is a more formal process with the presence of a Judge; gowns and wigs are sometimes worn and barristers need to be employed to present the case.

A Judge, sometimes in gown and wig, presides over a County Court

Attending court

If you are asked to attend court, you may like to identify someone who can attend with you as a support. When invited to attend you will be given the date, time and venue of hearing. Always arrive in plenty of time and report to the court reception where they will direct you to the court hearing the case. When you wait outside the court, make yourself known to the usher, who will tell you when you are required.

It is preferable that you do not wear casual clothing as an Early Years Practitioner in court. Ensure that your appearance is smart when giving evidence; this is to show respect for the legal process and also for the family who are participating in the hearing.

Giving evidence at court

When you are asked to give evidence you will be shown to a table or witness box by the usher and asked to state an **oath of truth**, which will be written on a card.

You can ask for a copy of your statement to refer to, if one is not already provided.

Listen carefully to the questions you are asked, and speak in a loud, clear, slow voice in reply.

Always turn to look at the Magistrates or Judge when you are giving your answers.

Ensure you answer the question asked, and try not to get side tracked into giving information that you think is relevant regardless of what you are asked.

TIPS FOR GIVING EVIDENCE IN COURT

1. Focus on why you are there. It is not about you but about the family and a very important decision about a child's future. Concentrate on the fact that you must give the best information possible to inform this process.

2. Take deep breaths and remember to pause for breath when speaking.

3. Take time to pause and think about a question and the answer before you reply.

4. If you do not understand a question, ask for clarification.

5. Try to adopt a neutral approach to your task and do not get into any antagonistic exchanges with those asking the questions.

6. Always give truthful answers. If the answer is that you do not know, then that is the answer you should give.

7. Make sure someone is available to you after court to review the process with you and to reflect on the evidence you provided.

8. Ensure that you are aware of the Social Services view and plans so that you can comment on them if you are requested to do so.

9. Do not use expressions appropriate for another profession, e.g. medical terms.

10. If you feel that something is unclear or missed in your evidence, you can ask to add information or to clarify something.

11. Address Magistrates as Sir/Madam, County Court Judges as Your Honour and High Court Judges as Your Lordship.

Human Rights Act 1998

Alongside the Children Act 1989, the Human Rights Act of 1998 has a direct bearing on how professionals work with children and families. The Human Rights Act 1998 came into force in the UK in 2000 and reflects the European Convention on Human Rights. The Act itself confers the same rights to children as it does to adults, in that it confers recognition to children as beings in their own right, capable of participating in decision-making about their futures.

There are two particular articles within the Human Rights Act that relate to the work of childcare professionals. These are shown in the table which follows.

Human Rights Act 1998 (articles relating to work of childcare professionals)		
Article 3	Right not to suffer ill treatment or cruel, unusual punishment	This article provides endorsement to the local authority role to provide services, Section 17 services to support families and prevent ill treatment, and to the duty to investigate circumstances when a child may be at risk of suffering significant harm or suffering significant harm.
Article 8	Everyone has the right to respect for his/her private and family life, his/her home and his/her correspondence	This article may seem a little at odds with article 3. It indicates that if a local authority intervenes in family life it should only do so with the consent of the family. In most cases of voluntary help, consent is sought and professionals are asked to seek consent before discussing the family with another agency – Social Services, for example. However, government guidance directs that consent should not be sought from a family if there is reason to believe that a child may be suffering, or at risk of suffering, significant harm, and to seek consent from the family would further endanger the child. For example, if there is a physical injury and the child indicates mother caused it intentionally.

The issue of consent

The Data Protection Act 1998 requires that:

> *... personal information is obtained and processed fairly and lawfully; only disclosed in appropriate circumstances; is accurate, relevant and not held longer than necessary; and is kept securely'*

Department of Health 1989: p. 113.

This statement, together with article 8 of the Human Rights Act, places a new onus on professionals' duty to respect family privacy, confidentiality and to recognise the need to seek consent when information is to be shared (the exception remaining, unless to seek consent would further endanger a child).

Most childcare agencies recognise the importance of having an explicit policy regarding **confidentiality**. Individual circumstances will determine how information is used and shared in each case.

Confidentiality

A general policy on confidentiality should include the points raised in the diagram below:

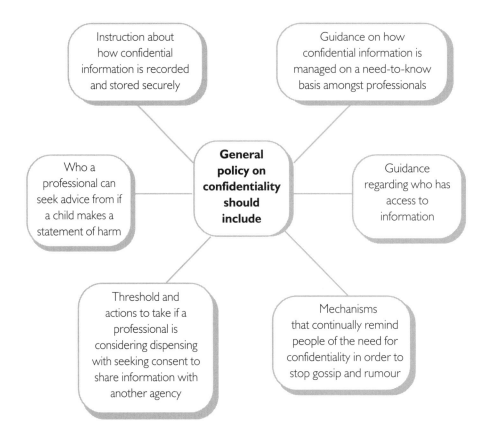

Points to be included in a general policy on confidentiality

Finally, it will help staff if there is a clear statement, agreed by your agency, to use if a member of the public approaches you with significant concerns about a child and then asks you to keep the information confidential. You will need to be clear with the person that information that suggests a child is suffering, or is at risk of suffering, significant harm cannot remain confidential and you will have to share it with the appropriate agencies. If this is made clear as a policy to parents and other adults using your service, it avoids difficulties in individual circumstances when they arise. As a professional you will want to remind people of this principle if they ask to confide in you. Not to do so will place you in a difficult dilemma if the information leads you to believe a child is suffering or at risk of suffering significant harm.

ACTIVITY

What would you do in the following situations?

This activity is intended as a thoughts and discussion exercise with colleagues and peers. It will enable you to think through strategies in hypothetical situations so you are prepared if they become reality. It may also help you identify possible areas of conflict that you might want to clarify in the workplace.

Scenario 1	Mr McKay has arrived to drop off four-year-old James. He informs you that James has a bruise to his arm and head. Mr McKay tells you it was an accident, as he caught him teasing the pet dog. He states he went a bit 'over the top' and grabbed James a bit too hard. Mr McKay states that James has been very badly behaved recently, and that he is stressed out trying to find a new job, having been made redundant. Mr McKay seeks reassurance that this does not have to go any further, as he doesn't want Social Services to be involved.
Scenario 2	Amanda, who is fifteen-years-old, approaches you in the infant school playground. She states that she is worried about Kate, who is a member of your class. Amanda babysits for Kate and says Kate informed her that her dad gets into bed with her and makes her do bad things. Amanda is anxious that you do not tell anyone, as Kate's dad is Amanda's uncle Paul, and her mother will be very angry with her if she thinks Amanda has got Paul into trouble. Paul is a parent school governor for your school.
Scenario 3	You are a childminder for Imran, a two-year-old boy. A neighbour approaches you in the street and asks how Imran is. She asks because she has heard information from a friend that the mother and her partner are heard fighting at night, and she has seen the mother with injuries in the past. The fights continue into the early morning and Imran is sometimes seen locked out in the back garden. The neighbour asks for the information to be kept confidential, as she does want to fall out with Imran's mother and partner, and anyway if the housing department knew, they would evict the family for causing noise late at night.

1. What actions would you take?

2. Who would you consult?

3. If you plan to dispense with consent, what would be your reasons?

4. Practise what you would say to these people, in order to address the issue of consent with them.

The professional and consent

It is important to keep in mind the conclusion in *Child Protection Messages from Research* (Department of Health 1995) that in most cases when there are concerns about a child, the child remains in the family. Note that it is in the interests of the child to identify difficulties early so that they can be dealt with and prevented from escalating into a more serious situation.

It is, therefore, important that a professional working with children should, if there are concerns about a child, raise them early and discuss with the family when seeking outside help from agencies such as Social Services. This action in itself may lead to the problem being resolved, particularly if you are able to offer advice and guidance. If you feel another agency could help, e.g. Health or Social Services, you should seek parental consent whenever possible.

If a parent will not give consent you need to consider the following options:

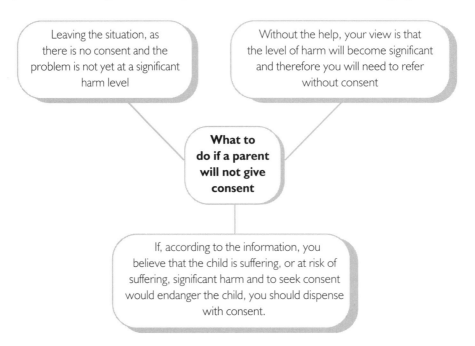

Options if a parent will not give consent

The recent outcome of the Climbie enquiry (Department of Health & Home Office 2003) into why Victoria Climbie died, and what professionals could have done to protect Victoria, emphasised that the issue of consent should not get in the way of professionals' sharing information to protect children.

However, as we know, child protection is rarely a clearly defined issue and dispensing with consent involves you in making a professional decision about the **level of harm** the child is suffering or is at risk of. In cases when there is uncertainty there are a number of actions open to you:

What to do when you are uncertain about the level of harm a child is suffering or at risk of

Do not feel that you have to make the decision on your own and always complete a written record of the action you have taken and why.

The Protection of Children Act 1999

Sadly, child protection inquiries indicate that children can be harmed within a professional setting by those whose job it is to look after children.

To provide measures to protect against such events the government introduced the Protection of Children Act 1999.

The Act has two main functions:

◆ referral of professionals to the Children Act 1999 list

◆ making checks against the Children Act 1999 list.

These are outlined below.

Referral of professionals to the Protection of Children Act 1999 list

This enables childcare organisations to refer people to the Protection of Children Act list. This is a national list held by the Secretary of State, against which checks are made in respect of those employees who are new to work with children.

It should be noted that the threshold for referral is not one of prosecution. The circumstances in which a referral should be made is as follows:

◆ the organisation has dismissed an individual on grounds which involved harm or risk of harm to a child

◆ an individual has retired in the circumstances above and if he had not retired he would have been dismissed

◆ on grounds of harm or risk to a child, the employee moved to a post which does not involve work with children

◆ the organisation suspended or transferred him on the above grounds.

The referral will be made by the employer of the person who is deemed to be a risk, to the Secretary of State for consideration of inclusion in the Protection of Children Act list.

Making checks against the Protection of Children Act 1999 list

The second action the Act covers is the need for childcare organisations to make checks against the Protection of Children Act list via the Criminal Records Bureau. The system is designed to build up a national database of those professionals who have placed a child at risk of harm, or harmed a child, to ensure that they are not employed to work with children again and repeat the incidents. As an Early Years Practitioner, you will have undergone a check against this list before commencing employment if you have been employed within the last few years.

In your role of working with children you may become aware of someone whom you think may pose a risk of harm to children. It is important that you are aware that this can happen and that there are measures in place to deal with any concerns you have. If you recognise issues about a professional you may discuss them with a line manager. If there are issues of significant harm then your workplace will need to make a referral to Social Services. A Section 47 inquiry may take place by Social Services and the Police. There will, of course, be the added dimension of employment issues for the professional concerned, and how to make all the children within the agency safe. At the end of inquiries the agency may decide to refer the person to the Protection of Children Act 1999 list, if the information suggests that the professional is a danger to children. Your workplace should have a procedure in place about what to do if you have concerns about a colleague or manager. It should include the following:

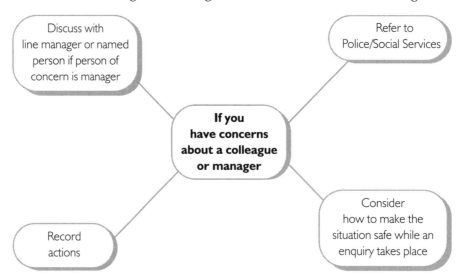

What to do if you have concerns about a colleague or manager

Before beginning an inquiry, the Police/Social Services will have a **strategy meeting**, which will include a representative from your organisation. Consideration will be given to how to keep children safe during any inquiry, as well as how to carry out the inquiry.

ACTIVITY

Consider the following actions by professionals.

Scenario 1   Mrs Gelormini, nursery manager, appears to be constantly stressed. She shouts a great deal at the children and often pulls them about roughly. She has singled out one child in particular, whom she constantly admonishes. He is always being sent out of the room and isolated. In an incident yesterday she pushed a child over in anger. Mrs Gelormini maintains this was an accident, but the child was taken to hospital for a medical check on the bump to his head.

Scenario 2   Mr Coughlin is the school caretaker, who is usually on site during school hours. Staff members have frequently seen him in his office talking with younger children when they should be out in the playground. He has been warned about this action, but he insists that they follow him into his office and he tries to get them to leave. You have recently walked into his office when he was talking to a young child who was upset. He had his arm around her and she was sat on his lap. Later in the week, the dinner lady informed you that the same child had told her that Mr Coughlin had asked to see her 'knickers'

Scenario 3   A fellow childminder has informed you of the stresses of looking after two young children for a working mother. During a conversation she states that there are some days when she finds it particularly difficult and has to leave the children in the house alone, lock the door and go and have a coffee with a friend. She says she feels much better afterwards.

1.   Would you consider the above actions to be of concern?
2.   Is there any action you could take in these circumstances?

Summary

- There is a clear legal framework that underpins the child protection system.

- The most significant element of the framework is the Children Act 1989. This act provides legal guidance in respect of both public and private legal proceedings. It also provides the local authority with legal duties towards children living in their area who are children in 'need' or 'children at risk of significant harm'. The key elements of the Children Act 1989 are:

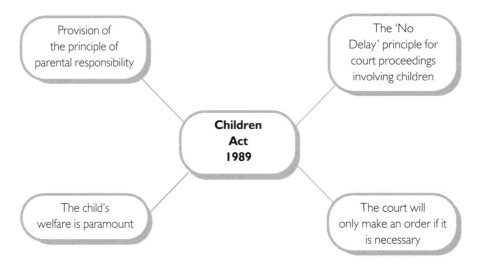

- In addition to the Children Act 1989, the Protection of Children Act 1999 makes it a legal duty to register people who have worked with children and who posed a risk of harm.

- The Human Rights Act 1998 and the Data Protection Act 1998 describes duties to be carried out towards children who are suffering, or at risk of suffering, significant harm.

- The Human Rights Act 1998 stipulates the basis on which governments can intervene in family life.

- The Data Protection Act 1998 guides professionals in the sharing and distribution of confidential information in such circumstances.

CHECKPOINT

1. Name two principles of the Children Act 1989.

2. What are Section '8' Orders?

3. What does Section 17 mean?

4. What is the legal basis for an inquiry into an instance of significant harm?

5. Who has parental responsibility?

6. Identify three important things to remember when giving evidence in court.

7. How do you address a Judge in court?

8. What does Article 8 of the Human Rights Act state?

9. What steps should you take if you are going to dispense with consent when sharing information?

10. What are the two main functions of the Protection of Children Act 1999?

Chapter 3

Recognition of harm

The quality of children's lives can only be improved if we can first identify when children and their carers are having difficulties. If we recognise early on that difficulties are starting to develop, then we may be in a position to provide support services to prevent further problems from arising

We can only do this if everyone in the community takes part and does not consider that making a report of harm is someone else's job. All of us have a responsibility to support vulnerable children and to discuss difficulties with parents and childcare workers.

> "
> *We have to do more both to protect children and ensure each child fulfils their potential. Security and opportunity must go hand in hand. Child protection must be a fundamental element across all public, private and voluntary organisations ... We need to ensure necessary intervention before children reach crisis point and protect children from falling through the net.*
> "
>
> Boateng 2003

It is only by talking to families and other workers that a picture of family difficulties can be put together, in order to plan support.

The aim of this chapter is to help you to recognise when children are at risk of harm. It considers those factors that we need to be aware of when thinking about whether a child's health and development are being affected by the care they are receiving. The chapter also looks at adult difficulties that might have an effect on children's care and what the effects of those difficulties might be.

By putting together worrying signs or behaviours in children with adult difficulties, it is easier to identify the most vulnerable children in our community and those that we should be targeting our resources towards.

Definitions of harm

Our views of what causes **harm** to children have developed, as more evidence from research has been available to inform us. Similarly, our views of what behaviour is considered to be normal and what is considered to be harmful to children have changed over time and been influenced by research.

THINK ABOUT IT

Consider the following extract from *Child Protection Messages from Research* (Department of Health 1995) of a study based on a random sample of children aged between four and sixteen, who had not been abused.

Think about the behaviours and situations and try to estimate what percentage occurred within the families studied.

'Parents report the child definitely or probably as having:

A   touched mother's breasts

B   touched father's genitals

C   drawn genitalia

D   been seen masturbating

E   seen 'simulated' sexual intercourse on films or TV

F   seen pornographic material

G   seen horror movies

H   bathed with parents.'

The figures shown (see foot of page for answers to the above) are intended to do two things: to highlight what we consider is abuse and what behaviours are potentially abusive.

'Overtly sexualised behaviour, such as excessive masturbation, sexual curiosity or touching genitals are sometimes thought of as indicators of abuse. However, the Institute of Child Health study shows that such behaviours do occur in moderation in the homes of 'normal' English families and do not in themselves suggest abuse. What is more important is the context of the behaviour: who else is present; what parents think about it; and the age of the child.' (Department of Health 1995: p13)

What is considered to be abusive behaviour?

Definition of abuse

Abuse is commonly recognised as any behaviour towards a child that causes harm to that child in some way. This behaviour may be deliberate, or the parent may not be aware of the effects of their behaviour. There are, of course, varying degrees of harm to children. The behaviour that we are most concerned about is that which will have a long-term effect on children. It is important to look at the

Answers:

A 63%   **B** 12%   **C** 35%   **D** 67%   **E** 31%   **F** 9%   **G** 30%   **H** 77%

severity of the harm and the length of time that a specific type of behaviour has been exhibited, along with the context (what else is happening in this child's life). There is a difference, for example, between a situation in which a child is living in a caring household, and may have been smacked once or twice, and one in which a child has been severely beaten, or is smacked on a regular basis and the parent or carer frequently tells that child that s/he is 'bad'.

Categories of abuse

Abuse is separated into a number of categories – physical, emotional, sexual and neglect. These are used by social workers and heard at child protection conferences, when discussing the category that a child's name should be placed in on the child protection register.

The definitions below are those used by the Department of Health and described in *Working Together to Safeguard Children* (Department of Health 1999: p.6):

Definitions of Abuse used by the Department of Health	
Category	**Definition**
Physical	Physical abuse may involve hitting, shaking, throwing, poisoning, burning or scalding, drowning, suffocating, or otherwise causing physical harm to a child. Physical harm may also be caused when a parent or carer feigns the symptoms of or deliberately causes ill health to a child whom they are looking after. This situation is commonly described using terms such as fabricated or induced illness. (This used to be known as Munchausen syndrome by proxy.)
Emotional	Emotional abuse is the persistent emotional ill-treatment of a child such as to cause severe and persistent adverse effects on the child's emotional development. It may involve conveying to children that they are worthless or unloved, inadequate, or valued only insofar as they meet the needs of another person. It may feature age or developmentally inappropriate expectations being imposed on children. It may involve causing children frequently to feel frightened or in danger, or exploiting or corrupting children. Some form of emotional abuse is involved in all types of ill-treatment of a child, although it may occur alone.
Sexual	Sexual abuse involves forcing or enticing a child or young person to take part in sexual activities, whether or not the child is aware of what is happening. The activities may involve physical contact, including penetrative (e.g. rape or buggery) or non-penetrative acts. They may include non-contact activities, such as involving children in looking at, or in the production of, pornographic material, or watching sexual activities, or encouraging children to behave in sexually inappropriate ways.

Category	Definition
Neglect	Neglect is the persistent failure to meet a child's basic physical and/or psychological needs, likely to result in the serious impairment of the child's health or development. It may involve a parent or carer failing to provide adequate food, shelter and clothing, failing to protect a child from physical harm or danger, or the failure to ensure access to appropriate medical care or treatment. It may also include neglect of, or unresponsiveness to, a child's basic needs.
Note: for children on child protection registers in England in 2001–2002, the highest number of children in any category is neglect.	

Working definitions of harm

Physical harm

This is a frequently recognised form of harm to children and can lead to physical injuries and in extreme cases, death.

SNAPSHOT: PHYSICAL HARM

Liam is aged two-and-a-half years and lives with his mother. His parents are divorced.

Liam was visiting his father for weekend contact. When his father undressed him, he noticed six red, circular marks on his chest and abdomen. These looked as though they were becoming infected and didn't seem to be of recent origin. Liam's father took him to the doctor straightaway. The doctor made a referral to Social Services. Following examination by a paediatrician, the injuries were confirmed as non-accidental and not consistent with Liam's mother's explanation that whilst walking along the prom in the summer with Liam in his buggy, someone had flicked cigarette ash on him. Liam's mother had no explanation for not going to the doctor's sooner. In this case, the concerns were both the cause of the injuries and the fact that Liam's mother had not sought treatment for them.

Emotional harm

Emotional harm is caused by persistent emotional ill treatment of a child. ('Persistent' means that it keeps happening and goes on for a long time, rather than being temporary or for a short time.) It may involve making a child feel worthless or rejected by ignoring him/her; calling the child names or belittling him/her; continually blaming one child for other children's behaviour; or being emotional; or, as parents and carers, being so involved in their own problems that they overlook their child's needs.

SNAPSHOT: EMOTIONAL HARM

Rosie, aged six months, lives with her parents, Jay and Alana. The couple describe themselves as 'Goths'.

The family were asked to go to a mother and baby home after concerns about their care of Rosie.

Staff at the home became concerned when Rosie was heard crying for long periods, and they had to intervene. When Rosie needed feeding, Alana was heard saying on more than one occasion that she would have to wait, as mummy and daddy were going to have their dinner first, or they were busy. Rosie's parents liked to stay up at night playing war and computer games and liked to sleep in the daytime. Rosie was often awake in the morning, lying in a wet nappy. On one occasion a worker didn't know where Rosie was, as she couldn't see her when she entered the room. Rosie was crying. Her parents indicated that Rosie had been placed on her changing mat under a chair. There was increasing concern for Rosie, who began to present a very 'blank' face, displaying no facial expressions or responses to adults talking to her.

ACTIVITY

In the example above, there are other indicators of possible harm as well as emotional harm, can you identify these and list what category they might come under?

In this case, the parents led an 'alternative' lifestyle. Consider whether your own background might influence your views.

Sexual harm

Sexual harm involves forcing or encouraging children to become involved in sexual activity. Younger children, in particular, may not be aware of what is happening, as the adult may present the activity as a 'game'. Adults may take photographs or digital images of children engaged in sexualised behaviours. Children may have physical symptoms of sexual harm, including sexually transmitted disease.

Neglect

Neglect occurs when a child's basic needs for growth and development are not consistently met. This includes:

◆ physical care: provision of food, bedding, warmth, cleanliness and hygiene

◆ protection from danger: fireguards, stair gates; supervision of the children by appropriate carers, not leaving children alone

◆ taking a child for medical treatment when required or for regular dental care.

Note: an appropriate carer is someone responsible for protecting children from danger and who would know what to do in an emergency. In addition, the carer is not someone who is known to be a risk to children, by having committed previous offences against children.

SNAPSHOT: NEGLECT

The Henry family are: Serena, Michael, Joe and Paul. They have moved home several times, moving between flats. They have, however, stayed in an area where they are close to Serena's family and where Joe and Paul, who have special educational needs, have been able to attend a specialist school where there needs can be met.

Family support services had been asked to visit the family following an anonymous referral about the very poor standard of care being received by the children. The support services visited Serena and Michael three times a week to help them with caring for the children, but the couple did not seem to be interested and did not cooperate.

Staff at the school that Joe and Paul were attending made a child protection referral, after the school dentist had expressed concern about the children's teeth; this was made following his removal of ten of Joe's teeth. The children also displayed sexualised behaviour towards staff and had severe scabies. Family support workers had also become concerned that the care of the children was not improving. They had asked Michael to remove twenty exotic pets from the home, which he had done, but he had again recently purchased a dog and there were pet faeces on the floor each morning.

The children's grandmother said that she was worried about the care of the children and that she had been unable to influence her daughter. She had helped them each time they had moved home hoping for a 'fresh start', but things seemed to be getting worse. She had recently bought the children new toys because she had thrown the last ones away, as they were covered in pet faeces. All of the family slept on mattresses, without bedding, in one room (bedding had been provided and there was another bedroom in the flat).

A report had also been received that an adult with convictions for harming children was looking after the children.

Indicators of harm

Children under the age of 1 year form the most vulnerable group of children; this is because of their physical vulnerability and reliance on adults to feed and care for them and to meet all their needs. Children of this age do not have the physical mobility to move out of the way if an adult is going to hit them and cannot tell anyone that they are being harmed. For example, babies cry when they are hungry, and need to be fed and changed, making their needs known. This behaviour makes them vulnerable to adults who have problems coping with stress and anger and who may hit or shake babies when they cry a lot. Demanding, colicky, difficult babies are more likely to be harmed. This is the age group with the highest incidence of child death.

Emotional harm is caused to children when their needs for care and attention are not met. A baby who receives no stimulation or play may be developmentally delayed.

THINK ABOUT IT

If you have experience of parenting or childcare, you may have had experience of caring for children who are more demanding. Caring for children, who may be colicky or have other difficulties, can be stressful, especially when you are tired. Adults who don't have good coping strategies, who have personal difficulties and who have little or no help with childcare may not be able to cope with this behaviour.

The table below identifies some of the signs and indicators of harm in each category, for two age groups – those children less than 1 year old and those aged 1 to 5 years: please note that these are signs or indicators, based on what has been seen, or observed.

Although some Early Years Practitioners might like a definitive checklist of injuries, recognising harm or potential harm to children is more complex than this and is about more than physical signs. It is important that the broader 'picture' of the child, in the context of her/his family is considered. In most cases, there will be other concerns about the child's care.

Category of harm	Signs and indicators of harm in children	
	Age less than 1 year	Age 1–5 years
Physical	Bruising	Bruising
	Children of less than six-months of age are generally not very mobile and therefore are not prone to getting bruises from falling, for example. Bruising that causes most concern occurs on 'soft' areas of skin, where there is no hard area of bone underneath. These include: ◆ hand or finger marks, caused by a slap ◆ bruises on the ear ◆ pinch marks ◆ facial bruising	As for younger children, but with concern for: ◆ unexplained or frequent black eyes ◆ facial bruising ◆ bruising of ear (pinch marks) and behind the ear ◆ grip marks (on the arms) ◆ slap marks on legs and buttocks (either a general area of bruising or linear marks) ◆ linear bruising: indicating child has been hit with a belt or stick

Category of harm	Signs and indicators of harm in children	
	Age less than 1 year	Age 1–5 years
	Other skin marks and injuries	Other skin marks and injuries
	Cigarette burns Burns and scalds anywhere on the body Bite marks Neglected skin conditions: weeping sores, broken skin, skin that looks infected	Cigarette burns Burns and scalds on the body (on the feet indicates possible 'dipping' in hot water, especially when it occurs on both feet) Any rash-like area that looks like bruising made up of red tiny pin-heads: small broken blood vessels Neglected skin conditions: weeping sores, broken skin, skin that looks infected Flinching or pulling away from sudden movement

➡

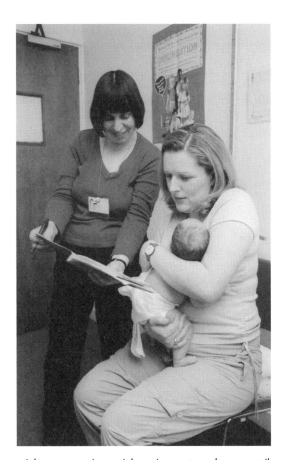

Low weight/not gaining weight or excessive weight gain compared to a centile chart can be an indicator of harm

Category of harm	Signs and indicators of harm in children	
	Age less than 1 year	Age 1–5 years
	General appearance	
	Low weight/not gaining weight/ excessive weight gain There would be concern where a child changes centiles, falling, for example, from the 50th to the 3rd.	Poor weight gain Delayed development
	Skin pale, dark rings around eyes Dirty/smelly Severe or persistent nappy rash Reddened, cold fingers and toes	Dirty and smelly, such that other children comment Ingrained dirt on hands or body, matted hair Clothing not appropriate for the time of year, e.g. thin, short-sleeved cotton dress in winter with short socks Several rotten teeth, decayed tooth stumps Thin, wispy hair
Emotional	Not smiling or reacting to parent's voice 'Blank' expression Poor weight gain Head banging/rocking	Withdrawn, solitary child in older age range of group, sitting or playing alone frequently, talking to self, rocking, head-banging. (It is usual for children as they grow older to engage in more social play, rather than playing on their own.) Behaviour of child is: ◆ aggressive, attention-seeking, hitting other children, verbally abusive to adults ◆ overly affectionate to people outside the family. Some children will 'model' family behaviour in play and this can be important in gaining an understanding of a child's life. Parent seen to be verbally abusive by name calling or persistently ignoring the child

➡

Category of harm	Signs and indicators of harm in children	
	Age less than 1 year	Age 1–5 years
Sexual	Indicators of sexual harm in children of this age may not be apparent, unless there are physical symptoms. These include: ◆ genital injuries ◆ unusual fear in some situations, e.g. bathing, nappy changing ◆ sexually transmitted disease	It is important to be aware that some childhood sexual experimentation is 'normal'. Inappropriate behaviour can include: ◆ Sexual experimentation which is unusual or excessive ◆ Evidence of detailed knowledge of adult sexual behaviour, outside that of his peer group; for example, using toys to demonstrate sexual behaviour, using sexual language outside that of the peer group, having seen adults engaged in sexual behaviour, either on TV, or through witnessing this ◆ Persistent inappropriate sexual behaviour towards adults or other children ◆ Abuse of other children ◆ Genital injuries, vaginal discharge, bleeding, soreness ◆ Sexually transmitted disease ◆ Bedwetting in older children
Neglect	Child being left alone, or with unsuitable carers Child being very dirty and smelly, having severe nappy rash, pale skin colour Inappropriate clothing for the weather Child seeming to be very hungry, e.g. drinking a full bottle with barely a pause and still appearing hungry Poor weight gain Failing to keep medical appointments for check-ups, or specific health needs Poor safety arrangements in the home, e.g. unguarded fire, child being left alone on sofa	Poor weight gain Child often hungry, taking or stealing food from other children Delayed development Physical appearance: ◆ dirty and smelly, such that other children comment, ◆ ingrained dirt on hands or body, matted hair, ◆ clothing not appropriate for the time of year, e.g. thin short-sleeved cotton dress in winter with short socks Several rotten teeth, decayed tooth stumps Thin, wispy hair Child not protected from danger: ◆ left home alone or with unsuitable carers ◆ child found out on street alone away from the home ◆ gates and doors left open

SNAPSHOT: SCARLETT

Scarlett is aged 11 months. Her mother, Eloise, is a heroin user. Neighbours have reported that Eloise goes out and leaves Scarlett on her own in the home, as they have heard the baby crying. Scarlett and Eloise are rarely seen out together. Eloise asks a neighbour to bring Scarlett to nursery, but the neighbour can't always wake Eloise up, even when she hears Scarlett crying. This is now happening more often. Staff at the nursery have reported that Scarlett has a severe nappy rash and looks very pale, and also that she is now smiling less often.

SNAPSHOT: INDICATORS OF SEXUAL HARM

Sara aged three, when playing with two soft toys, placed one on top of the other and said they were 'sexing'.

Billy, aged five, asked a boy if he would like to kiss his tail (penis).

CENTILE CHART

When health visitors weigh children, the measurement is plotted on a 'centile chart'. This shows a child's weight in relation to other children. The 50th centile shows the height and weight that one would expect to find for 50 per cent of children. The 3rd centile shows that only 3 per cent of the population are this height or weight. This chart is used as a guide for assessing children's progress. Children on or below the 3rd centile are likely to be monitored for growth, in case there are any difficulties.

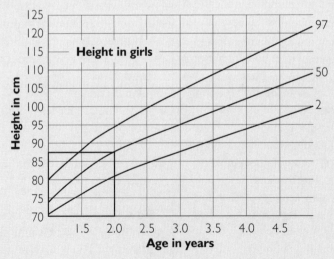

An example of a centile chart – the expected pattern of height gain in girls of 1–5 years

THINK ABOUT IT

Farzaneh, aged nine months, was found to have a bruise across the top of her ear, ending in a solid line. Her mother said she had fallen off the sofa.

◆ Does this explanation seem to match the injury?

◆ Would Farzaneh perhaps have had additional bruises?

◆ What might cause a straight line?

The doctor confirmed that this injury was a result of Farzaneh being slapped on the side of the head.

Note: Any injury to a child's head is particularly worrying owing to the risk of the force of a blow causing brain damage.

THINK ABOUT IT

Shane, aged four years, had a scald mark on his foot like a short ankle sock.

His mother told staff that he had burnt it on the hot tap in the bathroom.

◆ Does this explanation cause you any concern?

◆ What sort of mark would you expect to find if someone had stood on a tap?

This injury suggests that Shane was possibly 'dipped' into a very hot bath.

ACTIVITY

Think of a child about whom you may have some concerns that harmful behaviour has been directed towards them. What are the signs and symptoms that you have seen? Write them down under each category, for example, physical, emotional, sexual, and neglect saying what they are and when you have seen them.

Did this activity clarify your concerns? Did they increase or decrease?

Might you need to seek further advice, or discuss your concerns?

THINK ABOUT IT

Did you fill in more than one column in the above activity? It is recognised that most harmful behaviour towards children falls within two or three categories, rather than just one. In particular, all forms of abuse have an emotional impact on children. We know from many survivors of abuse about the long-term emotional effects, which can also affect adult relationships in the future. For example, many 'survivors' of sexual harm talk about having 'flashbacks'. These are symptoms of trauma.

The following information has been given to Social Services by the local school nursery, who have concerns about these children. Consider the case outlined below. Group the signs and symptoms that would give concern about the child under each category of harm.

The Thomson Family

Theresa and Jeffrey are white British. Becky, Marty and Louise are also white British. Tom is mixed race. Jeffrey is father to all of the children, except Tom.

Family structure		
Mum	Theresa	26 years
Dad	Jeffrey	34 years
Children	Tom	6 years
	Becky	4 years
	Marty	3 years
	Louise	1 year

Tom has been attending the school since nursery. Recently, staff have become more concerned about Tom's behaviour towards both adults and children and in relation to learning.

Tom does not play with other children. He tends to stay on his own, either sitting or running around the playground. Tom recently asked another child in the toilet if he would like to suck his willy. Tom often exposes himself to other children in the class. His speech and language are developed. He often swears in class and seeks attention by shouting out 'rude' words. Tom is on the special needs register. He sometimes touches female members of staff on the breasts, when they are working closely with him.

Tom was previously on the child protection register after receiving a number of bruises, including a black eye that he said daddy Jeffrey had caused.

Becky appears different to the other children in the family in the way that she is dressed and how her parents speak to her. Although she is never dressed in new clothing and her clothing is nearly always dirty, she always wears a frilly party-type dress to school. Becky often hits her brothers, but if they hit her back, their parents physically chastise them, but not Becky. Becky can be aggressive to other children in class when she wants something that they have.

Marty is in the nursery at the present time and staff are becoming very concerned about his behaviour. Marty has very poor speech and a poor vocabulary, which he strings together into phrases of two to three words. Marty is very aggressive towards other children in the nursery and parents frequently complain about this. Marty is fond of his sister and often plays with her at break. Sometimes in class, Marty rocks backwards and forwards. He has a limited attention span of only a few minutes before he loses interest and starts being 'naughty', by annoying other children or running around the classroom. Marty is not toilet-trained and often soils himself at school. He is often dirty and smelly. There was a child protection enquiry last year when Marty was seen by school to have a large linear bruise on his bottom. His parents said this was caused by his falling on the edge of an old sofa in the garden.

The health visitor only occasionally sees Louise, as her parents don't like her visiting and they don't answer the door. Louise has not yet received all her immunisations. Her development is age-appropriate. Louise is often dressed inappropriately for the weather, wearing either too warm or too thin clothes. She is always seen to look grubby.

Jeffrey is aggressive and threatening to both school and other parents if they say anything about the care or behaviour of the children. Theresa says that she can't do anything with the boys. They behave in the same way at home. Other parents are saying that Jeffrey is violent towards Theresa, who was seen with a black eye a few weeks ago.

Adult difficulties that may present a risk of harm to children

Some adults may have personal difficulties that have an effect on the care and protection of their children. They may have difficulties related to mental health or substance misuse, which might cause them at times to overlook, or be unaware of their children's needs or they may become violent, verbally abusive or aggressive.

It is important to state that it should not be assumed that because a parent has personal difficulties, that his/her child will be harmed in some way.

It is likely that the children in such a family might need additional support. Regular contact with and involvement of a partner, relative or friend may provide this. As with other risks of harm to children, there are a number of factors to think about, rather than assuming that there is a definite risk. These include: the type and severity of the difficulty, how often the problem occurs and whether the carer is stable on medication. It is important that we should be alert to considering the needs of children in this situation, as they can be overlooked, when support workers are primarily concerned with adults. Careful consideration should always be given to considering how the parent's difficulties might affect the care of their child.

The aim of the remainder of this chapter is not to make you an expert on adult difficulties, but to broaden your knowledge and understanding of the difficulties that adults face and their impact on the care of their children.

Mental illness

The term 'mental illness' covers a wide range of difficulties. A brief outline of a number of these and their possible effects on parenting is given below.

Depression

Many parents receive treatment for depression, but we are not always aware of this. Some parents receive treatment for a short time and recover, whilst others suffer from a longer-term and more serious condition. Those suffering from depression find it affects all aspects of their life: they may not sleep properly, suffer from a poor appetite, have poor concentration and difficulty in making decisions, low energy levels and feelings of worthlessness. Some parents may become agitated.

Typically, parents suffering from depression may be insensitive to their children's needs and may not respond emotionally to their children's needs.

Post-natal depression causes women to be less responsive to their children and less sensitive to their needs. This may cause difficulties in the attachment between the mother and her child. Attachment difficulties can cause problems both in the relationships between parents and children and also later in life, in adult relationships.

Some parents, when depressed, may have a chaotic lifestyle, with irregular mealtimes and difficulties in controlling their children. (Cox, 1988, from Reder & Lucey p.171)

Schizophrenia

Parents who suffer from schizophrenia may not be ill all the time, as schizophrenia occurs in episodes. During an episode, the carer may lose contact with reality and become absorbed with personal thoughts. They may suffer from one or more of the following:

◆ bizarre delusions, which make little sense to other people

◆ hallucinations, where they may hear voices or see things that do not exist

◆ disordered memory and thoughts and incoherent speech, muttering.

It is most worrying to professionals when children in the family become involved in these delusions, as there is a risk of physical harm.

Billy's mother, Lisa, became ill shortly after he was born. She had experienced one brief episode of illness ten years previously and had not received any ongoing support or involvement with health services. Social Services had no involvement with the family before Lisa stabbed Billy a number of times in the chest, when she 'saw' angels descending from heaven. Lisa thought that these were actually devils and in order to save the world, she needed to kill Billy.

Billy's mum was suffering from a severe mental health condition that had recurred.

Anxiety disorders

Adults suffering from anxiety disorders have irrational feelings of fear. Their feelings are not in proportion to the situation or occur in situations in which someone would not normally be frightened. Some people may have panic attacks.

Self-harming

Some parents who harm themselves may have a psychiatric disorder. Other adults may self-harm in response to stresses and relationship difficulties.

Isobel has three children: Carolyn (15 years), Lynn (12 years) and Jade (3 years). Isobel is married to Pete.

Isobel has a long history of self-harming and has been admitted to hospital on several occasions. The children have found Isobel in the process of slashing her wrists more than once and threatening their father with a knife. When she is ill, she can become abusive and threatening to both Pete and to the children. Isobel has made physical threats to staff working with her and has sought attention by making nuisance Emergency 999 calls. Sometimes, Isobel forgets to collect Jade from the nursery. Carolyn helps with household tasks and collecting Jade from school. Recently, Carolyn has said that she is fed up with Isobel's behaviour and no longer wishes to have her living in the house after she came home and found Isobel trying to hang herself.

THINK ABOUT IT

In the above snapshot how do you think it feels to be Jade, living in this family? What do you think Jade's experience of parenting is? Is it consistent? How are Jade's needs for security, and her other needs met? Are her needs met consistently? Who do you think is meeting her needs?

The family was never referred to other agencies for support until Carolyn told her mother's support worker that she had had enough of her mother's behaviour.

In families where there is a parent with personal difficulties, an early offer of support may help.

Substance misuse

Substance misuse includes the use of both alcohol and drugs.

It affects the way that we behave and our ability to carry out normal everyday tasks. The same drug may affect different people in different ways. Their behaviour or mood may be altered. For example, we are accustomed to seeing people who become increasingly tired after drinking large amounts of alcohol. Other people, when drunk, become aggressive and fight, as observed at night at weekends in town centres.

Substance misuse can affect our everyday behaviour

Categories of drugs

The main categories or groups of drugs are:

◆ analgesics (painkillers)

◆ stimulants

◆ depressants

◆ hallucinogens (perception altering drugs).

For more details and information on the psychological and physical impact of drugs see the reading by Cleaver, Unell and Aldgate (1999).

Domestic violence

Domestic violence tend to be a 'hidden' problem, with adults being reluctant to seek help or make complaints, although in recent years, the number of reported cases has been increasing. Police are also now more active in both providing support and advice to victims of domestic violence and in making incidents known to Social Services.

In most cases of reported violence, the victims are women. There is little information on the experiences of men and, therefore, the examples here relate to women.

Domestic violence involves both physical abuse and emotional abuse. Victims may be punched, kicked, slapped, burnt, kicked, and sexually abused and raped. They are also likely to be verbally abused, sworn at, belittled and humiliated. Their children may also have been involved in their abuse.

Women experiencing this type of behaviour typically suffer from low self-esteem, depression, lethargy, and isolation, and may use medication and alcohol to cope.

Women find it difficult to leave violent relationships, feeling financially dependent, afraid to leave their children and having no accommodation or family support.

Domestic violence may affect a parent's ability to cope with their children's behaviour, and meet their physical and emotional care needs.

Hester and Pearson (1998) discuss the effects of domestic violence in detail in their reading.

The effects of mental illness and substance misuse on parenting

The effects of mental health difficulties and substance misuse vary between individuals. It is, however, important to be aware of effects on mood and behaviour that may lead to harmful consequences for children. An early offer of support to a family at a time of difficulty may assist in reducing harmful long-term effects.

The way in which children's needs are met and the effects on their circumstances and standard of living are considered below.

Health and development

When parents are unwell they may have difficulty in prioritising their own needs. For example, they may not be aware when their children were last fed, or they may not have done any shopping. The same may be true where parents who are misusing substances prioritise their own need to go out and get drugs before the needs of their child.

SNAPSHOT: PHYSICAL HARM AND NEGLECT

Christine is thirty-years-old and lives alone. Her partner, Paulo, who is Italian, had returned to live in Italy.

When Christine's probation officer visited her at home, she could not get a response at the door. She heard baby Natasha crying and entered the house, as the door was usually open. She found Natasha lying on the sofa, crying. Christine returned twenty minutes later, having felt the need to go and get drugs to meet her craving. Christine was placing her own needs before Natasha's but did not see her actions in this way. She felt that if she did not go out, she would become irritable and go into withdrawal. Christine did not see that Natasha had been left inappropriately.

In contrast, Zoe, Christine's sister, who had a long history of heroin dependency, had sought support early in her pregnancy, having previously had two children taken into care. She kept regular appointments and had gone onto a methadone programme in pregnancy. She was managing her dependency in a fashion that did not affect her care of baby Reuben. Zoe only used methadone in the daytime, but, occasionally, Zoe would lapse and would want to use heroin. On these occasions, her partner would take on the full care and responsibility for Reuben.

The child's health and development may be affected if the needs listed in the above snapshot are not adequately met. There may be a risk of neglect and/or physical harm.

Neglect

Parents may not live a 'routine' lifestyle and may have difficulties in keeping regular appointments themselves. Health appointments for regular weighing and measuring may not be kept, and appointments for immunisations may be missed.

A parent may be less perceptive or sensitive to the child's needs and may not notice when the child is unwell, and fail to seek prompt medical treatment as a result. By contrast, some parents suffering from anxiety difficulties may be over-anxious and seek medical treatment when it is not always necessary. Similarly, the child's basic needs and routines may be overlooked.

Children's developmental needs may not be consistently met in a household in which adults have personal difficulties. They may receive a low level of stimulation and age-appropriate attention. Some parents may not be able to recognise the changing developmental needs of their children, as they naturally begin to make progress.

Effects of depression and low mood on parenting

Children living with a parent suffering from depression and low mood may have problems related to the quality of care and relationship with their caregiver. They may have difficulties with physical growth, self-esteem, the ability to form secure relationships and the ability to manage their feelings. These issues are more likely to be serious where the parent's depression affects all aspects of the family's life, where relationships are unreliable, or when the parent's lack of energy leads to neglect. The parent may also feel so irritated by their child's needs that they physically abuse them. (Reder & Lucey 1995: p.171).

Effects of disorganised/inconsistent lifestyle

When parents are suffering from disturbed sleep/are keeping irregular hours and are less able to concentrate, they are likely to have difficulty in organising their lives and providing consistent care for their children.

Young children and babies are vulnerable in that their parents/carers may forget to take them for regular health checks and immunisations, or may leave them alone, or with unsuitable carers. Where parents are over-sleeping or are sedated, they may not wake up in time to take their children to school, or may not realise the time. Children may get themselves up, but may not be old enough to take themselves to school. Children's attendance may be irregular. Likewise, some parents may not arrive on time to collect their children from school, or may regularly appear under the influence of alcohol or drugs when they do collect their children.

There is evidence that children are more likely to have accidents in households in which parents have substance misuse difficulties.

ACTIVITY

Identify a parent and child that you know reasonably well. Before you talk to them, write down the developmental stage that the child is at, in your opinion, and what milestones it is reaching. Think about age-appropriate play and interactions and write these down. Then ask the parent, firstly, about the child's development. Is the parent's view the same as your own? Secondly, ask them about what the child enjoys doing with them. Are their views the same on this? How similar are your views?

REFLECT ON YOUR PRACTICE

Questions to ask yourself when you are beginning to have concerns about a child's care include the following:

◆ Does the parent arrive on time to drop off/collect the child? How often is the parent late?

◆ Does the child attend regularly?

◆ Has the parent or carer made arrangements for someone else to collect the child? If so, has the individual been introduced to you and is it the same person who comes each day?

◆ Have the parent and child suddenly stopped attending, without explanation?

◆ Is the child often said to be ill?

◆ Does the child seem to be excessively hungry?

◆ Is the child clean and dry on arrival, or always brought in a very wet nappy, with nappy rash?

◆ How is the child clothed when brought to you? Is the clothing suitable for the weather? Is the child too warm/too cold?

Does the parent/carer arrive on time to drop off/collect the child?

GOOD PRACTICE GUIDE

- Ask about each child's health and development when placed with you and routinely afterwards.
- Encourage parents to chat with you about their child and to give you information to assist you in caring for them.
- Has the child had all appropriate immunisations? How was the child after having them?
- Do parent and child manage to see the health visitor or have arrangements been made for the child to sometimes be seen at nursery/childminders?
- Ask about the child's development. Is the child doing anything new? Comment on any developments that you have noted.
- It may be helpful to both the child and parent if you ask about anything that you have observed and are concerned about.
- If the parent seems to be looking for advice, make suggestions.
- If parent looks worried, ask if he/she is OK.

Effects of difficulty in controlling emotions

The effects of using alcohol and drugs have been described above. Some parents, when abusing alcohol, experience sudden mood swings. For example, someone may be described as a pleasant, calm person when not using alcohol to excess. When drunk, that individual's moods might swing from aggression and violence to deep depression. Such behaviour can be frightening and confusing to children, especially at a young age. Additionally, there is a risk that younger children, in particular, may be physically harmed when the parent/carer becomes irritated by their behaviour.

Women with opiate dependency have more complications during pregnancy, and neonates may experience withdrawal, irritability, fits and withdrawal symptoms. Unfortunately, these children consequently need extra care and may be more difficult to care for than other children, which places extra demands and more stress on parents.

SNAPSHOT: PHYSICAL AND EMOTIONAL HARM

Carl, aged two-years, was left in the care of his father while his mother went out to a nightclub. Following an afternoon in the pub with friends, Carl's father, Mike, spent the evening drinking. Carl woke up and began crying because he had wet the bed. Mike described seeing a red mist and took off his belt and hit Carl on the buttocks. Mike told Carl's mother what he had done when she came home.

Note: Children in this age group are more likely to be killed or severely injured, according to a study into child deaths, where abuse was confirmed as the main cause: seventy-four per cent of the group studied were under two years at the time of death for the year ending 1994. (Reder and Duncan 1999: p.35)

Effects of domestic violence

There is evidence to suggest that the first incidence of domestic violence for some women happens during pregnancy.

There is a physical risk during pregnancy that the foetus may be damaged by a violent attack. This results in an increased risk of miscarriage, premature birth, stillbirth, brain injury, and rupture of the mother's internal organs, including the uterus.

A key factor in relationships that are violent is control. Some men do not allow their partners to go out on their own, or may limit the time that their partner can go out without them. Others may be worried that their partner's injuries may be seen, or they may tell someone about what is happening to them.

This results in women booking late for antenatal care and not keeping antenatal appointments.

In some cases, women may become so depressed that they don't take care of their own health, which may have an impact on the baby.

SNAPSHOT: DOMESTIC VIOLENCE

Sharon, aged twenty-four, lives with her partner, Billy. Sharon has four children – Cindy, Ellie, Tina and Kieran. Billy is father to the youngest child Cindy, aged two.

Sharon had previously been in a violent relationship with Ellie and Tina's father. Her current partner, Billy, regularly assaulted Sharon when he was drunk. Sharon had on more than one occasion received medical treatment for fractures to her face and bones. Kieran was born ten weeks prematurely, the day following a violent assault by Billy. It was after this incident that Sharon decided to move away from the area and went to live with her sister. Owing to her experiences and fear of Billy, Sharon was unable to see why continuing contact with Billy might be harmful to the children. When Sharon got her own home, Billy 'persuaded' Sharon to allow him to stay in her home three days each week to have contact with the children, as he lived some distance away.

As children grow older, they may begin to 'mirror' adults' behaviour. Generally, this means that children pick up parents' language and copy some of their behaviours. Children also imitate abusive behaviours of adults perpetrating violence. They may call the victim names, or become violent in the same way they have seen adults behaving, as a reaction to something that displeases them. They may also display such behaviours as an 'unconscious' means of protecting themselves, by adapting their behaviour to the situation. They may call the victim names and laugh at her/him. Alternatively, they may mirror the victim's behaviour by developing behaviours that are intended not to displease the aggressor in any way. Both are maladaptive and emotionally harmful behaviours, in that in one, the child is learning aggressive behaviours, and in the other, the child is learning to become a victim.

REFLECT ON YOUR PRACTICE

- ◆ If you are concerned about a woman being a victim of domestic violence:
    - ◆ ask her about her injuries
    - ◆ give her advice about whom to contact for advice and support, and
    - ◆ if you have one, give her a card with details.
- ◆ In talking to a woman, it is important to convey to her that:
    - ◆ it is not her fault.
    - ◆ you are concerned about her and her children.
    - ◆ you are willing to help her by giving information about people who can help.
- ◆ Even if the children are not present in the room when violence takes place, they will still be aware of what is happening and will be affected by it.
- ◆ Be aware of the additional difficulties that children from non-white racial origins might face. For example, some Asian girls may be afraid to leave the family home with their mother, due to fear of being ostracised by the family.
- ◆ Institutional racism may mean that families fear that there may be a lack of action by professionals to help them.
- ◆ Children should not be used as interpreters for their mother, as she may not feel it is appropriate to disclose full details of her experience to her children.
- ◆ The effects on children may be greater where they are subject to racial abuse outside the home and home is not a safe place for them.
- ◆ Remember that children are at risk of physical and emotional harm in a violent relationship and that a referral should be made to Social Services when someone is aware this is going on.

Emotional needs

All children look to their parents for affection, attention and reassurance when they are worried. Children's tendency to seek closeness to particular people and to feel more secure in their presence is called attachment. Children display attachment behaviours in order to have their basic needs for development met. It is recognised that these are not just physical care needs. Without these needs being met, children will develop less secure relationships with their caregivers and, without this, may have difficulties in adult life in developing and maintaining close adult relationships.

Babies develop a secure attachment to their parents and carers when they display warmth and empathy and consistently meet their needs. Through this, children develop a secure base from which to begin to explore their surroundings.

Babies are, therefore, affected both by whether their care needs are regularly and consistently met and also by their parent/carer's responses to them. The moods and behaviours of those around them affect babies.

Relationships between older children and their parents are also affected by their parents' difficulties. Parents may not like to be physically close to their child when they are ill, or they may be less sensitive to their children's needs and problems. In addition, parents are more likely to respond with irritability and anger, or fail to respond at all, than parents who are not affected.

Children learn to adapt to their parents' behaviours in order to get the most from them and develop their own ways of behaving to reduce the harmful effects; even very small children learn to do this.

It is appropriate that children begin to develop some self-care skills as they grow older. However, some children of this age may begin to take on responsibilities in the household beyond their years. For example, when Raman's mother was having a psychotic episode, a neighbour found four-year-old Raman out in the street in his pyjamas at 11 a.m. When she took him home, she asked whether he had eaten. Raman pointed to the bottle of milk in the fridge and a packet of biscuits in a cupboard.

Some children prepare food for siblings before going to school.

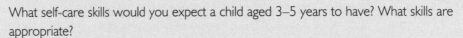

THINK ABOUT IT

What self-care skills would you expect a child aged 3–5 years to have? What skills are appropriate?

Examples may include:

◆ learning to wash and dress independently

◆ helping to tidy.

How do you think a child might feel, getting up on his/her own, without an adult available for advice or to help them?

Self-image/self-esteem

Older children, living with a parent who either has mental health difficulties, or misuses substances, are more likely to have a poor image of themselves and poor self-esteem. This is likely to be because when they are unwell, parents may respond less warmly and may even be verbally abusive towards them, or make negative or insulting remarks. This results in children beginning to view themselves as 'bad'. Some children who are less resilient may think that they are responsible for their parent's behaviour, reinforcing negative views of themselves. Others may have difficulty forming relationships with their peers.

SNAPSHOT: SUBSTANCE ABUSE

Patrick, aged six, lives with his mother, Eileen, and two older sisters. Eileen had a severe dependency on alcohol and when drunk was either unaware of what her children were doing, or was critical and abusive. Patrick began to display aggressive behaviours at school and had some learning difficulties. His speech and language skills were poor.

Where parents are hospitalised or are not living with the family for any length of time, older children are more likely to be distressed than younger children. A serious difficulty as children become older is that they may be ashamed or embarrassed by their parent's behaviour. Children may become unwilling to invite other children to visit and others may be reluctant to visit, which results in their having less social contact with their peers and leading a fairly solitary life.

Some children may begin to show signs of withdrawal and depression, as a consequence. Others may begin to resent their parent's behaviour.

Family and environmental factors

Parental difficulties can affect not only the relationship between the child and his/her parent, but also the circumstances in which the family lives.

Isolation

Many parents receive support from family and friends when bringing up their children. This is referred to as a family's support network. (See Chapter 4 on assessment.)

THINK ABOUT IT

Think about your own support network. Who assists you when you have difficulties? If you were ill, whom could you ask to take your children to school, apart from a partner?

When parents have mental health difficulties, or have difficulties associated with domestic violence or substance misuse, it is possible that these supports have been reduced. This may have happened because relationships became strained as a result of their difficulties and families may feel less able to support them.

SNAPSHOT: DOMESTIC VIOLENCE AND ABUSE

Kay is aged twenty-eight years and has separated from her partner, Paul, after suffering severe domestic violence and abuse.

Kay's partner regularly physically assaulted her. On one occasion, she was verbally and physically assaulted and had her clothing removed in the street by Paul, in front of Connor, aged six. On another occasion, Paul kidnapped both Kay and Connor. Connor has recently begun to swear at Kay and is physically aggressive. Kay has tried to leave Paul several times, but he always came to find her and took her home. Kay's relationship with her mother and her sister deteriorated, to the extent that her sister began to be verbally abusive towards her, and Kay was prevented from returning to the family home to visit her father, who was terminally ill.

Some parents may feel ashamed of their behaviours and may try to conceal them, as they are afraid of other people's reactions.

In the community, parents with difficulties may find it difficult to make friends, especially where their problems are known, e.g. a parent with a heroin problem, who may be referred to as a 'druggie' by neighbours. In this situation, a parent's only friends may be other drug users and opportunities for children to socialise with others may be reduced. Younger children of substance-misusing parents may not have friends outside the home and may be observed to play on their own or invent elaborate 'fantasy' worlds.

Where children are isolated, they are more vulnerable to abuse, as they have fewer contacts with 'trusted' adults that they could talk to if they had concerns.

Positive relationships with extended family members can reduce harmful consequences for children. Where a parent lives with a partner who does not have any difficulties of her/his own, harmful consequences are also reduced, where that partner deals appropriately with the other's behaviour and does not collude with any delusions or anxieties that the parent may have.

Income

Difficulties in the relationship between parents may cause children to be distressed. For example, where there are financial difficulties related to a parent spending money on alcohol or drugs, leaving insufficient money to buy food, pay bills or purchase clothing.

Where the use of alcohol or drugs affects a parent's ability to get up in the morning, the parent may lose his/her job. Some adults resort to stealing, drug dealing or prostitution in order to finance their addiction.

In a household in which drug dealing is a feature, there will be frequent visitors to the family home, some of whom may display aggressive or violent behaviours. Visitors to the home will turn up at all hours of the day and night, disturbing both adults and children. There is also a risk of violence from suppliers, where money is owed.

SNAPSHOT: SUBSTANCE ABUSE

Debbie lives with her children Max, aged 4, and Amy, aged 6. Debbie lives alone but has some support from her parents, who live a few miles away.

Debbie has a serious cocaine addiction and it was rumoured locally that she was involved in prostitution. Her household became increasingly chaotic and neighbours became concerned about the care of her children, Max and Amy. On one occasion, when Debbie owed money to suppliers, she was taken from the house in front of the children and driven off in the back of a van. Debbie was taken to London and dumped in an area known for prostitution, and told not to return until she had earned enough money to repay her debt. Neighbours called Debbie's parents to care for the children, when she had not returned after two days.

It was several months before Debbie returned.

Housing

If a family experiences financial difficulties, it is possible that rent may not be paid and they may be evicted, resulting in the family having to move to less suitable housing.

Property in the home may be damaged by violent arguments or threatening behaviour, or removed due to debts. The home may be dirty and unhygienic, due to parents being lethargic and uninterested in their surroundings or unable to motivate themselves to change.

CASE STUDY:

THE BROWN FAMILY

Below is an extract of a child protection conference report, where the children's parent has a heroin addiction. Try to identify and list difficulties, associated with the parent's substance misuse and the effects that these are having, or might have, on the children's care

Family structure		
Mother	Wendy Brown	36 years
Children	Lee-ann Brown	12 years
	Sherry Brown	10 years
	Tony Brown	7 years
	Alisha Brown	6 years
	JoJo Brown	3 years

Summary of events since last conference

At the last conference, it was reported that Wendy was waiting for an appointment with the substance misuse team. Wendy was pro-active in the plan at this time and had sought an appointment herself, having previously not been interested.

There are still concerns that the children have head lice. Social Services have provided support for this, as other children at school would not play with Sherry. Priority care team support was arranged, as Wendy felt that some assistance with combing the children's hair would be useful. When the team visited, they found conditions in the home to be poor: there were piles of wet washing around, which had mould on it. Wendy said the reason there was so much washing was that the children had been bed-wetting. It was noted that there were no towels, soap, flannels or toothpaste in the house.

On one occasion, Wendy was found making toast on the gas fire in the living room. Because Wendy did not have any money and there was no hot water and inadequate bedding, assistance was provided with bedding.

➡

On another occasion, the social worker was concerned that the front downstairs window was broken and there was glass on the floor and sharp pieces of glass were still attached to the window, within reach of the children.

The children were dirty and the house smelt of urine. The mattresses were all on the floor in the front room. Wendy said that she had moved the mattresses there so that the children were warm. The children appeared happy and related well to their mother. Wendy spoke warmly to each child during the visit.

At the core group meeting it was agreed that Social Services would provide new beds and bedding for the children and some kitchen equipment. The priority care team dealt with the backlog of washing and established some routines for household tasks with Wendy, who has worked extremely hard at improving the condition of the house.

Social Services paid to have the rubbish cleared out of the garden and the rats dealt with, but the problem is starting up again.

School reported that the children's personal hygiene and clothing had improved.

There continue to be concerns about Wendy's drug use. The substance misuse worker is involved with Wendy, but Social Services are concerned that the worker was not aware that Wendy's GP had concerns about her health, related to her drug use.

There have also been concerns about the number of visitors to Wendy's home and some of the individuals visiting the family. Wendy was assaulted by one visitor last week and the children have told the social worker that they don't like it when Ron visits, as he threatens their mum if she doesn't give him money.

Staff at the school are concerned that Lee-ann's attendance has dropped to 43 per cent and that her absence is generally unauthorised. Wendy says that the absence is due to head lice.

There had also been a bullying incident reported to the Bullying Council, when another girl made remarks about Wendy.

The school nurse reported that the standard of care of the children had improved and there were no concerns about their growth and development.

Tony had been referred for a hearing check, but Wendy failed to take him for two appointments.

Alisha had not been seen for a medical assessment. Three appointments had not been kept and when the nurse had visited the home to see Wendy, she was not in. Other health professionals reported that when they visited the home Wendy was never in and it was always someone different caring for the children.

Alisha is reported as being happy in school, but seeks more attention and affection than other children.

Summary

◆ The categories of abuse used by agencies to identify concerns are: physical abuse, neglect, emotional abuse and sexual abuse.

◆ The most frequently identified category is neglect.

◆ There is a wide range of significant signs that suggest that children may be the subjects of harmful behaviour towards them. More than one sign, or symptom, is likely to be observed.

◆ Parents' difficulties can have a significant effect on the care of their children and their ability to meet their needs. These difficulties include mental health, substance misuse, and domestic violence.

◆ Early support and intervention may assist in supporting families and reducing the risk of harm.

CHECKPOINT

1. Briefly describe (a) physical abuse and (b) neglect?

2. How might a parent's heroin dependency affect the care of a baby?

3. If you become aware that a woman might be a victim of domestic abuse, what would you do?

4. What type of parental or carer behaviour towards a child can be considered emotional harm?

5. What are the Department of Health's categories of abuse, as listed in *Working Together to Safeguard Children*?

6. Would you be concerned if a child's weight is below the second centile?

7. If a child's weight did fall below the second centile, what additional information would you look for?

8. What are the main categories of drugs?

9. How might a family's environment be affected by substance misuse?

10. Substance misuse in itself is not necessarily a cause for concern. What areas of a child's care would you be concerned about if a parent was known to be drinking throughout the day?

Chapter 4

Framework for Assessment

This chapter introduces you to the *National Framework for the Assessment of Children in Need and their Families* (Department of Health, Department for Education and Employment & Home Office 2000). It looks at the development of the *Framework for Assessment*, the principles of assessment, and the process of assessing children in need. The aim of the chapter is to explain what the *Framework for Assessment* is, identify how it applies to you as an Early Years Practitioner and to explore how you can contribute to the process.

Background and context

The 2001 Labour Government has a policy aimed at improving the life chances of disadvantaged and vulnerable children through the development of a range of inter-departmental initiatives and partnerships with voluntary and private agencies including SureStart, the Children's Fund, and Pathfinder Trusts.

The government is also committed to improving the provision of services to local communities, both in quality and effectiveness, by requiring local authorities to assess children's needs in both a systematic and timely fashion.

It is the intention in the future to:

◆ improve information-sharing between agencies

◆ establish a common assessment

◆ identify lead professionals to take the lead on cases where children are known to more than one specialist agency

◆ integrate professionals through multi-agency teams.

The government sees information coming to a common 'hub'.

> *A critical task is to ascertain with the family whether a child is in need and how that child and family might best be helped. The effectiveness with which a child's needs are assessed will be the key to the effectiveness of subsequent actions and services and, ultimately, to the outcomes for the child.*
>
> Department of Health, Department for Education and Employment & Home Office 2000

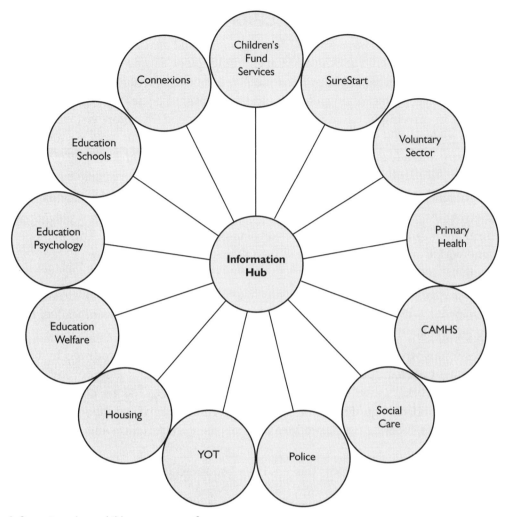

The circles contain: Children's Fund Services, Connexions, SureStart, Education Schools, Voluntary Sector, Education Psychology, Primary Health, Information Hub, Education Welfare, CAMHS, Housing, YOT, Police, Social Care

Information about children can come from many sources

It is intended that a common assessment framework will be developed, rather than using individual agency assessment tools.

This common assessment will be undertaken by any frontline professional, without the involvement of a social worker. North Lincolnshire is currently using such a process (www.northlincs.gov.uk for information).

For those families referred to Social Services, a framework has been developed which helps local authorities to involve families in collecting, recording and analysing information in order to decide what services can best meet the needs of a child and their family.

This guidance links together child protection guidance with assessment, in that children at risk of harm need to be seen as children in need. The wider needs of children and families involved in child protection processes should be considered.

Description of the Framework for Assessment

The Framework for the Assessment of Children in Need and their Families (Department of Health, Department for Education and Employment, Home Office 2000) is a guidance document aimed at professionals and staff who will be involved in carrying out assessments on children and their families. Social Services take the lead role in carrying out assessments of children in need, but there is a clear need for others to assist Social Services in doing this. It is only by all working together to identify and address the needs of children that good outcomes can be achieved. This includes Health and Education services.

The guidance is not a detailed manual, but provides a systematic framework for collecting information, involving the family and other agencies so that this information can be analysed and a clear plan of support produced. This framework can be adapted and used flexibly to suit individuals and circumstances.

The *Framework for Assessment* is a means of avoiding overlapping and duplicate assessments, which is a positive aspect for service users, who sometimes feel that they are constantly providing the same information.

Professionals working in Social Services can use specific forms produced by the Department of Health to assist in collecting information, but it is important to be aware that workers should not simply fill in these forms by asking questions; they are intended to guide the collection of information, involve the service user in the process, record details, produce an analysis of information and a plan based on this.

A pack of materials to support this has been produced in a training pack, called 'The Children's World: Assessing Children in Need ', (Department of Health, NSPCC, University of Sheffield, 2000) which includes questionnaires for service users to complete.

This guidance requires Social Services to regard children in need of protection as children in need and, therefore, all children referred to Social Services for a service are assessed using the *Framework for Assessment* guidance.

How are other agencies involved?

A key aspect of the assessment process is recognition of the contribution of other agencies and professionals who may have had considerable involvement with a family prior to a referral being made to Social Services. These agencies will have an important contribution to make to the assessment, provision of services and review of plans. It provides a way of assessing families that can be understood by everyone involved with them and provides a shared, common 'language'.

Another key aspect is that it provides a common approach to assessment, so that a single assessment can be completed, avoiding duplication and overlaps.

One of the strengths of the *Framework for Assessment* is that it provides a way of collecting information about all aspects of children's lives that clearly identifies needs and develops a multi-agency plan of support that will best meet the needs identified.

Roles and responsibilities of other agencies

The *Framework for Assessment* details the roles and responsibilities in Inter-Agency Assessment of Children in Need. (Department of Health, Department for Education and Employment & Home Office 2000: p.63)

It is the intention of the government to strengthen these roles in current proposals, detailed in *Every Child Matters* (Treasury Office 2003).

Social Services has lead responsibility for assessing children in need and their families, but they also work in partnership with other professionals, who contribute information to the assessment. Social Services plans and coordinates the assessment. Others may share the role in the future.

Day care services

Day care services are increasingly involved in the lives of younger children. Opportunities to access services have improved, and free places are offered to children from the age of three years. Staff who work in day care services are often the first to notice that a family or child may be beginning to experience difficulties. The paragraph below from the *Framework for the Assessment* outlines the role of day care services in assessment.

Day care services may contribute by

♦ Identifying and referring families to social services

♦ Contributing to the assessment of children and their parents or caregivers; sometimes providing a specialist assessment of family relationships

♦ Providing services which support the child's development and strengthen the parents' capacity to respond, through routine work or as part of a child care plan which is monitored and reviewed.

(Department of Health, Department for Education and Employment & Home Office 2000: p.74)

Initiatives such as SureStart and Children's Trusts may assist in a similar way.

Education Services

Education Services are recognised as having a key role to play in supporting children and in observing their development and progress. They are the agency that sees a child most frequently and may contribute significantly to an assessment.

Where a child has special educational needs, or is disabled, schools and other supporting professionals, e.g. educational psychologists will be able to offer advice on the child's development, level of understanding and the most effective means of communicating with the child. This information should be requested before Social Services begin an assessment. Those professionals may assist in seeking a child's views, by working alongside the social worker.

It will also be vital to consult with such professionals when formulating a plan.

(Department of Health, Department of Employment and Education & Home Office 2000: p.71)

Education services play a key role in observing a child's progress

Principles of the Framework for Assessment

The principles that underpin the *Framework for Assessment* are described here in some detail, as they form the basis for the way in which we approach working with children and families. They are key elements of assessment. It is important to consider these in some detail, as they underpin and guide thinking and practice.

The principles are outlined in the diagram opposite:

Principles that underpin the Framework for Assessment

The meanings of these principles in practice are set out below.

Child-centred

One of the key points of the *Framework for Assessment* is that assessments should be child-centred.

This means that:

- it is intended that children are the focus of assessments and the whole framework guides us to consider their needs and how they are met in the context of their family and community

- children should also be actively involved in assessments. We should see and speak to children and take account of their views. It is important to plan and carry out some direct work that is both age-appropriate and takes account of culture and gender

- children should not be overlooked, or become 'invisible' because the needs of their parents and the family situation take up most of the time

- we should think about things from the child's perspective, i.e. what does it feel like to be this child in this family?

Rooted in child development

Another key aspect of the *Framework for Assessment* is child development and it guides the assessor towards considering age-appropriate areas and stages of development. A separate booklet is available for assessing each age group. There are five age-specific booklets, which relate to the following age groups: 0–2 years; 3–4 years; 5–9 years; 10–14 years; and 15 years and over.

The areas of a child's development that are considered in the booklets in detail are:

Health; Education; Emotional and Behavioural Development; Identity; Family and Social Relationships; Social Presentation; and Self-care Skills.

The *Framework for Assessment* helps those using it to pinpoint where a child's unmet needs and areas of greatest need are. Likewise, for children who have specific needs related to disability, the document guides those using it to consider how the child's developmental needs may best be met.

Ecological in approach

This aspect of the *Framework for Assessment* requires us to think about each child in the context of his/her family and in relation to the wider community in which they are growing up.

The parent-child relationship has been a focus for work and research for many years in child psychology and social work.

However, less consideration has been given to thinking about a child in the context of his/her local community, which can also affect their development, both positively and negatively.

For example, most parents are conscious of whether they are living in what they consider to be a 'good' or 'bad' area for their children. Most parents would prefer not to live in an area in which there is a high incidence of criminal activity. They often have concerns that their child may either be a victim, or may become involved in offending. Many parents now try to move to an area where their child can attend a school that has a good record of achievement and is not identified as a 'failing' school. Parents recognise that their child's chances of educational success are better in a 'good' school.

Equality of opportunity

In the context of working with the *Framework for Assessment*, equality of opportunity does not mean that all children are treated the same. It means that we should have knowledge, and an understanding, of particular issues for a child, and work sensitively in addressing these in the context of both the child's family and community.

Working with children and families

Working with children and their families requires working in partnership with parents, in the best way that we can. This involves openness, honesty and consideration of and respect for the views of others.

It is important that we work with families in this way, from the outset.

Building on strengths, as well as identifying difficulties

It is important when contributing to or making an assessment that the assessment is 'balanced', i.e. it looks at both 'good' and 'bad' points. It is very difficult for anyone to read something that just picks out all of our weak points and doesn't recognise any strengths or things that we are good at.

CASE STUDY:

CASSIE, BRAD, LOLLY AND JAMES

Which of the two descriptions of scenarios, given in the table, do you think would be easier for a parent to hear and what might be their reaction to each?

	Cassie, Brad and Lolly's parents are separated and the children live with their father, James.
Scenario A	Cassie and Brad arrive late for school most days. Sometimes Cassie looks as though she has not washed: she still has jam and toast crumbs around her mouth. Her hair has been tied back, but not brushed. Brad's shirt often looks dirty and he also sometimes looks as though he hasn't washed. Neighbours report that they hear loud music and there are often visitors to the home late at night.
Scenario B	James finds it difficult trying to get all the children up in the morning so that he can get the two eldest to school. He has a routine of giving the two eldest children their breakfast, while he gets the baby, Lolly, washed and dressed. James prepares breakfast for the children each morning. Cassie and Brad are quite good at dressing themselves, but aren't so good at brushing their hair and washing; and sometimes James forgets to check them before they leave for school. James does a load of washing every day and tries to put clean clothes out for each of the children at night, but if he forgets, Tom will put on the same clothes he wore the previous day. James feels isolated, as the family are the only black family on the estate and he often invites black friends round to visit and they stay up late talking and listening to music.

1. How would you feel about working with the person who had written Example A?
2. Would you feel differently about the person who had written Example B?

Inter-agency approach

A key aspect of this approach to assessment is that it is based on an inter-agency model, in which other agencies, as well as Social Services, can complete assessments and provide services.

A continuing process, not a single event

This is an important concept in assessments. Assessments should not be static, but should work with families throughout the process to bring about changes. Assessments should be done *with*, not *to* families. We should assist families in looking at where the difficulties in their lives are and looking at where they can bring about changes in their lives.

THINK ABOUT IT

For example, how do you think it might feel to attend an interview, where the interviewer only asks the questions and does not give any assistance when you are 'stuck'? The interviewer then tells you at the end of this process that you have not been successful in getting the job.

Would it feel better if the interviewer asked some additional questions to guide you when you were 'stuck'? In which interview might you perform better and in which might the interviewers establish a relationship with you where you would perform best and illustrate your skills?

Actions and services are provided in parallel with assessment

Services should be provided when we identify a need for them. We should not wait to take action until we have completed our assessment. This means not only providing support when it is needed, but also taking action to protect children if we recognise that they are suffering significant harm.

Grounded in evidence

Each professional discipline has its own knowledge base that informs practice. For example, teaching children requires knowledge of child development and learning processes.

This approach requires us to demonstrate the use of our theoretical knowledge in practice.

The process of assessing children in need

The process of how Social Services carry out an assessment is described below.

Assessment has a number of 'phases', or stages.

These are:

◆ clarification of source of referral and reason

◆ acquisition of information

◆ exploring facts and feelings

◆ giving meaning to the situation, which distinguishes the child and family's understanding and feelings from those of others

◆ reaching an understanding of what is happening, problems, strengths and difficulties and the impact on the child (with the family wherever possible)

◆ drawing up an analysis of the needs of the child and parenting capacity within their family and community context, as a basis for formulating a plan.

(Department of Health, Department for Education and Employment, Home Office 2000: p.29)

In practice, this means,

◆ Collecting information from the person making the referral about where they have got their information from, what the information is and why they are making a referral now.

◆ Gathering information from other people involved with the family and the family themselves.

◆ Talking to the representatives of the agencies involved about their views and what their views are based on. Is it what they have seen themselves, heard from others? How long have they had concerns and what have their concerns been about?

◆ Talking to the family about the referral. What are their views?

◆ Identifying where the views of people are different and why. 'Weighing up' the situation.

◆ Developing a view on the whole family situation, the 'bigger picture'. What is happening in this family: what are their strengths and weaknesses and how do these affect the care of the children?

How is the family involved with other people and agencies? What support do they receive? What are their difficulties?

♦ Coming to a conclusion about the family's needs and developing a plan that clearly relates to their specific needs.

This process of assessment is a 'common sense' one, which recognises the process that we use when making decisions in our own lives.

EXAMPLE OF THE DECISION-MAKING PROCESS – CHOOSING A NURSERY PLACEMENT

The process might be:

♦ Making a decision that you wish to place your child in a nursery

♦ Gathering information leaflets and making telephone calls for information

♦ Making calls and visiting to see what the nursery is like, to see the children at play and to talk to staff about any queries that you have

♦ Talking to friends and family about their views of the placement and whether it will suit you and your child's needs

♦ Evaluating the advantages and disadvantages of the various placements and how they will affect you and your child. For example, establishing whether the 'best' nursery is too far away for you to be able to transport your child, or if there are no extended hours of care offered, and costs.

♦ Making your decision and making plans and arrangements for placement, and getting your child there each day.

Domains and dimensions

The *Framework for Assessment* is based on three systems or domains that relate to developing an understanding of a child in his/her family and community. This system collects information on different types and levels of need that are recognised as having an effect on a child's development. The three domains are:

♦ The child's developmental needs

♦ The parent's or carer's capacity to respond appropriately to those needs

♦ The family and environmental factors

Each domain is related to the others; they are not separate.

For example, in Chapter 3, we considered how parental mental health difficulties might impact on parental capacity (e.g. affecting emotional warmth and stimulation) and thus would impact on a child's development.

The domains guide our thinking about the holistic needs of a child and the extent to which they are met or unmet. They help in addressing the following:

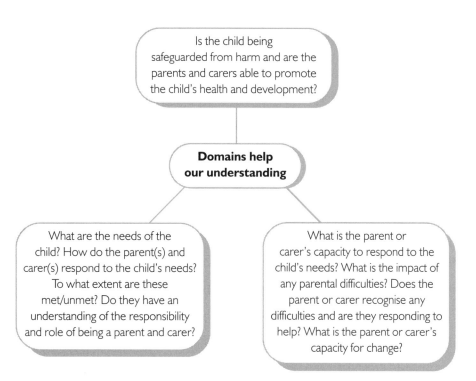

How domains guide our thinking about the holistic needs of a child

Each domain has a number of dimensions, which have been identified as being significant areas in considering the extent to which children's needs are met.

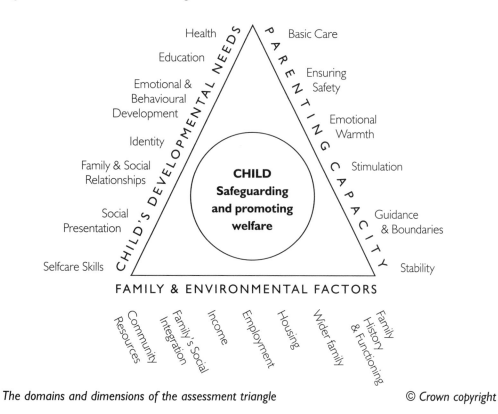

The domains and dimensions of the assessment triangle © Crown copyright

Child's developmental needs

In assessing children's developmental needs, there needs to be a careful consideration of the stage that the child is up to in respect of his/her age and the degree to which the child's needs are met, along with where support may be needed. There needs to be recognition of and understanding of what each child is capable of in order to be able to achieve their potential.

The dimensions of a child's development are listed below.

DIMENSIONS OF CHILD'S DEVELOPMENTAL NEEDS

Health

Includes growth and development as well as physical and mental wellbeing. The impact of genetic factors and of any impairment should be considered. Involves receiving appropriate health care when ill, an adequate and nutritious diet, exercise, immunisations where appropriate and developmental checks, dental and optical care and, for older children, appropriate advice and information on issues that have an impact on health, including sex education and substance misuse.

Education

Covers all areas of a child's cognitive development which begins from birth.

Includes opportunities: for play and interaction with other children; to have access to books; to acquire a range of skills and interests; to experience success and achievement. Involves an adult interested in educational activities, progress and achievements, who takes account of the child's starting point and any special educational needs.

Emotional and Behavioural Development

Concerns the appropriateness of response demonstrated in feelings and actions by a child, initially to parents and caregivers and, as the child grows older, to others beyond the family.

Includes nature and quality of early attachments, characteristics of temperament, adaptation to change, response to stress and degree of appropriate self control.

Identity

Concerns the child's growing sense of self as a separate and valued person.

Includes the child's view of self and abilities, self image and self esteem, and having a positive sense of individuality. Race, religion, age, gender, sexuality and disability may all contribute to this. Feelings of belonging and acceptance by family, peer group and wider society, including other cultural groups.

Family and Social Relationships

Development of empathy and the capacity to place self in someone else's shoes.

Includes a stable and affectionate relationship with parents or caregivers, good relationships with siblings, increasing importance of age appropriate friendships with peers and other significant persons in the child's life and response of family to these relationships.

Social Presentation

Concerns child's growing understanding of the way in which appearance, behaviour, and any impairment are perceived by the outside world and the impression being created.

Includes appropriateness of dress for age, gender, culture and religion; cleanliness and personal hygiene; and availability of advice from parents or caregivers about presentation in different settings.

Self Care Skills

Concerns the acquisition by a child of practical, emotional and communication competencies required for increasing independence. Includes early practical skills of dressing and feeding, opportunities to gain confidence and practical skills to undertake activities away from the family and independent living skills as older children.

Includes encouragement to acquire social problem solving approaches. Special attention should be given to the impact of a child's impairment and other vulnerabilities, and on social circumstances affecting these in the development of self care skills.

Some nurseries and schools now hold annual meetings where parents are provided with written information on their children's expected developmental changes during that year.

Parents might be given some advice and suggestions with supporting their children's needs

CASE STUDY:

MAYA, GOPI AND KIRAN

Maya is twenty-five years old and her family is from northern India. Maya's husband left her and returned to his family in India. Maya's husband worked for a relative, but she now claims benefits, as she does not receive any financial support from her husband, who has not contacted her since he left. Maya's family live in the local area and visit her and the children regularly. Maya is caring for four children under seven years of age. The youngest, Gopi, aged three has cerebral palsy and has some difficulty in walking. Recently, Maya has stopped taking Gopi to hospital appointments and the hospital has made a referral to Social Services. Kiran, aged four, has recently started school and staff have noticed that she does not mix with the other children at playtimes and does not seem to have good comprehension and language skills. She is having difficulty in writing and can only write her name.

1. List the developmental skills that you would expect a child of four years to have. How does Kiran compare? Is she in need of additional support? Would your views be different if Kiran was a white British child?

2. Whom would you speak to about your concerns?

Note: It is important when completing assessments, that stereotypical or cultural assumptions are not made and that you seek support when you are not clear about any aspects of culture or race, e.g. language.

Importance of self-awareness and cultural perspectives

What we see when observing a child is influenced by our own values / attitudes. In undertaking child observations it is important to be aware of the following:

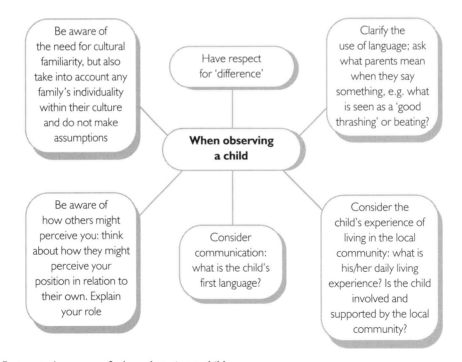

Factors to be aware of when observing a child

Evaluate the system in your workplace for assessing the developmental needs of children. How comprehensive is this approach? Does it address cultural needs and identity? Is the assessment used to inform future work? Do parents receive any detailed reports on their child?

Parenting capacity

The ability of parents to respond to their children's changing needs has a critical impact on their child's development.

The dimensions of parenting capacity are listed below:

DIMENSIONS OF PARENTING CAPACITY

Basic Care

Providing for the child's physical needs, and appropriate medical and dental care. *Includes* provision of food, drink, warmth, shelter, clean and appropriate clothing and adequate personal hygiene.

Ensuring Safety

Ensuring the child is adequately protected from harm or danger.

Includes protection from significant harm or danger, and from contact with unsafe adults/other children and from self-harm. Recognition of hazards and danger both in the home and elsewhere.

Emotional Warmth

Ensuring the child's emotional needs are met and giving the child a sense of being specially valued and a positive sense of own racial and cultural identity. *Includes* ensuring the child's requirements for secure, stable and affectionate relationships with significant adults, with appropriate sensitivity and responsiveness to the child's needs. Appropriate physical contact, comfort and cuddling sufficient to demonstrate warm regard, praise and encouragement.

Stimulation

Promoting child's learning and intellectual development through encouragement and cognitive stimulation and promoting social opportunities. *Includes* facilitating the child's cognitive development and potential through interaction, communication, talking and responding to the child's language and questions, encouraging and joining the child's play, and promoting educational opportunities. Enabling the child to experience success and ensuring school attendance or equivalent opportunity. Facilitating child to meet challenges of life.

Guidance and Boundaries

Enabling the child to regulate their own emotions and behaviour.

The key parental tasks are *demonstrating and modelling* appropriate behaviour and control of emotions and interactions with others, and *guidance* which involves setting boundaries, so that the child is able to develop an internal model of moral values and conscience, and social behaviour appropriate for the society within which they will grow up. The aim is to enable the child to grow into an autonomous adult, holding their own values, and able to demonstrate appropriate behaviour with others rather than having to be dependent on rules outside themselves. This includes not over protecting children from exploratory and learning experiences. *Includes* social problem solving, anger management, consideration for others, and effective discipline and shaping of behaviour.

Stability

Providing a sufficiently stable family environment to enable a child to develop and maintain a secure attachment to the primary caregiver(s) in order to ensure optimal development.

Includes: ensuring secure attachments are not disrupted, providing consistency of emotional warmth over time and responding in a similar manner to the same behaviour. Parental responses change and develop according to child's developmental progress. In addition, ensuring children keep in contact with important family members and significant others.   © Crown copyright

These dimensions have been based on evidence from a number of studies that have explored the link between parenting behaviours and effects on children, or outcomes.

The following areas have been identified as causing children to have behavioural and emotional problems:

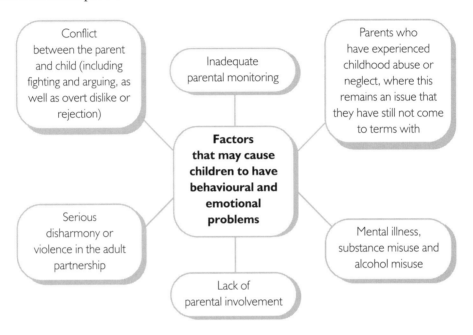

Parenting behaviours and effects on children, or outcomes

However, it is important to comment that other areas of a child's life and other individuals can compensate for the potentially harmful effects of parenting. These provide a 'balance' to any difficulties that may be present. We have discussed this in Chapter 3 in some detail, but compensating factors include situations where:

◆ there is another significant adult or adults actively involved in caring for the child

◆ the child is 'resilient'. This means that some children are more able to cope with difficult experiences than others are

◆ the child is involved in local community activities

◆ school is a positive experience for the child, who enjoys attending it.

Involving families in assessments

It is important that all of those who are part of a family are involved in assessments, as the contribution made by fathers to caring tasks and their role and influence on family life is often overlooked. If only part of a family are considered, then there will be an incomplete picture of family life.

For example, where a new partner has come into a family, there is likely to be an effect on other family relationships.

Where there are concerns about the care of children, further information is collected about their present circumstances and previous experiences, which may be affecting their parents and carers ability to safely and adequately care for their child.

Those working in a childcare setting could assist Social Services in this part of the assessment by providing the following information:

Information that Early Years Practitioner may provide to assist Social Services

---

CASE STUDY:

CHANTELLE

Chantelle has recently moved to a seaside town, leaving her violent boyfriend. The local substance misuse team have recently made a referral to Social Services, as Chantelle is pregnant and the baby is due in four weeks.

The specialist worker is concerned that Chantelle's drug use will affect her ability to meet her child's needs.

Chantelle has not attended any antenatal appointments at the hospital. She lives in a one-room flat and shares bathroom facilities with other residents. When workers call at the flat they often have difficulty in gaining entry. When they do get into the flat, there are often other people present and Chantelle is often asleep. No preparations have been made for the baby, but Chantelle says that she wants to look after it. She has told the substance misuse worker that she stopped using crack-cocaine for the first three months of her pregnancy. Chantelle has told her social worker that she is diagnosed as having hepatitis C and is using crack-cocaine, heroin, painkillers, diazepam, and amphetamines.

1. How might Chantelle's drug use affect the care of her baby?

2. What are the risks to this child?

Family and environmental factors

We all live as part of a community and are involved to varying degrees with others in it. All family members are influenced by the wider family, the neighbourhood and social networks in which they live.

The dimensions of family and environmental factors in the *Framework for Assessment* are detailed below.

FAMILY AND ENVIRONMENTAL FACTORS

Family History and Functioning

Family history includes both genetic and psycho-social factors.

Family functioning is influenced by who is living in the household and how they are related to the child; significant changes in family/household composition; history of childhood experiences of parents; chronology of significant life events and their meaning to family members; nature of family functioning, including sibling relationships and its impact on the child; parental strengths and difficulties, including those of an absent parent; the relationship between separated parents.

Wider Family

Who are considered to be members of the wider family by the child and the parents?
Includes related and non-related persons and absent wider family. What is their role and importance to the child and parents and in precisely what way?

Housing

Does the accommodation have basic amenities and facilities appropriate to the age and development of the child and other resident members? Is the housing accessible and suitable to the needs of disabled family members?
Includes the interior and exterior of the accommodation and immediate surroundings. Basic amenities include water, heating, sanitation, cooking facilities, sleeping arrangements and cleanliness, hygiene and safety and their impact on the child's upbringing.

Employment

Who is working in the household, their pattern of work and any changes? What impact does this have on the child? How is work or absence of work viewed by family members? How does it affect their relationship with the child? *Includes* children's experience of work and its impact on them.

Income

Income available over a sustained period of time. Is the family in receipt of all its benefit entitlements? Sufficiency of income to meet the family's needs. The way resources available to the family are used. Are there financial difficulties which affect the child?

Family's Social Integration

Exploration of the wider context of the local neighbourhood and community and its impact on the child and parents.
Includes the degree of the family's integration or isolation, their peer groups, friendship and social networks and the importance attached to them.

Community Resources

Describes all facilities and services in a neighbourhood, including universal services of primary health care, day care and schools, places of worship, transport, shops and leisure activities.
Includes availability, accessibility and standard of resources and impact on the family, including disabled members. © Crown copyright

---

THINK ABOUT IT

How are you involved with and supported by your family and local networks?

Do you have support? If so, who supports you? Who do you talk to about your problems?

For example, if you were ill and unable to collect your children from school, who might help you?

Try drawing a diagram with yourself in the centre and all those who support you round about.

Some families may not have support available to help them to reduce stresses, for example, where they have had to leave their country of origin. They may be asylum seekers who have experienced trauma in their past. They are likely to have more limited language skills and understanding and, therefore, may have fewer people to talk to about their difficulties.

A wide range of environmental factors can affect family life. Financial difficulties and worries can cause stress, which affects how we behave towards others. Unsuitable accommodation can also be a source of stress.

For those families who have left their home and are living in unsuitable housing, with no support, their difficulties are compounded.

Note: it should not be assumed that all family support is positive; this may also lead to increased stress. Some members of the wider family can cause difficulties because of their relationships and influences.

SNAPSHOT: O'DONNELL FAMILY

Family structure		
Mother	Tina O'Donnell	aged 25 years
Father	Sean O'Donnell	aged 20 years
Child	Sian O'Donnell	aged 9 months

Tina and Sean have been married for one year. Tina had been married before and her husband had been violent towards her. Tina had become very depressed and unable to care for, or protect, her children in that relationship and they had become 'looked after' by Social Services and subsequently adopted. Tina had recently had another child and wished to succeed in caring for her. Tina's care of Sian was good and she had a good relationship with Sean. The only difficulties that Tina needed help in resolving related to her stepfather, Jim, who had physically abused her in the past and who continued to live

➡

with her mother. Tina did not take Sian to visit their home, but was unable for a long time to say that she no longer wished to see Jim. Tina was anxious and constantly asked professionals for advice and reassurance. With support from a community worker, May, a black domestic violence worker, Tina began to go out more in the community and after some months felt able to attend personal therapy sessions. Tina finally made the decision that she no longer wished to have any further contact with either her mother or stepfather again, after her stepfather visited her home in a drunken state and made threats towards her.

Tina felt that she had new friends in the community and could seek support from May's project if she had any concerns.

In the example above, family factors had previously affected Tina's care of her children. Tina had been the victim of abuse as a child and was in a violent relationship. She had become depressed and not able to recognise or meet the needs of her children. In caring for Sian, some years later, Tina was in a supportive relationship and able to work in resolving previous problems so that she was successful in parenting Sian.

This is an example of how one dimension of parenting affects another, i.e. family factors affected parental capacity and the ability of the parent and carer to meet her children's needs: the children from her previous relationship had developmental delay, which was believed to be related to the care and stimulation that they had received.

Involving and focusing on children

In the *Framework for Assessment* the child is located at the centre of the system. It has been observed that children are sometimes overlooked when families are being assessed and that children don't feel involved in decision-making, or do not understand what is going on. Although we are clearly asked to see and speak to children when completing an assessment, it is still possible to overlook this fact, as we spend much of our time speaking to adults. In this way, we can make assumptions both about the care of a child and their views.

For example, *The Victoria Climbie Inquiry* (Department of Health & Home Office 2003) revealed little evidence of anyone talking to Victoria Climbie. There was very little contact with either Victoria or her aunt and it is worrying that where there was some opportunity to talk to her, no one seemed to engage. For example, 'The first agency they visited on leaving hospital was Ealing Social Services' Acton Area office. Kouao left Victoria in the waiting room on her own for over an hour, much to the annoyance of a social worker.'

(Department of Health & Home Office 2003)

'A number of staff who saw Victoria and Kouao together during May 1999 noticed a marked difference between Kouao's appearance (she was always well dressed) and that of Victoria (who was far scruffier).

One worker went so far as to comment that she thought Victoria looked like an advertisement for Action Aid.' (Department of Health & Home Office 2003)

THINK ABOUT IT

How could working with children in completing assessments be improved? How could children's views be explored and considered and how can these be reflected clearly in the assessment report?

Those experienced in play may have a lot to offer Social Services in working with children to ascertain their views.

REFLECT ON YOUR PRACTICE

The knowledge that an Early Years Practitioner working with the child every day may offer in carrying out an assessment includes the following:

◆ Does the child have good communication skills?

◆ Is the child an easy one to engage with, or does it take time for the child to feel able to talk about him/herself?

◆ Does the child prefer to talk or to write and draw?

◆ What are the child's interests?

◆ How long is the child's span of concentration?

◆ Does the child talk about his/her family or home life?

This knowledge and the fact that the Early Years Practitioner has a relationship with the child, may enable you to carry out a piece of work on the child's views, through discussion and play.

Initial and core assessments

This system of assessment recognises that timely responses to children's needs are critical. Before the introduction of the *Framework for Assessment*, there were timescales in place for responding to child protection referrals, but none for responding to children in need and no expectation for planning.

There are now specific timescales for Social Services to respond to referrals and to make assessments. This means that families' needs may be assessed and a service provided quickly, where it is available.

Social Services response to referrals and initial and core assessments	
Timescales	Social Services response
1 day	Within 1 working day of a referral being received, or new information about an open case, there will be a decision about what response is required
7days	An initial assessment should be completed within a maximum of 7 days, but could be less than this, depending on the child's circumstances
35 days	A core assessment should be completed within 35 working days of the completion of the initial assessment, or of a strategy discussion decision to undertake a S47 enquiry, or the point at which new information on an open case indicates that a core assessment should be undertaken

(Department of Health, Department for Education and Employment & Home Office 2000, p. 31)

This process is illustrated on the next page.

In Chapter 3, the process for making a referral to Social Services is described in some detail. A large number of authorities now have a common assessment tool for individual agencies to carry out a simple needs assessment themselves, in order to make a decision about whether a local child in need meeting should be held, or whether it is more appropriate to make a referral to Social Services for an assessment. These referrals will most likely be made where there are child concerns (see Chapter 3 for details).

In this chapter, we are looking at the process of assessment for referrals that have been made to Social Services.

What is an initial assessment?

An initial assessment is defined as a brief assessment of each child referred to Social Services with a request for services to be provided. It should include some, or all, of the elements shown in the diagram on page 104.

'Note: as part of any initial assessment, the child must be seen. This includes observation and talking with the child in an appropriate manner.'

(Department of Health, Department for Education and Employment & Home Office 2000: p.32)

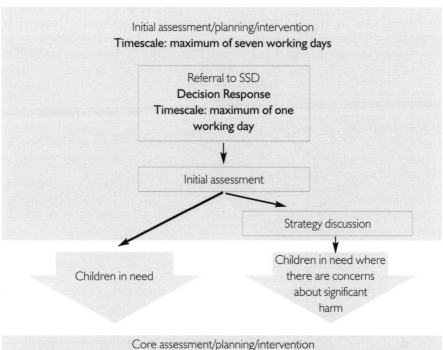

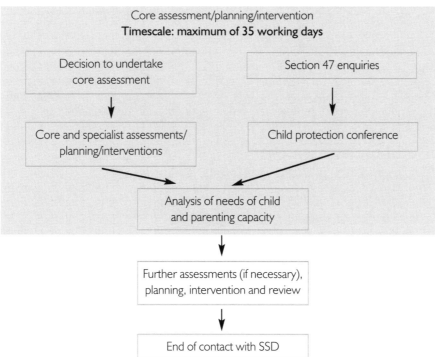

Maximum timescales for initial and core assessments

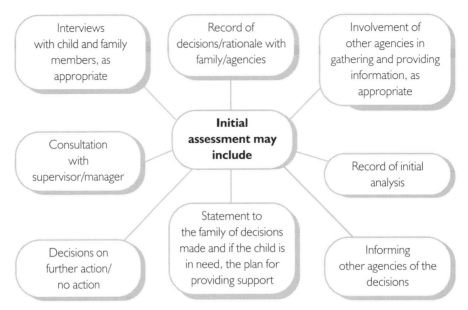

Elements of an initial assessment

> **COMMENT**
>
> It was identified in the report into the inquiry into the death of Victoria Climbie that it was assumed from the information given that Victoria could speak and understand English. When she was interviewed in child protection inquiries, no one established her level of understanding of English and hence she was denied the opportunity to express her pain and fears.
>
> The recommendations of the inquiry have been outlined in Chapter 2, but they clearly impact on the assessment process, requiring careful consideration and planning.

Purpose of the assessment

The purpose of the assessment is to ascertain the following:

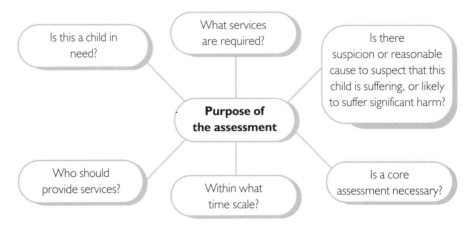

Purpose of the assessment

Note: If at any time during the assessment, there are concerns about a child suffering or likely to suffer significant harm, 'there must be a strategy discussion and inter-agency action in accordance with the guidance in *Working Together to Safeguard Children* (Department of Health 1999: p.34).

In these circumstances, the inquiry and the assessment take place at the same time. While urgent action may be needed to protect a child in the first instance, there should then be a wider consideration of the child's circumstances. The period of initial assessment in these circumstances may be very brief.

The Department of Health has published an Initial Assessment Record, to assist staff in recording information and assessing needs and risks. An extract of this is shown on the next page. Many authorities, however, use their own form, which still reflects the domains and dimensions.

Role of Early Years Practitioners

During the period of assessment, where a person from another agency is actively involved with a family, it may be appropriate for that person to assist with the initial assessment through joint work, where they have:

◆ previously completed a common assessment

◆ knowledge and information about a family

◆ current contact with the family.

That person's involvement will be discussed and agreed with the allocated social worker. Social Services will be responsible for ensuring the completion of the assessment.

At the end of the assessment, a decision will be made about whether:

◆ the child is a child in need and should receive services from Social Services, or whether another agency or group might provide support

◆ the initial assessment should proceed to a core assessment.

◆ a S47 enquiry (child protection inquiry) should be undertaken

◆ a child in need or multi-agency meeting should be held to agree a plan of support.

It is important that when other agencies and those working with children are asked to provide information, it is done quickly. Remember that the timescales for completing an assessment are seven and thirty-five days.

What is a core assessment?

A core assessment is defined as an in-depth assessment that addresses the central or most important aspects of the needs of a child and the capacity of his or her parents and carers to meet them.

Framework for the Assessment of Children in Need and their Families

INITIAL ASSESSMENT RECORD

In completing this initial assessment, if it is known a core assessment will be required, social work staff should make a professional judgement about whether it is necessary to complete all sections before beginning a Core Assessment.

Name

Gender   Date of birth

Address

Telephone number

Date Initial Assessment commenced   Date completed

The Government's Objectives for Children's Social Services (1999) requires an initial assessment to be completed within 7 working days.

Agencies contacted/involved during Initial Assessment (please tick)

G.P. ☐	H.V. ☐	Nursery ☐	E.W.O. ☐	School ☐
Community Mental Health ☐	Community Paediatrician ☐	Dentist ☐	Y.O.T. ☐	Police ☐
School Nurse ☐	Other ☐		Other ☐	

Reason for Initial Assessment, including views of child/ young person and parents/carers

Example of page from Initial assessment record   © Crown copyright

The purpose of the core assessment is:

◆ to gain an understanding of the child's developmental needs and the parents' and carers' capacity to respond within the wider family and environmental context

◆ to provide an analysis of the findings, to inform planning, case objectives and the nature of service provision.

Whilst Social Services is the agency responsible for the completion of the assessment, it will involve collecting information from other agencies or professional individuals, who will either provide information or may provide specialist advice and assistance in completing the assessment, e.g. substance misuse workers, and the developmental assessment of a child with disability.

The Department of Health has published a core assessment record, in the form of a 32-page booklet, which guides those completing assessments. Each age range has its own specific booklet and guides those completing the assessment to consider those specific aspects of care that should be considered within each age range.

Many authorities have modified these documents and may not be using this exact format.

ACTIVITY

Ask your local Social Services department for copies of their initial and core assessment forms.

Specific guidance

The Department of Health has provided specific guidance for use when considering black children and those with a disability.

(Department Of Health, Department for Education and Employment & Home Office 2000)

Disability

The practice guide states that the following should be considered when assessing a child with disability:

◆ direct impact of a child's impairment

◆ any disabling barriers that the child faces

◆ how to overcome such barriers.

The practice guide provides a number of suggestions, to assist in completing assessments.

It is recognised that some sections of the records may be inappropriate to the needs of children who may have profound difficulty, but there is still the capacity to look at whether their progress is at their expected level. The advantage of using this 'social' model of assessment is that it considers the wider needs of a young person, rather than those that relate purely to education or health. For example, what opportunities does the child have for socialisation?

Ethnic minority children in need and their families

The practice guide includes a chapter on assessing black children in need and their families. It does not give specific guidance on other ethnic groups, but the guidance can be transferred. This guidance states that two key questions should be addressed:

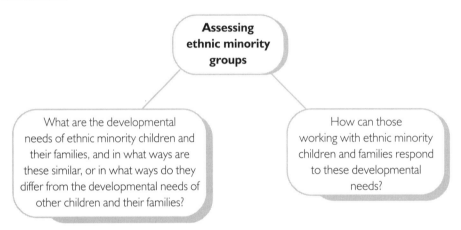

Key questions to ask when assessing ethnic minority groups

It is important that children should not be used as interpreters for their parents in difficult family circumstances, as parents may not feel able to disclose problems in the presence of their children; for example, women suffering domestic violence.

For children from diverse cultural groups, it is important that children and families are assessed in the context of their community and that support and conversely, racism and hostility are considered, the last being an additional source of stress to a family.

Relationships within a family should also be considered. For example, racism may be used as part of a pattern of abuse, by calling children names.

Conclusion of assessment

At the conclusion of the assessment, the parent and carer should be informed in writing (or other means, if more appropriate) of the decisions made and be offered the opportunity for their views on the assessment to be recorded, along with a request for any corrections to be made that are necessary.

Early Years Practitioners and agencies involved with the family should receive a copy of the plan of support agreed, which should clearly identify the action to be taken, by whom and within what time scale.

A review date for the plan should be set and everyone involved in the plan should be invited.

THINK ABOUT IT

A family that you are working with informs you that Social Services are coming to do a core assessment. They ask you what this is.

What would you say to them?

Hint:

◆ What do you think you would want to know about an assessment?

◆ What is it?

◆ Why is it being carried out?

◆ What will happen?

◆ How will you be involved?

CASE STUDY:

THE CROSS FAMILY

The family below was referred to Social Services, who, at the end of the initial assessment, felt that a core assessment would be appropriate.

Social Services have asked for your assistance in providing information to them. The family have given their agreement to this.

This is the information that you have.

Primary School Report on Stephen Cross, aged five years

Family structure		
Mother	Christine Cross	age twenty-four years
Father	Dave Johnson	age thirty years
Children	Stephen Cross	age five years
	Ben Cross	age four months

Stephen joined Moor Road School in 2001, in the Reception class. At that time, he was experiencing some difficulties in adapting to the school routine. He would often leave the classroom in order to draw attention to himself. He spoke to everyone aggressively, had poor concentration and very low self-esteem. He spoke a lot to other children and adults about violence, for example, people being blown up, blood on the ceiling, being attacked by sharks and asking why the windows of the classroom didn't have curtains to keep out burglars. Playtimes were difficult and he was often involved in aggressive activities with other children.

Periodically, Stephen would soil himself.

In his second term at school, Stephen had made a great deal of progress. The class teacher had used a variety of methods and techniques to support Stephen. Stephen's mum came to the school on several occasions to discuss his progress and tried using some similar behaviour management techniques at home, e.g. smiley faces for good behaviour with a prize at the end of the week.

Stephen was more settled in the classroom and he began to show signs of consideration for other children, e.g. letting them play with his toys and bringing them tissues if they were upset. His attention span was still short, but the only time that he still displayed inappropriate behaviour was when he was asked to carry out a specific task, e.g. simple number work or a piece of writing.

During his final term in Reception, Stephen began to need less attention and he settled more into normal school routines and seemed to enjoy school. There were still incidents of fighting with other children in the playground, but Stephen could talk about these. We also spoke to Stephen about his mum's second pregnancy and Stephen began to look forward to the birth.

After the summer holiday, Stephen moved into his Year 1 group, which is a mixed Year1/2, due to the small numbers of children in each year. It was immediately obvious that Stephen's behaviour had regressed. He refused to remain in the classroom, shouted abuse at the class teacher and was not interested in mixing with the other children. Stephen appeared angry and soiled himself on a daily basis. An individual programme was set up for Stephen, which proved to be successful, and his mother, Christine, said that she would like to try the programme at home.

However, after the half term, Stephen's behaviour deteriorated again. His mother said that she could not manage him at home and he had become aggressive towards herself and the baby. She had been too busy to fill the chart in and her partner, Dave, said she shouldn't be rewarding Stephen for bad behaviour and that he should be smacked more often. Christine is unsure about this, as her father used to hit her and she was in care for a time. Dave was too busy at work to come into school and talk about the programme.

Stephen was becoming more difficult to manage and had become angrier. Although he continues to go to school each day, he was not happy about this and argues with his mother in the cloakroom, calling her names. At the end of the day, he refuses to go home with Christine, saying that he hates her and he asks staff to stay with him. This has become a serious issue, and Social Services are now involved.

Stephen has a support assistant in school to work with him, but his behaviour is having an effect on the whole school at times. Christine still speaks to staff at school when asked to, but is no longer keen to try things out. Stephen doesn't do his homework and spends all his time watching TV or on the Play Station. Stephen doesn't get invited to play with other children and Christine feels that other mothers don't like talking to her.

Stephen is well-dressed and generally clean when he comes to school. Christine is looking increasingly tired and says that she doesn't think she can care for Stephen much longer, as she and Dave are arguing all the time about Stephen and she isn't sleeping well.

Tip

Before you write up your assessment it is sometimes helpful to set information under headings where you identify strengths and difficulties, based on your observations. (See below.) This will help you in coming to a view about the family that you are working with.

Example

Child's developmental needs		
	Strengths	Difficulties
Health	Stephen appears well-nourished	Stephen soils himself almost every day
	Stephen is clean and well-dressed	
Education	Stephen attends school regularly on time	Christine says Stephen spends most of his time at home on the Play Station
	Christine attends parents' evenings	Christine tries, but struggles to manage Stephen's behaviour
	Christine always collects Stephen on time	Stephen is behind his peer group in meeting milestones
		Stephen doesn't have friends at school
		Stephen finds it difficult to concentrate and is disruptive
		Christine isn't able to get Stephen to do his homework
		Christine is now saying that she can't cope with Stephen
		Stephen seems to spend time at home on his own
		Dave not involved in the support programme

1. Think about how it feels to be Stephen, living in his family.

2. Try to write a diary of his day, thinking about what people say to him, what he does and how he feels.

THINK ABOUT IT

In working with children, do you routinely consider and talk to children about their views? For example, in the case of Stephen, it would be useful to have some view from him about his home life. This may come from a direct one-to-one or group discussion in the classroom, or may come from a piece of project or written piece of work, such as describing a 'day in the life of…'. This can raise awareness of children who may need additional support.

If you were to start working with Christine in relation to Stephen's behaviour at school, you might explore difficulties by talking to her about life at home and describing situations.

REFLECT ON YOUR PRACTICE

The Home Inventory (Cox and Walker 2002) has been written to assist practitioners. The method described is useful in engaging those being assessed through looking at events in the past week.

The extract below is from *The Home Inventory*.

Were you able to spend any time with…?

What did you do?

Did you play with any toys?

What toys did you play with?

What other toys has … played with in the last week?

Which ones have you played with him/her?

Are there any activities that you have particularly enjoyed doing with…?

For example, did you play any games?

What about number games?

Does s/he know any numbers?

Does s/he know any songs or rhymes? How did s/he learn them?

Does s/he know his/her colours? How did s/he learn them?

(Cox and Walker 2002: p.18)

Summary

◆ The assessment framework provides a common or shared approach to assessment.

◆ There are 10 key principles underlying the Framework. These principles should guide our thinking and practice.

◆ An assessment is a *process*, not an event.

◆ There are three domains that are used to develop an understanding of a child in their family and community context. Each domain is related to and impacts on the others.

◆ Each domain involves a number of different dimensions – each are significant in assessing children's needs.

◆ An initial assessment should be completed within seven working days of a referral being accepted.

◆ A core assessment should be completed within 35 working days of the initial assessment, or of a strategy dicussion decision to undertake a s.47 enquiry.

◆ At the conclusion of an assessment of the family, and those working with them, should receive a copy of the plan of support – with clear actions and timescales identified.

CHECKPOINT

1. What are the principles of the *Framework for Assessment*?
2. Could you explain to someone what an initial assessment is?
3. What are the three domains of the *Framework for Assessment*?
4. What are the dimensions of a child's developmental needs?
5. What are the timescales for an initial assessment?
6. When would a core assessment be carried out?
7. What are the timescales for a core assessment?
8. What is the role of your agency in assessment?
9. How might you be asked to contribute to an assessment?
10. What happens at the conclusion of an assessment?

Chapter 5

The child protection process

In the last chapter we considered in detail how you may recognise behaviour towards children that is harmful. This chapter addresses the questions of when to take further action and what action to take. Typically, those caring for children on a daily basis need to decide whether or not to make a child protection referral. Common concerns are identified in the illustration below.

Common concerns of an Early Years Practitioner

This chapter addresses each of the above questions in detail to give you a clearer understanding of the referral process, the type of information to give and an awareness of what actions Social Services take when they receive a referral.

The areas considered after a referral has been made are:

◆ Initial decision-making

◆ Initial assessment

◆ S17 and S47 inquiries

◆ Strategy discussion

◆ The assessment/inquiry

◆ Concluding the inquiry and planning further action

Responsibility to safeguard children

Government guidance states that everybody shares some responsibility for promoting the welfare of children, as a parent or family member, a concerned friend or neighbour, an employer, staff member or volunteer.

Everybody shares some responsibility for promoting the welfare of children

> *Everybody shares some responsibility for promoting the welfare of children, as a parent or family member, a concerned friend or neighbour, an employer, staff member or volunteer. Members of the community can help to safeguard children if they are mindful of children's needs and willing to act if they have concerns about a child's welfare.*

Department of Health 1999: p.29

Professionals working with children and families

Recent guidance (Department of Health 2003) advises that those who come into contact with children and families in their everyday work, including people who do not have a specific role in relation to child protection, are likely to be involved in safeguarding and promoting the welfare of children in the following three main ways:

You may have concerns about a child and refer those concerns to Social Services or the Police (via your designated child protection teacher in the case of schools)

You may be asked to carry out a specific type of assessment, or provide help or a specific service to the child or family as part of an agreed plan and contribute to the reviewing process (including attending child protection conferences)

Early Years Practitioner

You may be asked by Social Services to provide information about a child or family to be involved in an assessment or to attend a child protection conference. This may happen regardless of who made the referral to Social Services

Early Years Practitioner's role in safeguarding children

Joined-up services

The Children Act 1989 gives every local authority the general duty to: 'safeguard and promote the welfare of children within their area who are in need; and so far as is consistent with that duty, to promote the upbringing of such children by their families.'

This general duty to provide services is the responsibility of the local authority as a whole and does not rest solely with Social Services. Also, government policy is that local authorities, health services and voluntary agencies should work together to provide services for children in need and their families.

In response to government guidance about providing more 'joined up' services, i.e. services working together to provide for local need, many authorities are now developing a multi-agency response to children in need. This means that a referral to Social Services may not be the first thing that happens where there are child welfare concerns, unless they are serious concerns or the possibility that a crime has been committed.

An increasing number of areas now have local multi-agency procedures in place that have a common method of assessing needs by all agencies in the community; and a common procedure where agencies can meet with families to agree coordinated support plans. This support to families may be led by agencies in the community and may not involve Social Services. In cases where there are needs, but not protection issues, a child in need meeting may be held. In cases where there are child protection issues, a S47 inquiry will take place and a child protection conference may be held.

Referrals of concern

Many Social Services departments now have systems in place that allow for referrals of 'concern' to be discussed by local professionals, or referred through a local multi-agency team, or Children's Trust. Social Services generally provide guidance to agencies in assisting them to decide when a child protection referral should be made. The following questions are an example of the type of guidance that may be available in local child protection procedures:

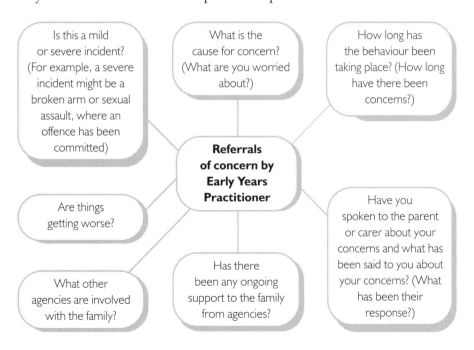

Referrals of concern

By considering the answers to the above questions, it is possible to develop an opinion on the most appropriate response to concerns.

Local authorities and Area Child Protection Committees are now developing guidance for those making an initial judgement about whether a concern they have suggests a need for an immediate child protection inquiry, or whether a local response by those agencies most involved with the family is more appropriate. In these circumstances, a 'child in need' meeting would be held.

ACTIVITY

Make enquiries about local child protection procedures in your area. These are generally available in the local library and most are now available on local government websites. To find these on the Internet, type in the name of your local authority and use a search engine to find its website. Find the heading for Social Services and when you click on this, services for children will then come up, with reference to local procedures.

The case study exercise below guides you through the questions you will need to consider in deciding on the most appropriate response to your concerns.

It is divided into three parts:

◆ Part one describes a number of potentially harmful situations and asks you to think about your views of their seriousness.

◆ Part two provides additional information about the child or family context that further informs your opinion, such as whether you have become concerned very recently by something that has been seen or heard or whether your concerns have been increasing.

◆ Part three considers parents' and carers' responses to concerns and guides thinking on informing parents and carers that a referral is being made to Social Services.

CASE STUDY:

PART ONE

In the examples below, read quickly down the list and circle either 'Yes' or 'No' according to your first thoughts (using the above guidance):

Scenario	Is this situation harmful to a child?	Please circle
1	You become aware that a parent/carer is a heroin addict. The parent/carer starts to arrive late in collecting the child from school. You notice that the child, aged four, frequently looks tired in the mornings and is often hungry on arrival.	Yes/No
2	A four-year-old child, with poor speech, has a burn that covers the whole of his foot up to the ankle. The skin on the sole of the foot is weeping. His mother doesn't tell you about it.	Yes/No
3	A neighbour tells you that a two-year-old child and a three-year-old child are left at home asleep on their own at night while their mother goes to the pub.	Yes/No
4	A mother comes to drop her three-year-old off and tells you that he went into the kitchen on his own the previous night and burnt his hand on the cooker. The mother has a black eye.	Yes/No
5	A three-year-old child has rotten front teeth and fleabites that are infected. The child has poor speech and a vocabulary of about ten words. The family have recently moved house for the third time.	Yes/No

Are any of these a severe incident?

All of the scenarios in the case study are situations that give cause for concern. Some are more severe than others. How might you rate them in terms of levels of concern – low, moderate or high?

No absolute criteria for significant harm

There are no absolute criteria on what constitutes significant harm and it is this that causes difficulties when trying to give specific guidance. Each case is different and it is the whole picture, rather than just a part of it, that really informs decision-making for social work professionals. The role of others who have contact with children is to be aware of indicators of concern and to help social work professionals by providing information that will help them in making a good assessment. This information provides part of the picture and it is only by putting all the pieces together that a clear picture emerges.

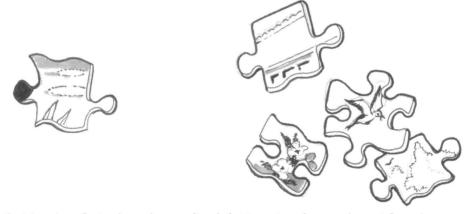

Social work professionals need to see the whole picture in order to make an informed assessment

Harm is sometimes caused by one serious event but is also caused by a series of events and circumstances that build up over time. In both cases, as an Early Years Practitioner, you will probably be aware of other information about the family that you have seen yourself or have learned from other people. In the case of a single event, you may be surprised by what has happened, or you may realise that you have concerns and this event has led you to think that you need to talk to someone about your concerns.

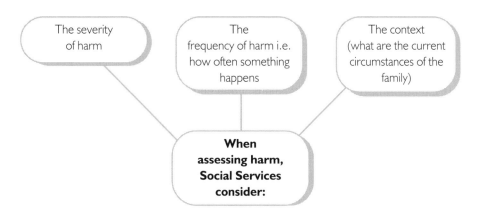

Information Social Services need to consider when assessing harm

CASE STUDY:

PART TWO

In part one of this case study, you were asked to consider situations that give some concern about the care and protection of children in the community.

You are now asked to consider the difference that additional information might make to those same scenarios (adding more pieces to the jigsaw).

Add the following information to the scenarios given in part one of this case study. Does it make any difference to how you see the situation?

	Scenario (recap)	New information
1	You become aware that a parent/carer is a heroin addict. The parent starts to arrive late in collecting the child from school. You notice that the child, aged four, frequently looks tired in the mornings and is often hungry on arrival.	The child's attendance has reduced considerably and other people often come to school to collect the child. On one occasion, the child appeared not to know the person who came to collect her at all. Another parent who recognized the child took her home.
2	A four-year-old child with poor speech has a burn that covers the whole of his foot up to the ankle. The skin on the sole of his foot is 'weeping' and looks very red and inflamed.	The child's mother doesn't tell you about this injury. You have noticed that the child's teeth are brown stumps. His language is very poor. The child's mother has recently had another baby. She lives on her own.
3	A neighbour tells you that she thinks that another parent in the street is leaving her two- and three-year-old children at home at night while she goes to the pub.	The neighbour tells you that she has heard the children crying and the sound of shouting when their mother returns home.
4	A mother comes to drop her three-year-old child off and tells you that he went into the kitchen on his own the previous night and burnt his hand on the cooker. The mother has a black eye.	The mother tells you that she and her partner had an argument the previous night and this is why they didn't see what was happening.
5	A three-year-old child has rotten front teeth and fleabites. Her speech is poor and she has a vocabulary of only three or four words.	The child tells you that her dad keeps five dogs, two snakes and a rat in their room (you know the family all sleep in one room) and that she could only have chips for tea last night because mum didn't have enough money left after buying dog food.

Next steps: sharing your concerns

Where there are concerns these should be discussed with parents, 'unless permission-seeking may itself place a child at risk of significant harm' (Department of Health 1999: p.41).

As an Early Years Practitioner, Social Services will ask you whether the parents have been informed that a referral is going to be made and whether you have sought the parent's consent to make this referral.

THINK ABOUT IT

How do you think a parent/carer might feel when someone from Social Services, whom they have never met before, turns up at their door to talk about their children, without having any knowledge of this? Many parents/carers are worried or become angry when they feel that someone who sees them every day has not told them about their concerns, or that they were making a referral to Social Services. Parents/carers report that in working with agencies, they prefer people to be open and honest with them about problems.

CASE STUDY:

PART THREE

In this part of the case study, parents' responses to an Early Years Practitioner's sharing of concerns are considered.

For a recap of the five scenarios, see previous page.

When you talk to the child's parents about your concerns, this is what they say:

Scenario	Parents' responses to Early Years Practitioner's concerns
1	The child's father says that he doesn't think it matters whether or not the child goes to nursery and might stop going altogether.
2	The child must have gone into the bathroom and burnt his foot on the tap, or he might have got into the bath himself.
3	Mum says that she has a part-time job at the local club and her babysitter left the house before she arrived home, leaving the children alone. She tells you that she was very angry and rang the babysitter and shouted at her.
4	The mother tells you that her partner hit her because she went out on her own. She says it hasn't happened before. The children were staying at her mother's when it happened.
5	The child's parents tell you that they have just moved house and haven't got a washing machine yet. They say that their children eat lots of sweets but the dentist says their teeth will be OK.

2. Do the responses of parents and carers make any difference to what you think? Note where your concerns are increased/decreased.

3. As you can see from the examples above, you may feel comforted after you have spoken to parents and carers, or what they say may cause you more concern.

Making a referral

While you should, in general, discuss any concerns with the family and obtain their agreement to making a referral to Social Services, this should only be done where it will not put a child in a position of increased risk.

If you feel that talking to parents will increase the risk to a child, you may make a referral without agreement, but this is the only time that you can do this.

Such circumstances might include the following situations:

◆ the child is in immediate danger, e.g. requiring medical treatment, or returning to a situation that will place the child at greater risk of significant harm.

◆ there is an allegation that a parent or family member living in the same household is implicated and it is your view that discussing the matter with parents would place the child or other family members at risk of significant harm.

◆ talking to parents might put yourself at risk.

Where you are unsure about what you should do, you should initially speak to your line manager for advice, or if you are not an employee of a childcare agency, you can ring Social Services or there may be a Children's Trust in your area that provides advice. If you are unsure about whom to contact for advice, Social Services can 'signpost' you to the correct contact point.

Levels of concern

An individual who has contact with a child every day is a key person in providing Social Services with information to guide them in planning the most appropriate response to the family. For example, whether an initial assessment is most appropriate, or whether a joint police/Social Services inquiry should take place.

Below is a table showing three levels of concern that might be used by agencies working with children when assessing concerns. This is intended as a guide to you when thinking about what is the appropriate level of concern for a family and whether the outcome should be a local child in need meeting, or a referral to Social Services. Remember, it is always possible to ring Social Services to talk through your concerns.

Note: the table here is intended as a guide only. Social Services, or the assessing agency will make decisions based on the information given, after they have spoken to other agencies and gathered a fuller picture of a family. (See Chapter 6 on assessment.)

Children's needs		
Low concern	Moderate concern	High concern
Physical harm Occasional bruises seen in places where you don't think they would happen accidentally in an older child. Bruising on a child with a physical disability.	Bruising in a baby. Frequent bruises where you wouldn't expect to see them in an older child (e.g. not on knees, shins) Parent fails to give an explanation or gives an explanation that doesn't seem to match the injury	Severe bruising, either large bruises or multiple bruises over a child's body. Handmarks, pinchmarks on ears. Burns Frequent broken bones. Frequent hospital admissions.
Neglect Child does not seem to be gaining weight. Child's physical appearance is poor, e.g. often dressed in the wrong clothing for the weather and not always clean. Baby with frequent nappy rash.	Child is not reaching developmental milestones, e.g. has very limited speech compared to other children. Child is mostly dirty and does not smell clean. Child is not toilet trained when beginning school. Child seen to be hungry.	Child's height and weight have fallen to below the third centile and the child is not putting on weight. Child is not meeting developmental milestones. Concerns as in mild and moderate, plus other children are name-calling and do not play with the child. Child has rotten teeth that require attention. Child is seen to be hungry when arriving at school and takes food from other children
House is often dirty and untidy. The home is not suitable for the number of people living there. There is inadequate heating.	House is always dirty and untidy. There is seldom food in the cupboards. There isn't enough bedding and bedding is often wet and smelly. There is no heating or hot water	Faeces on the floor. Decaying food. Garden full of rubbish. No bedding. No cooker or fridge. Evidence of drug use seen in the house. Large numbers of pets living in the same accommodation as the family. Toilet is broken or leaks.

➡️

Children's needs		
Low concern	Moderate concern	High concern
Emotional harm Parents are critical of the child's behaviour, 'blaming' the child for problems, conflicts and arguments. Ignoring the child when he/she is looking for attention. Lack of boundaries. Parent does not seem aware of child's needs.	Rejection by a parent. Child's behaviour is attention-seeking, difficult, or child is emotionally 'flat'.	Child is displaying difficult and challenging behaviours that are not just a 'phase': ◆ aggression towards others ◆ poor socialisation or isolation ◆ 'blank' expression.
Sexual harm Sexual behaviour that is unusual for a child of a similar age.	Concerns about sexual behaviours towards other children. Inappropriate sexual behaviour.	Adult with history of sexual offending against children living with family. Child seems to have knowledge of adult sexual behaviours and displays sexualised behaviour towards adults or children. Sexual assault.

Parental factors		
Low concern	Medium concern	High concern
Parents involved in substance misuse, who are receiving treatment. A single, isolated incident of domestic violence. Parents with moderate learning difficulty who receive support. Parents with mental health difficulties who are stable on medication and in a supportive relationship. Previous experience of poor parenting. Limited social contacts.	Parents involved in substance misuse, who are not receiving treatment. More than one report of domestic violence, or one serious incident. Parents with moderate learning difficulty who receive no support. Experience of neglect/abuse as a child. Socially isolated/no network of support.	Unstable, chaotic substance misuse. Offending related to drug use. Severe financial difficulties. Repeated incidents of domestic violence. Parents who receive support, but care of the children is deteriorating. Experience of neglect/poor parenting as a child and current or previous concerns of own parenting. Socially isolated/no network of support/negative family support.

CASE STUDY:

THE THOMAS FAMILY

Below is an example of information that an Early Years Practitioner may have about a child and its family.

Family structure		
Mother	Pam	29 years
Children	Bethany Thomas	8 years
	Sam Thomas	7 years

Sam Thomas lives with his sister, Bethany, and his mother Pam.

School report to a child in need meeting

Sam Thomas

Mrs Smale reported that Sam is currently going through the statement of special education needs and saw a paediatrician last week as part of the process. His behaviour is not good and he can be disruptive. He shouts a lot in class and can be rude and disruptive. He can be quite aggressive and there are difficulties in gaining his cooperation. Verbally, he is bright and enjoys one-to-one conversation, but he has a short attention span. He is constantly hungry and has also taken food from other children, although his mother has said that he does have breakfast. He often wets himself at school. The other children tend to pick on Sam, as he often smells of stale urine. The children sometimes arrive at school without coats on days when they should be wearing them.

Bethany Thomas

Mrs Smale reported that Bethany is lovely, helpful, bright and keen to do well, although she can be very withdrawn and does not have many friends. Her appearance deteriorated last term and this was discussed with her mother, as the smell was alienating her from other children. The school provided Bethany with a new sweatshirt, which she is very pleased with. Bethany's attendance at school last term was poor, but has improved a little recently. Bethany does seem to take a lot of responsibility for her brother. Mrs Smales stated that Bethany is a pleasure to have in the classroom, but there are concerns that she is not reaching her potential.

There have been recent reports about the number of drug users visiting the family home and the children's mother was recently assaulted in the home.

1. How would you assess Sam's situation, using the information above?

2. Write down your concerns, as outlined above, under the following headings:

Sam		
Low concern	Medium concern	High concern
	Aggressive	Constantly hungry, taking food
	Learning difficulty Short attention span	Pam's drug use
	Wetting himself. Smelling unpleasant	

When a child tells you they have been harmed

Sometimes children want to tell someone that they trust about what has happened to them. Often children feel able to tell a teacher that they like and feel safe with. Staff are often unsure about what they should say to the child when this happens.

GOOD PRACTICE GUIDE

What to do if a child tells you that he/she has been harmed:

◆ Listen carefully to what the child tells you

◆ Take what they are saying seriously (it is very difficult for children to get to the stage of deciding to talk to someone)

◆ Allow the child to tell you about what has happened, without stopping them or asking for more details. You may repeat things that the child has said in an enquiring tone, where you are not sure about something, but do not ask them any questions

◆ Stay calm and reassure the child that they are doing the right thing in talking to someone. Try not to be negative towards the child and do not suggest that they are not telling the truth or that you do not believe them

◆ Explain to the child that you need to talk to someone else about what has happened and that someone else may need to speak to him/her

◆ As soon as you can, write down as much as you can remember, using the child's words. Try to be as precise as you can. Record the time and date that the child informed you and anything else that you remember that led up to the child speaking to you

Note: The reason for writing this information down is so that there is a clear written record. This information could be used later in Court.

Support services

It can be distressing listening to details of the experiences of children and adults who have been abused at first hand. It may be especially difficult for those adults who may have been abused in the past.

In these circumstances, talk to your manager, or if you do not feel comfortable in doing this, talk to Social Services, who will be able to advise you about local counselling services and how to access them. Your GP will also be able to assist in signposting and accessing services.

A GP can assist in finding counselling services

SNAPSHOT: RAVI

Ravi, aged six years, lives with his mother and father and four siblings.

Report by an Early Years Practitioner

Date 4th March 2003

Time 2.30 p.m.

Ravi arrived at school this morning looking tired. An uncle had brought him to school. Ravi appeared to find it difficult to concentrate in class in the morning. At lunchtime, I was on playground duty, when Ravi came up to me and started to cry. I took Ravi to a quiet corner and sat down with him and asked what was wrong. He told me that he didn't like staying with his uncle and didn't want to go any more. Ravi said that when he was in bed, his uncle had come into the room and had touched his 'privates'. He said he didn't like this and was scared because his uncle had told him that he would get into trouble if he told his mum and dad. He said he didn't know what to do.

I reassured Ravi that he wasn't in any trouble and said that we needed to talk to someone else about this.

REFLECT ON YOUR PRACTICE

◆ Where there is a 'build-up' of concerns, it is sometimes difficult to decide at what point a referral should be made to Social Services. In these circumstances, you may have already spoken to parents about your concerns and suggested a referral to support services to help them. If parents aren't receiving help, or your concerns are continuing, you should talk to someone else.

◆ If you work somewhere where there is a child protection coordinator, speak to that person.

◆ If you are a childminder and have a link worker, speak to him/her. You can ring Social Services for advice.

◆ After you have spoken to someone else, it is important that you should confirm your referral in writing within 48 hours.

◆ Social Services should then confirm receipt of your referral; so if you do not hear from them within 3 working days, contact them again.

◆ It is important to note that in those cases in which there is an early offer of support or intervention, further harm/risk of harm may be reduced. Current government initiatives are aimed at increasing early intervention and inclusive services. Seek support for families from other agencies at an early stage.

THINK ABOUT IT

If you were having difficulties at work, would it help you if someone who noticed this offered you help and advice?

Making a referral to Social Services

Local Area Child Protection Procedures provide guidance on how to make a referral to Social Services and include details of telephone contact numbers. Generally, specific guidance is available for pre-schools, day nurseries, out of school clubs, SureStart, and childminders; this is outlined on the next page.

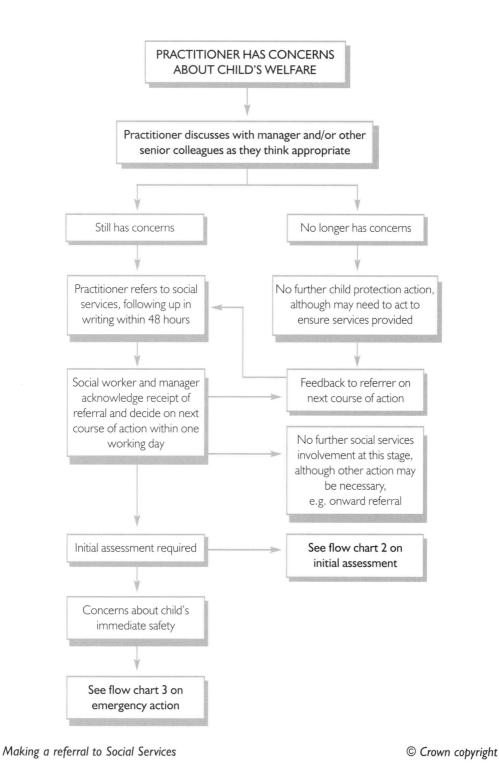

Making a referral to Social Services   © *Crown copyright*

Teaching and non-teaching staff in schools

All schools must have a designated **child protection coordinator**, who has received specific child protection training and will advise and assist staff. This will generally be a senior member of staff in the school, but where possible, should not be the head teacher.

If you have a child protection concern, you should contact the child protection coordinator, who will make a referral on your behalf. If the child protection coordinator is not available, you should contact the head teacher.

If no other senior member of staff is available and the referral is urgent, in that a child has been injured, seriously harmed or is at immediate risk of harm, you should make a referral yourself to Social Services.

If you are unsure about who to contact, ring Social Services or the main council telephone number for advice, saying that you wish to make a child protection referral.

In the event that you feel that a concern that you have passed on has not been referred to Social Services, or no action has been taken by Social Services, and you continue to have concerns, you should contact the Senior Education Officer who has designated responsibility for child protection at the Authority Headquarters.

Child protection coordinator or head teacher

When receiving a child protection allegation, the child protection coordinator or head teacher should make a referral to the local Social Services team, who will liaise on your behalf if the child lives in another area. The procedure is as follows:

- ◆ They should record the date and time of making the referral and follow this up in writing within 24 hours.

- ◆ You should gain a detailed outline of concerns from the person making the referral. At this stage, it is important to provide Social Services with as much relevant detail as possible to assist their decision-making, to avoid misunderstandings and help in planning an inquiry sensitively, with consideration for the needs of those involved. (See the section below on information requested.) Try to be clear about anything that has been seen or said.

- ◆ In the event that the situation is urgent and you cannot contact Social Services, a referral should be made to the local police child protection unit, who offer a specialist service, or if they cannot be contacted, to any police station.

- ◆ If no contact has been made with you and it is nearing the end of the school day and there are concerns about a child returning home, contact Social Services for advice. A child cannot be prevented from returning home unless the Police have sought a police protection order (PPO) or Social Services have an emergency protection order (EPO) where a child is in immediate danger.

Allegations against a member of staff

Where an allegation has been made against an employee of the Local Education Authority (both teaching and non-teaching staff) the head teacher should contact Social Services and the Designated Local Education Authority Child Protection Officer immediately.

This person will then contact Social Services and consider any immediate action that is necessary to safeguard other children.

Where the allegation is against the head teacher, the Designated Local Authority Child Protection Officer should be contacted immediately.

Early Years Education and Childcare, SureStart, out-of-school clubs and playschemes

Each of these schemes should have a designated senior or other member of staff to act as a responsible person for child protection. The designated staff member who has received some training in child protection should follow the steps described above for the child protection coordinator.

Allegations against a member of staff or assistant

Where an allegation is made against a member of staff, or helper, the matter should be reported to the designated member of staff, or most senior person on duty, unless the allegation concerns them, in which case, the person who has received the allegation should either contact Social Services directly, or if known, the local Early Years link worker.

Crèche workers

The most senior member of staff should hold responsibility for child protection and should have attended child protection training. This senior member of staff should report any child protection concerns to Social Services or, where they cannot be contacted, the local Police.

Urgent and non-urgent cases

When Social Services are contacted, they will ask for information to help them to decide whom to contact for further information and how they should deal with the referral. The information that is given will assist Social Services in deciding whether a referral is urgent or non-urgent.

Examples of an urgent and less urgent referral:		
Urgency	Scenario	Reason for decision
Urgent	Samir (aged two) has arrived at nursery today with a large number of bruises on his body, including across the top half of his ear, on both arms and a large bruise on his buttock. His mother said Samir had fallen off the sofa and suffered the bruising as a result. Samir seems unhappy and cries more than usual.	Samir may have sustained further more serious injuries and needs to be assessed by a doctor. A crime may have been committed and the Police may need to make enquiries and gather evidence.
Less urgent	There have been concerns for some time about Carmel and Sean's parents misusing drugs. Sean's father has recently been arrested for drug dealing and other adults, not known to the school, have started to collect the children, who have begun to attend school less regularly and have been arriving late. Sean is often very hungry when he arrives at school. The head teacher has attempted to contact Carmel's mother, but she does not answer her mobile or letters.	There are no serious urgent problems that require an immediate response. The situation has been getting worse over time and needs to be assessed.

Providing information to assist Social Services (or agency taking referral)

It is very helpful for the agency in deciding what to do next if the referrer provides as much of the information given in the checklist below as possible, but do not delay in making an urgent referral when you don't have all the information.

The reason for this is that Social Services need to make a decision on what should happen next and the more information they have, the easier it is to make the right decision.

It is helpful to Social Services if the person making the referral has information about other agencies having contact with the family, so that they can make contact with them.

Social Services rely on other people to help them by sharing information so that they can make a well-informed decision. Your information will assist in developing a picture of a child in relation to their family and community. You may hold a key part of the picture.

THINK ABOUT IT

Where a child has been injured or you have serious concerns about his/her returning home, it is important to make a referral as soon as you can in the day to Social Services. The reason for this is that in circumstances where children need to be interviewed or have a medical examination, it is not good for them if this takes place when they are tired and need to go to bed.

Also, in some circumstances where the risk of harm is so serious that the children should not return home, the children need to be placed with other carers in enough time to allow them to settle in before bedtime. It is not helpful when someone rings up to make a referral after they arrive home from work, if the information was available earlier in the day.

In the event of a child requiring urgent medical attention, he/she should be taken to the nearest Accident and Emergency Department. Staff there should be informed discreetly of your concerns that the child may have been injured as a result of abuse.

Information required when making a referral

The type of questions that Social Services or the agency taking the referral might ask include the following:

a. Your details:

   ◆ Your name, telephone number, and your position, where you work for an agency

b. Factual information:

   ◆ The names of people living at the family home

   ◆ The family's address and telephone number, if known

   ◆ Gender, ethnicity, first language and any special needs

   ◆ Dates of birth of any other children living at that address

   ◆ Who the birth father of the children is and whether parents are married.

   ◆ What school the children attend

   ◆ Who the family GP is

   ◆ The names of other agencies that you know are involved with the family

c. What your involvement is with this family:

   ◆ How long you have known them?

   ◆ How you know them?

   ◆ How often you see the children/parents/carers?

   ◆ Reason for making contact now

d. What are your concerns?

  ◆ Is it something that you have seen or heard? (You will be asked for details: please give as much accurate information as you can. If you don't know, say so)

  ◆ Is it a serious incident that needs urgent attention today?

  ◆ Is it based on something that someone else has told you? If so, who is it and how are they connected to the family?

  ◆ Has this concern happened due to an incident today, or have you been concerned for a while?

e. Who do you believe is causing harm or is a risk to the child?

f. Are you concerned about other children in the family?

g. Have you spoken to the parent or carer about your concerns and informed the parent or carer that you are making a referral?

h. What would you like to happen as a result of your referral?

A pro-forma of this information, like the one on page 239, may be available in your agency to assist you in making a referral.

SNAPSHOT: REFERRALS TO SOCIAL SERVICES

The two scenarios outlined below demonstrate the difference between a poor referral to Social Services and and a better quality one

Example of a poor quality referral to Social Services	Aisha, aged 12 months, has recently started nursery. This morning, staff noticed a large purple-reddish mark on her lower back/buttocks. They did not ask the child's mother about this but are ringing to make a child protection referral. The referrer doesn't know who the child's health visitor is.
Example of a better quality referral to Social Services	**Referral made by school child protection coordinator** **Urgent referral:** due to child having an injury. **Information from the class teacher, Mrs Rashid** Kiera, aged six, has attended school for the past year. **Reason for making a referral now** This morning, Kiera arrived at school with a black eye. Her mother said that her elder brother swung a door back against her, hitting her in the eye. The teacher noticed another large bruise on Kiera's arm later in the day when she took her cardigan off and asked her what had happened. Kiera said that Brendan (her mother's partner) did it because she dropped her milk on the carpet. **Who is risk of harm from** Mother's partner, Brendan

➡

> **Previous concerns /background**
>
> Over the past month or two, a change has been noticed in both Kiera and her mother's appearance and demeanour. Kiera had become more withdrawn and often looked unkempt and tired in the mornings. Her mum, who was previously very chatty to other mums and staff, had started to avoid conversation. Staff at school have heard that neighbours have been complaining that they often hear Brendan shouting in the evenings.
>
> Kiera has a younger sister, aged three, who has just started school in the nursery. Like Kiera, they have also noticed a change in her appearance and demeanour in the last two months.
>
> **Consent**
>
> Permission has not been sought for making this referral

Note: When a referral has been made to Social Services, it should always be confirmed in writing within 48 hours.

At the end of the discussion, you should be clear about who will be taking what action or that no further action will be taken.

REFLECT ON YOUR PRACTICE

In the snapshots above, staff had started to see some deterioration in the children's appearance two months before one of the children was assaulted.

- If you notice changes that give you concern, it may be helpful to talk to colleagues about what you have noticed and ask them if they have noticed anything.

- When you see the child's parent or carer, you could ask to speak in private and share your concerns. Explain that you have noticed a change in the children, talk about the changes you have seen and ask if anything is wrong; or if something has changed and the parent or carer is having difficulties in coping, suggest that a referral for some support may help them.

- Write down what you have seen, along with details of your conversation, including the date and the parent or carer's response.

- If the parent or carer doesn't wish to receive any further support and you remain concerned about the care of the children, you should inform them that you are making a referral to Social Services.

- Remember, that you should always inform parents or carers of this, unless doing so will place the child at increased risk of significant harm.

Social Services' response on receiving a referral

When Social Services receive a referral, they have 24 hours to decide what action should be taken.

There will be a decision made within one working day about what action should be taken and this decision will be recorded.

Possible responses or outcomes of the referral are:

◆ Provision of advice or information

◆ Referral to another service or agency

◆ No further action

◆ Completion of an initial assessment

◆ S47 inquiry (Social Services will make an initial assessment under S17 of The Children Act, except where the referral is so serious that there needs to be an immediate S47 inquiry.) If a crime might have been committed, the Police should be involved at the earliest opportunity, in order to make investigations.

Note: where a referral is received from a member of the public, personal information about referrers, including anything that might identify them, should only be shared with the family or other agencies with the agreement of the person who has made the referral. (Department of Health 2003: p.8)

Section 17 of the Children Act

Section 17 of the Children Act defines a child in need as follows:

Section 17 of the Children Act defines a child in need as follows:

He is unlikely to achieve or maintain, or to have the opportunity of achieving or maintaining, a reasonable standard of health or development without the provision for him of services by a local authority under this Part

His health or development is likely to be significantly impaired or further impaired, without the provision of such services

A child in need

Section 17 of the Children Act also requires authorities to safeguard and promote the welfare of children in their area and to support this by providing a range of services to children in need.

First steps: initial assessment

Knowledge recap (for a full discussion see Chapter 4).

The matters to be addressed in an initial assessment are:

◆ What are the needs of this child?

◆ Are the parents able to respond appropriately to the child's needs?

◆ Is the child being adequately safeguarded from significant harm, and are the parents able to promote the child's health and development?

◆ Is action required to safeguard and promote the child's welfare?

An initial assessment is a 'brief' assessment of each child referred to Social Services to determine:

◆ whether the child is in need

◆ the nature of any services required

◆ and whether a further, more detailed core assessment should be undertaken.

The assessment should be completed within a maximum of seven working days from the date of the referral. (Note: children at risk of harm are also children in need.) The initial assessment period may be very brief where the criteria for a S47 inquiry are met. An initial assessment should be carried out in all cases, but the assessment period may be very brief where the criteria for a S47 inquiry are met.

An initial assessment may be carried out where:

◆ An assessment is needed to clarify information about a child where child welfare concerns, rather than child protection concerns, have been expressed.

◆ No harm or injury is suggested or where it is suggested that there is a need for support, without which the care of children in the family would deteriorate.

The process of assessment

Following an initial assessment, Social Services should decide on the next course of action, following discussion with the child and family, unless such a discussion may place a child at risk of significant harm.

Suspected actual or likely significant harm

What is a S47 inquiry?

The local authority has a duty to make inquiries into allegations of harm under S47 of The Children Act 1989. This is referred to as the statutory duty of the local authority. It is something that they are required to do by law.

The authority shall make, or cause to be made, such inquiries as it considers necessary to enable it to decide whether it should take any action to safeguard or promote the child's welfare in the following circumstances:

(a) where a local authority is informed that a child who lives, or is found, in its area is:

   ◆ the subject of an emergency protection order; or

   ◆ is in Police protection; or

(b) where a local authority has reasonable cause to suspect that a child who lives, or is found, in its area is suffering, or is likely to suffer significant harm.

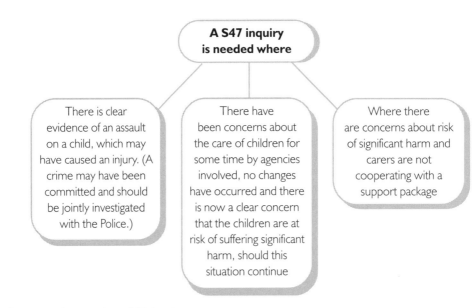

A S47 inquiry is needed where

There is clear evidence of an assault on a child, which may have caused an injury. (A crime may have been committed and should be jointly investigated with the Police.)

There have been concerns about the care of children for some time by agencies involved, no changes have occurred and there is now a clear concern that the children are at risk of suffering significant harm, should this situation continue

Where there are concerns about risk of significant harm and carers are not cooperating with a support package

Situations that require a S47 inquiry

SNAPSHOT: LEE TAN

Lee Tan is seven-years-old and lives with his father, stepmother and two half-sisters, aged two and three years.

Lee arrived at school one morning and looked to be in some pain and discomfort. The teacher had previously noticed that Lee had been looking pale and unhappy. At break-time, Lee's teacher asked him if anything was wrong.

Lee became very tearful and said that his father had hit him with a stick the night before and his back hurt. He pulled up his shirt to show eight linear red lines across his back. The teacher reassured Lee and said that they needed to speak to someone else about this. Lee said that he was frightened of his father and he did not want to go home.

The teacher spoke to the child protection coordinator and a decision was made to contact Social Services, who consulted the police and it was agreed to hold a joint S47 inquiry, following a planning meeting.

What happens in a S47 inquiry?

The decision to proceed to a S47 inquiry is taken jointly by Social Services and the Police. A senior police officer (Detective Inspector) and a senior social worker or team manager will make a decision on whether an inquiry should be carried out jointly with the Police, or by Social Services alone. Where there are concerns that a crime may have been committed, Social Services will inform the Police at the earliest opportunity and it is good practice for the inquiry to be carried out jointly with the Police. Similarly, the Police will inform Social Services of any alleged offences when there is a child victim. The inquiry will involve staff who have received specific training in interviewing children. (This is called Best Evidence training – see Chapter 2.)

The two agencies will make a decision about how to proceed in the best interests of the child. The possible outcomes of the discussion are shown in the diagram below:

Possible outcomes of discussion in S47 inquiry

Strategy discussion

Where the outcome of the consultation is that a S47 inquiry is required, a strategy discussion should take place. The decisions reached and actions planned will be recorded.

A strategy discussion may take place as a meeting, or in some cases by telephone. The discussion should be used to plan enquiries under S47 in more detail.

The people who may be involved in a strategy discussion are shown in the diagram below:

People who may be involved in a strategy discussion

The purpose of a strategy discussion is to:

◆ share information

◆ agree on the need for any immediate action

◆ decide who should be interviewed, by whom, where, for what purpose and when

◆ consider race, ethnicity, special needs, disability, gender issues and how these can best be addressed

◆ consider the needs of other children in the family, or other children who may have contact with the alleged abuser

◆ identify who has parental responsibility and who may give consent for the interview and any necessary medicals

◆ decide on an appropriate person to support the child during the inquiry process, if this is not to be a family member

◆ consider and decide the level of family participation in the inquiry. Exceptionally, it may be appropriate for suspected child victims to be spoken to without parental consent, e.g. where the child might be coerced into not saying anything, if police evidence might be destroyed or where the child did not wish his/her parent to be present and were felt to be competent to take that decision.

Obtaining parents' permission

The permission of parents or carers should be sought before discussing a referral about them with other agencies, unless permission-seeking may itself place a child at risk of significant harm. Exceptionally, a joint inquiry/investigation may need to speak to a suspected child victim without the knowledge of the parent or carer.

This meeting:

◆ should not make assumptions that a disabled child is unable to be interviewed or give credible evidence; and

◆ should carry out a full assessment of the child's abilities and needs, e.g. accessibility, chosen method of communication, specialist interpreter.

Example of a strategy meeting

Strategy Meeting held in respect of Lee Tan

Date of Meeting: 2/4/03

Attendance : Mrs Bird, teacher; Ms Dunn, School Child Protection Coordinator; Tariq Raman, social worker; Detective Inspector Nagra, Detective Constable Fox.

Discussion

Mrs Bird informed the meeting that Lee had told her that his father had hit him during the previous evening with a stick. He had eight linear red marks across his back that looked to confirm what Lee was saying. Lee had told her that he was afraid of his father and did not want to go home.

Mrs Bird said that she had been concerned about Lee for a couple of months. He had been looking very pale and tired and was having difficulty in doing his homework. Mrs Bird knew that the family has a takeaway business and that Lee sometimes sits in the shop, as he has been seen there. Lee does not look well cared-for. His clothes are often grubby and he does not smell clean when he comes to school.

Mrs Bird said that the family originated from Hong Kong, but she was not clear about which dialect they spoke. She was aware that Lee's father speaks some English, as do his stepsisters. Lee speaks and understands English well.

Ms Dunn said that the eldest of Lee's sisters had just started school. In contrast to Lee, she is well dressed, clean and appears happy. Her language skills and vocabulary are limited and her teeth are brown. There are no particular concerns about her.

➡

The social worker reported that the health visitor had not seen the girls for some time, but there had been no concerns.

Actions agreed:

- an interview with Lee should take place immediately
- inquiries to be made about a translator, independent of the family, but from a similar cultural background.
- Lee will be supported in the interview by his teacher
- inquiries should be made by Social Services about other family members
- parental consent will not be sought, due to the possibility of the child not wishing to see his father and the child being coerced into not saying anything
- inquiries should be made concerning the other children in the family and their safety considered
- Lee should be medically examined.

THINK ABOUT IT

If a strategy meeting was being held on a child that you know well, what information would you have that might be useful to those interviewing the child?

Information that might be useful in a strategy meeting

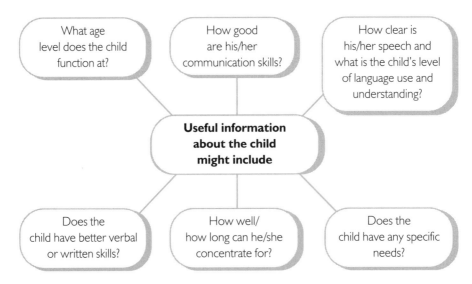

Information about a child that might be useful in a strategy meeting

Interviewing children

Where there is a need for an interview to take place, with a view to gathering evidence for criminal proceedings, *Achieving Best Evidence in Criminal Proceedings* (Home Office 2001) will be followed as a recognised guide for all video-recorded, evidence-gathering interviews with children. (See Chapter 4.)

Child protection inquiries should be carried out in a way that minimises distress to children and ensures that families are treated sensitively and with respect.

Parents and carers should be given the appropriate information (usually a leaflet produced by the local ACPC), which explains the inquiry process and their rights in this process. Separate leaflets are generally available for children and adults.

After the inquiry

At the conclusion of inquiries, a decision will be made about the need for further action. The decision-makers in the Police and Social Services may make this decision jointly. The following information will be discussed in order to make a decision:

- all information gathered during the initial and core assessment to date
- details of the allegation of harm / suspected harm
- content of the interview with the child and any interviews with the child's parents and carers
- child's views
- outcome of any medical examinations
- interviews with any other significant persons
- where the person against whom the allegations have been made is now living.

See the flow chart on page 149 which outlines what happens after a strategy discussion.

Outcomes of a S47 inquiry

Concerns not substantiated: this means there is little or no evidence to support the allegations

In cases where concerns are not substantiated, it is probable that the family would benefit from support to meet needs identified in the course of the inquiry

It may be appropriate for a child in need meeting or a family group conference to take place. In these circumstances, the meeting will be convened by Social Services.

The family should be informed by Social Services, in writing, that child protection concerns are not substantiated. This is particularly important to families who may feel that they are still 'under investigation' without this. Many families have commented that their distress caused by the inquiry does not cease until they receive this letter, as there has been no 'ending' for them. This letter should acknowledge the distress that may have been caused by the inquiry.

Consideration should be given to the child's/family's need for further support or counselling and information given about possible sources of support.

The person who made the referral should be informed of the outcome by the social worker in the case.

Concerns are substantiated and the child is assessed not to be at continuing risk of significant harm

There may be cases where there are substantiated concerns, but it is agreed between the agencies involved and the family that a plan for ensuring the child's safety and welfare can be agreed without the need for a child protection conference. Parents and carers may acknowledge difficulties and request support or be willing and able to work in partnership with agencies.

Family circumstances may have changed and it may be judged that there is no further risk of harm, e.g. where the perpetrator has permanently left the household.

In these circumstances an inter-agency meeting should be held to agree a plan of support. This may be called a child in need meeting.

A decision not to proceed to a child protection conference when a child has been significantly harmed should be taken carefully and recorded. If those agencies most involved with the family have serious concerns that a child may not be adequately safeguarded, they can request that a conference is convened.

Concerns are substantiated and the child is judged to be at continuing risk of significant harm

Where those agencies most involved with the family judge that a child may continue to suffer or be at risk of suffering significant harm, Social Services should convene a Child Protection Conference. (See Chapter 6)

SNAPSHOT: CINDY, KELLY, CHLOE, KARL AND RAMAN

The case study below describes a case in which agencies had been working with a family for some time, providing support. At a review meeting to discuss the child support plan, agencies felt that the plan was not improving the care of the children and that there were issues of significant harm. A decision was therefore made that a S47 inquiry should be carried out.

Family structure		
Mother	Cindy	age 30 years
Children	Kelly	age 11 years
	Chloe	age 8 years
	Karl	age 6 years
	Raman	age 2 years

Relevant others

Cindy and her children have very little contact with their extended family, even though Cindy's mother and sister both live in the area.

Cindy's main source of support is her friend, Mrs Suleman, who Cindy calls 'nana' . This support is very limited, however, as Mrs Suleman is physically disabled and has limited mobility.

Background

The family has been known to Social Services for a number of years.

April 2002

The current social worker became involved with the family.

Concerns at the time were:

◆ the children were being bullied and teased at school due to the smell of stale urine, dirty clothes and head lice

◆ Karl and Raman were bed-wetting and bed linen was not being changed: soiled, wet bedding was being used

◆ Cindy reported Chloe was having temper tantrums

◆ Problems with Housing Benefit

A child in need meeting was arranged and a support package was agreed with Cindy.

This included a volunteer visitor (Homestart), a referral to Children's Health services for advice with behavioural difficulties and bed-wetting, advice from Welfare Rights and laundry assistance.

Conditions in the home seemed to improve, as beds were stripped and soiled bedding was put into plastic bags.

Arrangements were made for rubbish to be removed from the garden, so that children could play.

June 2002

A fire occurred in the family home. Allegations were made that Cindy had left the children at home alone when the fire started, but this information could not be confirmed. This resulted in the family living in temporary accommodation for two months, firstly with a friend in over-crowded conditions and then in bed and breakfast accommodation.

September 2002

The family returned to their home. Assistance was given with refurnishing and the provision of clothing and bedding. Volunteer visits continued, but there was never anyone at home when the volunteer called. Cindy said that she didn't need any support.

Professionals visiting the home have seen the children regularly and all have commented on the positive relationship between Cindy and the children.

November 2002

Children were seen walking home in the rain, not wearing coats, and Karl was seen playing outside without wearing shoes. A report was received from school that the younger children had turned up without wearing underclothes.

Three health appointments for Karl and Chloe were not kept. Cindy said that she had lost the appointment cards.

A child in need meeting was held and a new support plan agreed, with Cindy agreeing to take the children to health appointments and Social Services continuing to provide a laundry service. Money for additional clothing for the children was provided.

December 2002

The volunteer visits ceased in this month due to there repeatedly being no one at home when volunteers called. Three referrals were made to Social Services, two by members of the public and one by Housing Services, alleging that Cindy was using illegal drugs and had various known drug users in her home. Cindy denied this.

January 2003

Referral made to Social Services out of hours team that Cindy had been assaulted in her home and Kelly had been involved. A S47 inquiry took place, as Kelly had been injured.

A referral was received from a member of the public who had seen Cindy in a public house injecting heroin in front of her children. Cindy was in the company of other adults and Kelly was seen to be caring for the younger children.

Decision to progess to S47 inquiry.

Joint decision-makers agreed there should be a Social Services alone inquiry.

When the social worker visited, Cindy was in the company of a friend and both appeared to have been using some substance. The house was dirty, with mouldy food on the table and little food in the cupboards. There was a strong smell of urine in the house and the beds had not been changed. Raman was strapped into a pushchair crying, wearing a soaking nappy, and Cindy did not know where the three elder children were.

Joint decision-makers agreed that a child protection conference should be held.

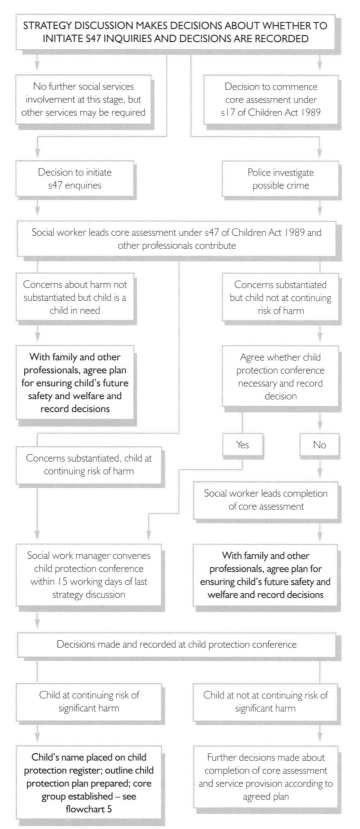

Flow chart showing what happens after the strategy discussion   © *Crown copyright*

REFLECT ON YOUR PRACTICE

In the previous case, an Early Years Practitioner will have attended child in need or multi-agency meetings. In such situations, it is useful to bring a written report on the family along to the meeting.

You should contribute to the discussion and to the plan. If any actions are allocated to you, it is your responsibility to report on these in the next meeting.

Summary

In this chapter, the child protection process has been described in detail. Here, the questions illustrated at the beginning of this chapter are used to summarise key points.

Question: What should I be worried about?

Answer:

◆ a single serious injury or incident of harm to a child. This may be an incident of physical or sexual harm

◆ a build-up of concerns about the care of a child

◆ a deterioration in the care of children to a standard that gives cause for concern: this may be sudden or happen over time

◆ involvement with an adult who may present a risk to children.

Question: Should I make a referral?

Answer:

◆ Everybody shares some responsibility for promoting the welfare of children, as a parent or family member, a concerned friend or neighbour, an employer, staff member or volunteer.

◆ Harm is sometimes caused by one serious event but is also caused by a series of events and circumstances that build up over time. In both cases, you will probably be aware of other information about the family from what you have seen yourself or from other people. In the case of a single event, you may be surprised by what has happened, or you may think that you have started to have concerns and this event has led you to think that you need to talk to someone about your concerns.

◆ It is important to note that in those cases where there is an early offer of support or intervention, further harm/risk of harm may be reduced. Current government initiatives are aimed at increasing early intervention and inclusive services. Seek support for families from other agencies at an early stage.

Question: Do I tell the family anything?

Answer: You should discuss your concerns and seek consent to making a referral, but this should only be done where such discussion would not be contrary to a child's welfare and place them at increased risk.

Question: How do I make a referral?

Answer:

School employee: refer to Child Protection Coordinator, or the Headteacher

Child protection coordinator: refer to the local social services team. Provide as much information as possible when making the referral.

Nursery staff, SureStart, childminders: the person with responsibility for child protection or the most senior member of staff on duty should contact the local Social Services, or where they can't be contacted, the Police.

Question: What happens when a referral is made to Social Services?

Answer: Social Services will make a decision within 24 hours about whether the referral should be followed as a child in need assessment, or a S47 inquiry. In the case of a serious concern, the initial assessment period will be very short. Social Services will gather information from other agencies to inform their assessment. Where there is to be a S47 inquiry, this may be carried out jointly with the Police, or by Social Services alone. An inquiry is carefully planned by Social Services and the Police, who consult other agencies as part of the planning process. Children in a family where there is a S47 inquiry will always be seen and spoken to.

Following a visit to the family, or interview with the child(ren), a decision will be made about further action and will consider the need for support services and whether a child protection conference should be held.

CHECKPOINT

1. Who has responsibility for safeguarding children?
2. How might you become aware of harm to a child?
3. What are the signs or indicators that a child aged six years is being neglected?
4. Who, in the setting that you work in, should make a referral to Social Services?
5. What information might you be asked to provide when making a referral?
6. When should you not seek parental consent to making a referral?
7. What is the difference between an initial assessment and a S47 inquiry?
8. Who might be involved in a strategy meeting?
9. What information could you provide to a strategy meeting, in your current role, that other agencies would not have?
10. What are the possible outcomes of a S47 inquiry?

Chapter 6

The child protection conference and the child protection register

As an Early Years Practitioner you may be invited to a child protection conference at some point during your work. This chapter provides basic guidance about what you can expect at a conference, what the conference does and what your role is in the process.

A child protection conference (often referred to as a case conference) takes place following a S47 inquiry, if there are concerns that a child may be at continuing risk of significant harm. The conference is organised by Social Services, but it is a meeting that takes place on behalf of the Area Child Protection Committee and is chaired by an independent person. It is an inter-agency meeting that represents the new agency body overseeing child protection locally.

The purpose of the conference

The purpose of the conference is for family members and professionals to meet to:

◆ share information

◆ consider any risk there may be to the child's safety and welfare

◆ identify any actions to safeguard children.

The conference will consider all the children in the family, not only the child that has been the subject of the inquiry. This is based on the principle that if one child in a family is felt to be at risk then other children living in the family may also be at risk.

The only decision a conference can make is whether or not a child's name is placed on the child protection register. Everything else is a recommendation that the family is encouraged to work with, although the family can choose not to do so. If the family refuse to carry out the recommended work, Social Services will need to assess whether or not the risk to the child is increased and any further action should be taken to ensure the child's safety, i.e. legal proceedings.

Conference participation

Parents and key family members, as well as any children (that are of an appropriate age and understanding) are invited to the conference.

Professionals who have a role in the child's life will also be invited.

The invitation itself should usually include some or all of the following information:

- names and dates of birth of any of the children and family members
- date, venue and time of the meeting
- chairperson and contact details
- names and professions of other persons invited.

Attendance at conference is not compulsory. However, if you have been invited it will be because the social worker thinks you will have a contribution to make towards considering the safety of the child, as a result of your professional role.

If for any reason you are unable to attend the conference you should contact the chairperson and send your apologies. It is good practice to send written information if you are not able to attend the meeting, and to bring a written report with you if you are.

A case conference will decide if a child's name is to go the Child Protection register

THINK ABOUT IT

Consider when you have had to attend a meeting or important interview. What would have helped you to make it a positive experience?

Quoracy

The conference is an inter-agency meeting and, as such, most local authorities will have a quoracy policy. The policy will usually state that a conference can only proceed if there are representatives of at least two agencies besides Social Services, e.g. Health, Police, and Education. This principle is to ensure that the meeting reflects the composition of the ACPC on whose behalf the meeting is taking place. It ensures the conference is truly an inter-agency responsibility and not a Social Services meeting. You may find that you attend a conference and it is cancelled because it is not quorate. Try to be patient if this is the case.

You should send your apologies to the chairperson and not the social worker if you are unable to attend. This enables the chairperson to check if the meeting is going to be quorate. If the number of apologies received beforehand indicates that the meeting is not going to be quorate, the chairperson can rearrange the meeting with some notice if needs be, without causing too much inconvenience. This averts a situation arising in which everyone, including the family, arrives at the meeting to discover that it cannot go ahead because of a professional's non-attendance.

Safety issues

You should contact the chairperson if you feel threatened or worried about how family members will react to your attendance, or the information that you will be providing at conference. Sometimes professionals have to share information that is difficult for family members to hear but is necessary to the consideration of safety for the children. The chairperson can make arrangements for your contribution to be made in a safe way.

People can be nervous about attending a conference, not least the family. However, the chairperson will seek to ensure a supportive environment in which everyone has a contribution to make and all contributions are valued.

Exclusion of family members

There may be some parts of the conference when it is necessary to exclude some or all of the family members. The chairperson will make this decision.

The reason for this exclusion may be that a professional present needs to share third-party information. For example, it may be necessary to consider medical information about the father in a conference that is confidential to him and cannot be shared in front of mother, unless the father gives his permission. Or there may be a Police record in respect of the mother that cannot be shared with her partner or extended family present.

If you think you may have third-party information that is confidential to one of the family members you should contact the chairperson before the meeting to discuss it.

The chairperson may also exclude family members if there is a threat of violence or intimidation toward other family or professional persons present.

The conference process

The conference has three distinct stages, which are as follows:

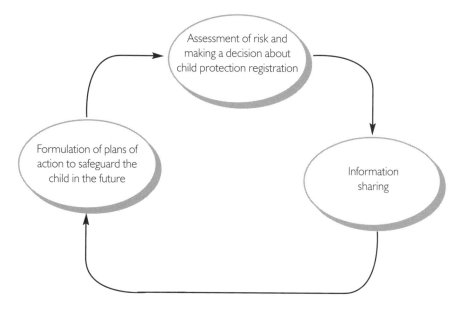

Stages in the conference process

Agenda

Different local authorities will have a different format for the conference meeting. Some will be more formal than others. However, here is an outline agenda, components of which you will probably be able to identify at any child protection conference you take part in.

Outline Agenda

Third party information

This includes information about a person or child not named as subject to conference but that is relevant to the consideration of risk to a child who is being discussed in conference.

Statement about purpose of conference/ground rules

The chair will remind all participants of the purpose of the meeting and the ground rules that members are expected to abide by, e.g. information remaining confidential and focusing on the welfare of the child.

Introductions

You will be given the opportunity to state your name, profession and nature of your involvement with the child and family.

Apologies

Notification of those persons invited who are not able to attend.

The chair will decide if it is important that the persons who send their apologies should receive a copy of the minutes. For instance, GPs are often unable to attend all conferences, but it is still important that they know what is happening for their patients and so the chair may decide to forward a copy of the minutes. If you do not send your apologies, however, it is unlikely you will receive a copy of the minutes.

Social work report/summary

The chair will usually begin by introducing the social worker's information about the nature of the concerns that have led to the conference taking place. This may involve the chair summarising the main issues from the report or the social worker speaking to the meeting, highlighting the important points for discussion.

Family information

It is good practice to involve family members in the conference as soon as possible. This is to help them become more comfortable with speaking in such a forum and to provide a balance through being allowed to answer the concerns early on in the meeting. The chair will often then return to the family for responses following each agency's information.

Information from agencies

All professionals present will provide their part of the information.

Summary

When all the information has been shared, the chair may take the opportunity of summing up the meeting to highlight the issues discussed and help professionals when they are considering whether or not registration is appropriate.

Decision

Professionals will be asked their view on whether there is a continuing risk of significant harm and consequently a need for child protection registration. The chair will seek to obtain a consensus view regarding this decision.

Child protection plan

Once a decision has been reached, and if it is one of registration, the chair will work with members of the meeting to draw up the outline of a child protection plan. Throughout the meeting, as information is shared, people usually identify work that should be carried out and actions that can address particular problems. At this point in the meeting, the chair will draw these actions together and make formal recommendations for work to be completed. This may include actions for many of the professionals present.

Core group

The chair will identify membership of a core group to ensure implementation of the plan and regular review of its progress.

Review conference

The Chair will usually set a date for the next child protection conference.

Information sharing

The child protection conference is a mechanism for professionals to work together to offer support to families in order to safeguard children. It is only by sharing information amongst family members and professionals that it is possible to begin to provide safety for children. Each person will hold pieces of information that when drawn together provide a truer picture of family functioning and the risk, or lack of it, to children. It is rather like each person holding a piece of a jigsaw that when put together provides the whole picture.

An Early Years Practitioner has an important part to play in this process. Outside of the family you will probably be one of the few people to see the child on a regular basis. Therefore, you can provide information that builds a picture over time about the child and you will know the child well enough to describe any changes in presentation or behaviour.

CASE STUDY:

CHILD PROTECTION CONFERENCE

Consider the following examples of reasons for convening a child protection conference:

Scenario 1: Louise	Louise is a two-year-old child, who has reportedly been left alone on many evenings while her mother is at the pub. Louise's development and growth appear normal, although a health visitor noticed a burn to the child's leg. Medical examination concluded it was consistent with a burn from a radiator or electric fire. While the health visitor has witnessed some good parenting of Louise and her mother maintains she never leaves her at night, she is concerned about the mother's presentation, as she often appears low and depressed. Grandmother has been in touch with Social Services, stating she is now offering support to her daughter. You have been invited to conference because mother sometimes brings Louise to your parents and toddler group.
Scenario 2: Megan	Megan is six-years-old. Lucy, the seven-year-old daughter of a neighbour, has made allegations of sexual assault against Megan's father. A conference has been convened to consider concerns about any sexual risk to Megan. You have been invited because Megan attends your after-school club. (Note: Lucy also attends your club and any information you offer about Lucy at conference will be third party, as it is confidential to Lucy and her family)
Scenario 3: Graham	Graham is a six-month-old baby, who appears to be failing to gain weight. Paternal grandparents have made reports that Graham's mother is using drugs. The mother's GP has confirmed that she is currently on a monitored detox programme and is in receipt of methadone. Police were recently called to an incident in the home when neighbours reported a row. They investigated and found that Graham's father had assaulted the mother, who was holding Graham when the assault occurred. You are invited to the conference as Graham's health visitor. (Note: This may be a conference which involves the chair excluding Graham's father for some or all of the conference in view of the domestic violence incident with mother)

| Case 4: Martin | Martin is a five-year-old deaf child. Neighbours have seen him outside, unsupervised, with his older brother Barry, who is seven. One anonymous caller informed Social Services that she has seen Barry encouraging Martin to play a game of 'chicken' with traffic on a busy road. Police picked Martin up a few nights ago at 11 pm, when he was found wandering the streets. Mother did not realise that he had gone missing and stated that he is always wandering off and she will keep a closer eye on him. There are six other children in the family. |
| | You have been invited to the conference as Martin's teacher. |

In each of the above cases:

1. Whom would you expect to be invited to the meeting?
2. What information might they bring?
3. What questions might you ask at the conference before you could make a decision about the child's safety and welfare?

Presentation of information

When providing information for a conference you should consider the *Framework for Assessment* as discussed in Chapter 4. Information should be organised into the three areas of the Assessment triangle:

◆ child development

◆ parenting capacity

◆ environmental factors

Guidance on the type of information that an Early Years Practitioner might provide for each area is given in the table below.

Providing information for a conference: points to consider		
Child development	*Physical presentation*	Dress Cleanliness Build and weight
	Emotional presentation	Happy or sad Anxious or withdrawn Social maturity Levels of distress
	Behaviour	Generally good or has difficulties Response to boundaries/rewards Ability to communicate with peers, adults Play Ability in keeping with age

Parenting capacity	Observations	Child and parent/carer together Nature of affection and language between child and parent/carer Evidence of routine
	Safety needs	Does child have an awareness of danger that is age appropriate? Are there clear arrangements for a responsible adult to bring and collect child from service?
Environmental factors		Information regarding housing, finance, wider family.

As an Early Years Practitioner you may not be able to provide information regarding all three categories, particularly the environmental factors. However, it is helpful if the information you provide can be organised into these categories.

When providing information it is important that you '...distinguish between fact, observation, allegation and opinion.' *Working Together to Safeguard Children* (Department of Health 1999: p.54). While it is not necessary to know every detail of the child's time with you, it helps if you give examples of any comments you wish to make. It is also important to bear in mind that the purpose of the conference is to gain a balanced view of the child and family. Therefore, you should include examples of positive care of the child if they are available, as well as any areas of concern you may have.

In the table below are two extracts from information provided by an Early Years Practitioner to a conference. Both give the same information about the same child to the meeting.

Examples of information presented about a child named Ryan to a conference:	
Example A	In my professional view Ryan's parents are unable to care for him appropriately. They are too young and do not know how to parent him. Ryan is always late and is naughty throughout his session at nursery. The other children in the group do not like him and the staff are unable to control him.
Example B	Ryan has attended fourteen sessions at nursery and for seven of these he has been brought late. When I discussed the problem with mother she explained her difficulties in getting his older siblings to school and Ryan to nursery in the morning. Since this discussion, mother and I have agreed that Ryan's sessions should be in the afternoon. Ryan has not been brought late for any afternoon sessions. Ryan can be defiant and does not respond to rules at the nursery. He has on several occasions thrown toys at other children and has tried to run out of the building twice. Ryan can be aggressive to other children and often kicks and bites others in the group. I have discussed my concerns with the parents, who recognise the behaviour but are at a loss about how to address it at home. It is my professional view that parents would benefit from advice about managing Ryan's behaviour.

Example B provides the more balanced constructive view for a Conference.

Assessing risk and making decisions about child protection registration

As a member of the child protection conference you have a responsibility to contribute to the assessment of whether the child is at continuing risk of harm. The assessment should be based on consideration of all the information provided at the conference.

The decision about whether a child's name should be placed on the Child Protection Register is the only decision a child protection conference can make. It indicates that professionals present believe the child is at continuing risk of significant harm and that a child protection plan is required to address the risk, and make the child safe.

Working Together to Safeguard Children states there is only one question that conference should consider when deciding whether or not to register a child:

Is the child at continuing risk of significant harm?

The test should be that either

The child has suffered ill treatment, impairment of health/development as a result of emotional, physical, sexual abuse or neglect. There is a likelihood this significant harm will continue.

Or

Professional research/opinion is that the child is likely to suffer significant harm as above.

(Department of Health 1999: p. 55)

Key factors

The key words in this guidance are *significant* and *continuing*.

You will remember from previous discussions that for a child to warrant a child protection response the harm will be of a significant level. Therefore, participants at the conference must be confident from the information presented that the harm is of a significant level. The second key word is continuing. Once the conference has established that it is confident the harm is of a significant level, it must discern whether the harm will continue.

The following table gives two examples of the same situation, in which the harm has reached a significant level.

Two examples of a situation involving a child called Sarah, in which harm has reached a significant level:	
Example A	Sarah has suffered sexual harm from her mother's male partner. The mother is extremely distressed to find out what has happened. Sarah's mother has immediately separated from her partner and does not have any contact with him. She is fully supportive of her daughter and wishes to ensure that Sarah will receive all the help she can to cope with the abuse.
Example B	Sarah has suffered sexual harm from her mother's male partner. The mother, while concerned at the news, has asked her partner to leave the home for a period. However, information suggests that mother is still seeing her partner and may have the children with her when she does so.

In Example A, the response by mother ensures there is no continuing risk of significant harm and, therefore, a child protection response is not required. In Example B, the response by mother raises concerns about continuing significant harm and warrants child protection registration.

It will *not* be helpful if you attend conference having already made a decision that child protection registration is appropriate, as you will not have heard all the information available. It is better to approach the meeting with an open mind and consult the chairperson for guidance if you are unsure of your view.

If a decision is made that the criteria for placing a child's name on the child protection register is not met, but there is information that suggests the child may need help and support (such as in example A above, when the child needs therapeutic help), the conference can still agree recommendations to ensure this service is offered.

The chairperson will provide conference participants with advice and guidance on whether thresholds for registration are met. The chair will usually seek a consensus of agreement for the decision made at conference. Each local authority will have its own procedure for dealing with disagreement at conference. This can involve an adjournment period to give participants the opportunity to seek advice from a manager and then return to the meeting for further discussion, perhaps after a period of a day or so to allow consideration of the situation.

The table below is offered as a guide when considering continued risk of significant harm. It is not intended to be exhaustive and each conference will have its own specific individual particulars. However, the following may help professionals in the analysis of the information shared.

Reduced risk	Continuing risk
The incident is not life threatening and is not one of sexual harm.	The incident may have resulted in loss of life or serious injury. The incident was of a sexual nature.
There is low significant impact to the child. The child continues with positive relationships, friends and achieves at school and in personal life. Demeanor is one of content or happiness. Achieving in accordance with age and development. There are no significant health issues.	The child is displaying emotional difficulties/distress. There are problems with school/nursery progress. There are development/health issues.
The child is resilient and has a support network of friends and extended family. There are interests outside of school and the home. Child shows signs of confidence and positive self-image.	Child is young, isolated. There is no extended family support or friendships/activities outside the home. Child is poor communicator with low self-esteem.
The person who is the source of harm no longer has contact with the child and will not have contact with the child in the long-term future.	The person who is the source of harm continues to be a carer for the child or has continued contact with the child.
The person who is the source of harm acknowledges the harm or risk of harm and intends to work with professionals/family to prevent future harm.	The person who is the source of harm does not acknowledge responsibility or future risk. There is no cooperation for future work.
There is a protective parent/relative who is fully aware of any future risk and can offer protection to the child.	There is no parent/relative that acknowledges the harm or is able to offer the child protection.
The family have few if any environmental stresses, e.g. finances are OK, the home is secure, relationships with extended family/friends are positive. There is a supportive network in place.	There are pressures to the family, e.g. debt; housing problems, possibly eviction; extended family pressures, perhaps family feuding.
Parents are cooperative and work with professionals.	There is evidence of some closure of the family. They are not receptive to professional involvement and do not demonstrate cooperation.

If most of the information shared at conference is compatible with the first column in the table, then as a professional you may consider non-registration and perhaps a support plan. If most of the information shared complies with the second column then clearly there is a need for child protection registration. There will always be exceptions to the above, but the table is a useful general guide to the kinds of information you should be looking for when considering registration or de-registration.

When a child's name is placed on the child protection register the chairperson will agree with conference the appropriate category under which the child's name will be placed.

The category will indicate the nature of the concerns, to anyone consulting the register in the future. There are four categories to register a child under:

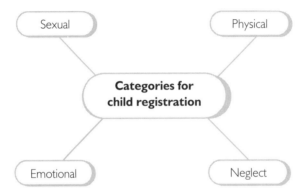

Categories for child registration

Definitions for each category are included in Chapter 3 (see pages 52–55), which addressed signs and symptoms of harm. You should familiarise yourself with these definitions, as they will be helpful to you in making a decision about child protection registration.

Child protection plans and actions to safeguard children

If a child's name is placed on the child protection register, the final task required of members of the conference will be to contribute to the outline of a child protection plan.

> *Where a child's name is placed on the register, the act of registration itself confers no protection on a child, and should always be accompanied by a child protection plan*
>
> Department of Health 1999: p.55

Child protection registration notifies professionals that the child is at risk of significant harm, when they consult the register. However, the act of protection and reduction of risk lies in professionals and family carrying out actions identified in the child protection plan.

The chairperson will engage with the meeting in compiling recommendations that will form the outline of the child protection plan.

A key worker will be appointed to the child to coordinate the inter-agency response to child protection and to visit the child regularly in order to monitor welfare. The key worker, who will be a person from Social Services, is the individual you contact if you have any concerns about the child during child protection registration, or you have concerns about the progress of the child protection plan.

The chairperson will also appoint a core group. The purpose and functions of the core group is discussed in more detail in Chapter 7. The core group is a smaller group made up of relevant family members and key professionals. Its purpose is to add detail to the child protection plan.

The group identifies who will do what and when. It also monitors and reviews the progress of the plan.

When a key worker and core group have been appointed, the chairperson compiles the main tasks of the child protection plan. The initial task will normally be one of assessment. A further assessment will need to be completed with the family and this will form the core assessment, as discussed in Chapter 4. This assessment might include specific specialist work, such as an assessment to look at a mother's ability to protect her children or an assessment of a father's physical risk to a child. As a provider of a key service, an Early Years Practitioner will normally be asked to contribute to the assessment. The key worker will coordinate this information.

The participants of the meeting and the chair will then look at ways to address any difficulties that are considered to pose a risk to the child.

As a participant, you should consider what you may contribute to the child protection plan. The following are examples of ways in which Early Years staff have played a part in child protection plans.

EARLY YEARS PRACTITIONERS AND CHILD PROTECTION PLANS

Part played by Early Years Practitioners

- A nursery offered extra sessions for a child, whose mother was having difficulty in coping with older siblings, following separation from her husband as a result of domestic violence.

- A childminder was able to give mother advice about behavioural management techniques for a toddler, as mother appeared to be having difficulty parenting the child.

- Nursery offered to monitor the well-being of a child who had suffered significant physical harm in the past and was now being returned to his mother.

- A mother and toddler group agreed to act as a venue for health visitor checks of a child, as the parent was unable to attend playgroup and the health clinic.

When considering what should be recommended as an action in the plan you do not have to confine yourself to the services you provide. You may also have ideas about other help that can be offered to the family, and it is appropriate to suggest any ideas you have to the meeting. For instance, you may have heard that the family are having financial problems, and you may wish to recommend that the Citizens Advice Bureau be contacted.

When the child protection plan has been completed the meeting will draw to a close. The chairperson should be expected to set a date for the next child protection conference within three months of the initial meeting. He/she will also agree who will receive minutes of the meeting.

Actions following an initial child protection conference

Following conference you will be provided with a copy of the decision and recommendations of conference. This document will be a useful reference for the Core Group, when detailed arrangements about the enactment of the plan will be made. You will also eventually receive minutes of the conference, although you may not receive these as soon as the document containing the decision and recommendations. If you disagree with anything stated in the minutes, you should contact the chairperson. Both the decision and recommendations, and the minutes of the conference are confidential and should not be shared outside the meeting unless you have sought permission of the chairperson. You should also ensure they are stored in a private, secure place.

Below is an example of what a child protection plan might look like:

Child Protection Plan

Name of child: DoB   Address

Date of Registration   Category   Date of conference

Key worker

Recommendation	Purpose	To be completed by
Core assessment	To ensure all the needs of the child and family can be met.	Key worker with the family and partner professionals
Advice regarding managing David's temper tantrums to be offered to mother	To help mother find alternatives to physical punishment to manage David's temper.	Nursery staff and mother.
Psychological assessment of mother	To have a clearer idea of mother's cognitive abilities to learn and her attachment to David.	Psychologist
David to receive a full medical check up and to be brought up to date with his immunisations	To ensure David's medical needs are met.	Health visitor and GP
Support to be given to mother at breakfast and tea time	Short-term work to help mother establish routines and an appropriate diet for David	Social Services priority care team
Mother to attend parenting class	Support and guidance regarding specific parenting tasks	Social Services parenting programme.

Core Group: Mother, Nursery, health visitor, Priority Care Team, Key worker and Social Services parenting programme worker.

Sample extract of minutes involving a case of neglect

Rose House Nursery

Ms Campbell informed members that James was three-years-old and attended the nursery three days a week. Ms Campbell stated that James was not a difficult child and seemed to fit in with his peers. James attends from 8.45 am to 5 pm. He does need firm boundaries and can display temper tantrums. However, Ms Campbell said that she had not observed the difficulties mother has identified at home.

In answer to a question from the chair, Ms Campbell said that James's progress with words and speech seemed to have slowed down recently. Staff have difficulty in understanding what he is saying and he does find this frustrating. She felt that there needed to be more interaction between mother and James at home to reinforce his speech skills. He does not play well with his peers and has difficulty sharing toys.

Ms Campbell had noticed that mother has appeared more stressed since the birth of her second child, Christopher, recently. James has been arriving late for nursery and on several occasions staff have had to remain behind with James because mother has been late picking him up. His physical appearance has deteriorated and he often appears at nursery in dirty clothes. He has had a difficulty with head lice, but mother has addressed this problem following advice.

Ms Green (chairperson)

Asked mother if she would like to make any comments.

Ms Roberts

Stated that she has struggled recently in the morning now that she has Christopher, but has always made sure that James is clean and tidy.

The child protection register

What is the child protection register?

Every local authority Social Services Department holds a central child protection register for their area. The register holds the names and details of every child resident in their area, including those placed by other authorities and agencies, who is considered to be at risk of continuing significant harm and for whom there is a Child Protection Plan. The register will usually contain the child's name, date of birth, home address, details of parent/carer and the category under which the child's name is registered.

What is the purpose of the child protection register?

The main purpose of the register is to inform professionals and agencies of those children who are viewed as being at continuing risk of significant harm and in need of a protection plan to safeguard their welfare. It is therefore important that professionals make use of the register and make checks against it when there are concerns about a child.

How to check the child protection register

A custodian of the register will have been appointed in each Social Services department. The custodian's task is to keep the register up to date and ensure the details contained on it are accurate. However, a professional can make a check by contacting the referral point in Social Services; outside of office hours a check can be made with the Social Services emergency duty team.

GOOD PRACTICE GUIDE: CHILD PROTECTION CONFERENCES DOS AND DON'TS

Do

1. Notify the chairperson of attendance or apologies. Also discuss with the chairperson if you wish to be accompanied by a colleague, who needs to observe a conference, or by a manager.

2. Compile your information in a report and send to the chairperson in advance of the meeting.

➡

3. Share your report with parents and carers if possible well before the meeting.

4. Arrive early for the meeting to have the opportunity of reading all reports available.

5. Turn up smartly dressed for the conference. It is an important meeting for family members and many will have made the effort to be smart in appearance. It is therefore out of respect that professionals should do the same and it reflects that professionals take the meeting seriously also.

6. Listen attentively and carefully to all information shared, as this will form the basis of your view regarding child protection registration.

7. Ask questions through the chairperson to clarify issues and help you in your assessment.

8. At the close of the meeting offer a view regarding continuing risk or harm and an explanation of how you reached your view.

9. Be prepared to alter your view if the discussion leads to the majority of the meeting agreeing a view different to your own.

10. Contribute actively to the formulation of the child protection plan.

11. Note the date and time of the next review child protection conference and the date and time of the initial core group meeting.

Don't

1. Arrive late for the meeting, accompanied by someone who has not been invited and whom you have not discussed with the chairperson.

2. Read directly from your report when asked to deliver your information to conference. Provide a verbal summary of your report and include examples that support your comments about the child and family.

3. Interrupt others when speaking; ask the chairperson if you can comment, when the person has finished.

4. Make provocative or judgemental comments that are likely to antagonise parents in what is a very difficult and sensitive meeting.

5. Withdraw your attention or participation when you have completed your task of giving information. All professionals present have a responsibility to listen to all information and make a judgement about child protection registration.

6. Leave the meeting before the end, as the final stages are the most crucial in terms of making decisions and formulating plans. Leave yourself plenty of time to attend the conference. Conferences vary in length but an average time scale is an hour to an hour-and-a-half.

Agency _____

Child protection conference report Re: _____

Child's name _____

Date of Birth _____

Address _____

(It is important to include the above facts you have about the child. Often at conference, checks regarding factual details such as date of birth, address, and so on, reveal there are differences in the information held by professionals. Conference is an opportunity to ensure factual details are correct.)

Date of involvement

This establishes how long you have known the family and child for conference.

Nature of involvement

What your role is with the child and family.

Significant events

List under this heading the date and event of any significant incident that has occurred during your involvement with the child and family.

Examples are as follows:

- period when the child was constantly late for a nursery
- mother presenting with an injury
- child describing difficulties at home
- child reporting changes in the family composition at home
- child moving to live at a different address
- any accidental injuries child may have had.

Child information

Information organised under headings given in *Framework for Assessment*

Family/parent and carer information

External factors/stresses

Summary concerns

Views how to address concerns

Signatures of report – Author & Manager

Indication as to whether report has been shared with parents

Highlight any parts parents disagree with and what the nature of their dissatisfaction is.

The suggested format for an agency child protection conference report

CASE STUDY:

MS SMITH'S REPORT

Consider the report provided below written by a nursery worker, Ms Smith, for a conference in respect of two young children, one of whom attends nursery three times a week.

Ms Smith reported that Jennifer has attended nursery from the age of six months. She is settled and there are no problems or concerns. Staff have noticed that Jennifer's behaviour has changed since her older brother Tim has left nursery and started school. Her link worker at nursery felt that Jennifer was frightened of her older brother. Jennifer is sometimes withdrawn around conflict and is frightened when other children have temper tantrums. Ms Smith reported a good relationship with both parents and on 10 May Mrs Parker informed staff that Jennifer had burnt her hand. Nursery contacted Mrs Parker to ask her to take Jennifer for medical attention, as she was showing discomfort during her session.

1. What questions might you have asked the mother?

2. What action do you think you might have taken?

You have been informed there will be a Child Protection Conference following a S47 inquiry into the burn to Jennifer's hand, as her parents were unable to offer an explanation for the injury.

3. What are your initial thoughts regarding the safety and welfare of Jennifer?

4. What further information would you like to have before you gave a view regarding child protection registration or not?

The following information was provided at the child protection conference, in respect of Tim and Jennifer.

Mr and Mrs Parker have had two older children removed from their care and placed for adoption. The assessment at the time concluded that the parents were unable to meet the developmental needs of the children when the children reached a certain age, usually around five years. The children who were placed for adoption displayed signs of severe developmental delay. The children had low self-esteem, were lacking in confidence, did not respond to boundaries, demonstrated aggressive behaviour and were unable to behave positively in social situations.

Health information in respect of Tim indicated a child who is aggressive, hyperactive and exhibits challenging behaviour.

There appear to be no concerns with Jennifer at this point in time.

School indicated Tim had not settled well and did not respond to instruction. His educational ability is low and he will require special needs support. Recently they have observed great displays of anger from Tim and the use of foul language.

➡️

Parents state that they can cope with Jennifer but are unable to manage Tim. Mother has decided that Tim is a bad child who will not change. However, they do not feel his behaviour is anything to do with their parenting. Tim's behaviour did deteriorate after Jennifer was born. Mother would like Tim taken into care.

Social Services provided past history regarding the older siblings and stated they did not discover the source of the burn to Jennifer.

5. Following the above information has your view regarding child protection registration changed?

6. What recommendations would you make regarding this family?

ACTIVITY

Contact your local Social Services Department:

◆ Find out who the chairpersons are and where they are based.

◆ Ask for a copy of the format for an agency report for conference.

◆ Ask for an agenda or conference format.

◆ Is there a specific venue for conference?

◆ Ask who is the custodian of the child protection register in your area, as this is the person you are likely to have to contact to make a check of the register.

Find out what your local ACPC policy is regarding family participation in child protection conferences.

Summary

◆ The purpose of a child protection conference is to share information, consider risk and identify actions to safeguard children.

◆ The only decision a conference can make is whether or not to place a child's name on the child protection register.

◆ Parents, children (if age appropriate) and key professionals will be invited to conference.

◆ If you have any queries about attendance or have issues of safety you will need to discuss these with the chairperson prior to the meeting.

◆ Once all the information has been shared and a decision has been reached regarding registration the chair will draw together recommendations from the meeting. If the decision is that the child's name is placed on the child protection register then the recommendations will form the outline of a child protection plan. A key worker from Social Services will be appointed and members of the core group will be identified. If the decision is one of non-registration, recommendations can still be made to offer support to the child and family if appropriate.

CHECKPOINT

1. What is the purpose of a child protection conference?
2. What information might you be expected to provide in your role as an Early Years Practitioner?
3. What should you do if you feel you may have difficulty in sharing information with the family present?
4. What is the threshold for child protection registration?
5. What should you do if you find inaccuracies in the minutes when you receive them?
6. What is the child protection register?
7. How do you make an inquiry to the child protection register?
8. What actions will the chair take if the child's name is placed on the child protection register?
9. What are the categories under which a child's name can be registered?

Chapter 7

Safeguarding children together

Most professionals who take a lead role in child protection would agree that placing a child's name on the child protection register does not in itself protect a child from significant harm. While it does mean there is a register that professionals can check as an indication that the child is at risk and that a child protection plan is in place, it is the inter-agency work with the family, post registration, that actually addresses the harm and can lead to improved safety for a child.

This chapter encourages you as an Early Years Practitioner to participate in the child protection process by thinking about the kinds of activity you will be involved in when there is a risk to a child you work with.

The stages in the child protection process are considered here, following a decision by a conference to place a child's name on the child protection register. This chapter looks at the work of such groups and includes an example of a child protection plan. There are useful tips for those taking part in the core group and guidelines for good practice by core groups so that, as one of its members, you can contribute towards ensuring that it is a positive process. The chapter concludes by considering those factors that, might be involved when deciding whether or not a child is no longer at risk of significant harm and whether removal from the child protection register is appropriate.

Child protection plans

When a child protection conference has made a decision to place a child's name on the child protection register the meeting will formulate an outline of a child protection plan. This will consist of a series of recommendations that to some extent will arise naturally out of the discussion in the meeting, or will be the result of suggestions from professionals and family present. If you attend a child protection conference you will be expected to make a contribution to the child protection plan.

Achieving a child protection plan

The following case studies are designed to lead you into the thought process required to achieve a child protection plan. They will draw on the knowledge of child protection you have acquired so far in this book.

CASE STUDY:

THE JESSOP FAMILY

This example is used to demonstrate how a child protection plan is formulated in conference.

Concerns

Jay is a twenty-one-year old woman, who lives in her own accommodation. Her parents are separated. Her mother has married again to a Mr Lewis. Jay's stepfather, Mr Lewis, has been convicted of sexual assault to two young girls. The assessment by Police and Social Services indicates that Jay's mother may be helping to procure young girls for her husband. Jay herself has made an allegation of rape against her stepfather but withdrew the allegation before the case went to court. Jay's natural father, Mr Jessop, lives in Bolton. Mr Jessop has a reputation for violence and misusing alcohol. He lives with his partner and Jay's sister, Mol, who is aged five. Recently, Social Services have been involved with Mol and are concerned about her care. Jay went to visit her sister and became concerned about her safety. Jay returned home with care of Mol. Concerns have arisen as Jay became threatening in a local benefits office with Mol in her company, when she was unable to make progress on her housing benefit claim. The local health centre has tried to visit Mol but have been met with hostility by Jay. Finally, Police have observed on one occasion Jay visiting her mother and stepfather with Mol and are concerned about the sexual risk posed by the stepfather.

Information shared at conference

Mol has been subject to a child protection conference following concerns about her care and the risk of sexual harm.

Social Services

The social worker has had an opportunity to visit Jay and Mol, as well as their mother Mrs Lewis and natural father Mr Jessop, who lives in a neighbouring town. Jay, although initially hostile for fear that Mol will be taken into care, calmed down and accepted that she will need help to care for Mol. The social worker feels that there is a risk to Mol from the stepfather, which the family has not yet fully acknowledged and that further information should be gathered about Jay's natural father, given his alcohol abuse and violent behaviour, if he is to have contact with his young daughter.

Social Services observed that Mol is settled with Jay and obviously is very attached to her sister. However, Jay does need to ensure that she can meet Mol's health and development needs and there is still time for her to establish this. The home is quite messy and there is little evidence of Mol's belongings. Mol did look well and played happily during the social worker's visit. She had a difficult temper tantrum and Jay indicated that these seem to be increasing and she would like some advice about how to deal with them.

The social worker considers that the plan will continue to be that of Jay caring for Mol with support but that Mol may be at risk of neglect and sexual harm until Jay's care is tested out.

Family

Jay attended conference with her father Mr Jessop; both stated that Jay would be caring for Mol with the support of her mother, Mrs Lewis, and father, Mr Jessop. Jay stated that she realises that this is a big responsibility and that she now needs help. She was originally hostile, fearing Mol might be taken into care but now she is willing to cooperate. Mr Jessop wishes to visit and have contact with both his daughters.

Jay acknowledges the risk posed by her stepfather to Mol and is clear that she will not allow any contact to take place between the two. Mol does not have any relationship with Mr Lewis and there is no reason why the two should meet.

Health visitor

The health visitor commented that Mol is behind with health checks and immunisations. She understands that Jay has not yet enrolled Mol in a school and considers that as Mol is behind with her speech she would benefit from attending school. The health visitor has visited Jay's home several times and left cards, but has not received any response. However, yesterday she managed to find Jay at home and they had a very positive discussion about Mol's health and development.

Education welfare

Education has been trying to contact Jay to help with the enrolment of Mol at a school. The infants' school close to Jay's home still has some places available.

Police

Jay has several convictions for dealing in drugs and theft from a local shopping centre. There are no recent police issues. An outline was given to conference regarding Jay's allegation of rape made against her stepfather. Police confirmed that Jay withdrew the allegation before the matter could proceed to court. Local police information is that Jay has been seen visiting her stepfather several times. There is a recorded event that Jay had a young child with her on one occasion.

Conference decision

Conference made a decision to place Mol's name on the child protection register under the categories of sexual harm and neglect.

Issues/information that led to conference decision

During a conference you will listen to all the information about the family and then you will move on to the next step of analysing the information. Below is a suggested way of organising the information to help you draw a conclusion about whether or not the child is at continuing risk of harm. It will inform your view if you note the strengths of a situation as well as the weaknesses. Then take a view on balance of information whether or not a child is at risk of continuing significant harm.

Information about the child

◆ Mol is not meeting all milestones.

◆ She has a speech delay.

◆ She is behind with immunisations.

◆ Mol is not yet enrolled with a school.

◆ Mol will be at risk of sexual harm if she has contact with the stepfather.

◆ Mol is attached to her sister Jay, and they have a good relationship.

Parenting/carer capacity

Jay is a young woman with no previous parenting experience.

Jay states that she is committed to Mol.

Although initially uncooperative Jay states that she would like help.

Jay is clear there should be no contact with stepfather. Although Police observation is that she may have taken Mol to her stepfather's home.

As yet the cooperation and commitment of Jay is untested.

Environmental factors

There are some financial pressures on Jay, hence the difficulties at the Benefits Office.

Based on the issues identified above, conference members came to the conclusion that there is a risk of significant harm in the form of possible neglect by Jay, as her care is untested, and the sexual risk of stepfather until Jay's ability to protect is clear.

Example recommendations made at conference

An outline child protection plan was formulated at conference to address the concerns as follows:

Child protection plan

Recommendation	Purpose of action
Key worker to be Meekle Jesso Social Services	To ensure regular visiting to family to check Mol's welfare and to coordinate the implementation of the child protection plan
Social Services to organise support to be offered to Jay in caring for Mol	To help Jay meet Mol's basic care needs, to establish routines and boundaries for Mol
Jay to enrol Mol in school	To provide education for Mol
Jay, with health visitor, to ensure Mol has a health check and is up to date with immunisations	To ensure Mol's health needs are met
Agreement that Mol should not have contact with stepfather	To ensure Mol is safe from risk of sexual harm
Core assessment to be completed	To assess areas of strength within the family care of Mol and offer support in areas of weakness
Assessment to include natural father	To look at safe contact between Mol and father given the issues of alcohol abuse and violence
Written agreement between family and Social Services regarding child protection plan	Clarify what is expected of all parties regarding the child protection plan

The recommendations made at conference should address the issues that have arisen from the information. For example, the Jessop conference identified a risk of sexual harm to Mol from Jay's stepfather and, therefore, made a recommendation that there should be no contact with Mr Lewis, as a means of protecting her. Equally, conference identified that Mol is not yet in school and made a recommendation that Jay should enrol her as soon as possible. The plan should consider all the needs of the child and family, not only the immediate presenting risk but also any support services required.

REFLECT ON YOUR PRACTICE

◆ It is helpful if you consider the three dimensions when looking at the information in conference.

◆ Make notes as the meeting progresses to refer to as you are thinking about registration.

◆ The important part to remember is that you are not just there to deliver your information. You are present as a professional to consider all the information provided and give your view about whether there is continuing risk of significant harm given the information shared by all members.

CASE STUDY:

THE GRAVES FAMILY

Concerns

Ryan arrived in school and informed his teacher that his father had hit him with a bat. Police and Social Services undertook an investigation into the allegation. A social worker and police officer visited Ryan at his home. Paul, Ryan's father, went to fetch Ryan from his bedroom so that he could speak to Social Services. Ryan clung to his father and would not speak. When asked by his father if he would speak to Police and Social Services on a video statement, Ryan said no. Ryan appeared to have a number of marks on both sides of his face. Ryan and his mother accompanied Social Services and Police to hospital. Father became upset and walked out of the house. Ryan eventually spoke on video and stated that his father had slapped him on his face for playing and 'messing up the computer'. Ryan's mother Cheryl indicated that she was afraid of her husband, stating there had been domestic violence in the past. Ryan and Mother were taken to a women's refuge. Mother and Ryan eventually moved in with grandmother as a temporary arrangement. Mother had informed police that Ryan sustained the injuries when she went out shopping and left him with his father. However, mother has since retracted this statement.

Cheryl is still in contact with Paul and would like them to reunite as a family as soon as possible.

Information shared at conference

Social Services

In addition to the above information outlining concerns, Social Services summarised their investigation, stating that mother had been in contact with father but that she had not allowed him to see Ryan at this stage. Social Services has concerns that mother will reunite with father and Ryan will be at risk of further harm as a consequence.

Police

Police confirmed that father has been charged with assaulting Ryan and has current bail conditions not to approach the home of grandmother, or Ryan. Police stated that Paul was particularly aggressive during the interview and had to be calmed down several times. There have been a number of calls to the home for domestic violence incidents. There have never been any injuries evident on Cheryl, and Cheryl has never wished to make a formal complaint.

Paul

Paul, who was previously in the army and served in the Gulf War, is currently unemployed. Paul stated that he has had difficulties with depression and had stopped taking his medication at the time of the incident. He isn't sleeping or eating and has now been prescribed medication by his GP. Paul would like the family to get back together and he is willing to undertake any work on parenting or anger management to make sure this happens.

Cheryl

Cheryl said that she often had problems managing Ryan and she thought he was hyperactive. She felt Paul to be the only person who could control him. Ryan was often aggressive to her friend's children. Cheryl would like the family to be together and said she was not afraid of Paul.

GP

The family GP confirmed that he knew all family members. He had seen the child only for minor difficulties. Both parents were on antidepressants and he felt they were victims of social problems, as they lived in a one bedroom flat on income support.

Education Services

Ryan's teacher indicated that Ryan has difficulty concentrating in class and can be aggressive with other pupils, although he does have some friends. He usually arrives on time and appears clean and well presented. Ryan has had some absences from school that have not been explained by parents, but on the whole his attendance is good. School have had some concerns about father's behaviour at school when he picks Ryan up. He fights with him in play in a fairly aggressive way.

School nurse

There are no particular health concerns.

Housing

The family are currently in a council flat, which they keep in good order. They have requested a move to a house and are a priority on the waiting list, but nothing suitable has yet become available. Paul remains living in the family home.

Consider the above information about the Graves family.

1. Draw together the main issues in the information in respect of the child, parenting capacity and any environmental factors such as housing, in the manner outlined for the Jessop family above.

2. When you have completed the task consider the issues and decide whether or not, on balance, the child is at continuing risk of significant harm and why.

CASE STUDY:

THE MARKS FAMILY

Concerns

Terry Marks is three-years-old. Social Services received an anonymous referral stating that parents were injecting drugs and a number of drug dealers were visiting the house. The house had been smashed up and there was a dispute with the neighbours at the time of referral. A police officer and social worker had attended the home and were concerned about the apparent depressed state of mother. Mother was very aggressive about Social Services and her mood went up and down from extreme anger to hysterical upset. Terry was removed to the care of his grandmother, where he currently remains.

Information shared at conference

Social Services

The social worker reiterated the concerns about the parents' lifestyle including drug use and the impact this had on Terry's care. It was stated that Terry was doing fine with his grandmother. However, there had been some animosity between mother and grandmother, and as a consequence mother and father have not had contact with Terry since his placement.

Views of parents

Both parents were adamant they did not use drugs apart from smoking the 'odd bit' of cannabis. The parents did agree that a drug user visited the home, but he apparently neither used drugs during the visit, nor did he attempt to inject any drugs.

While Terry's father denied there were problems, his mother stated that they had difficulties. She said that they often argue and this can result in violence. Mother also said that they drank heavily. Both wanted to attend courses for anger management to resolve their difficulties.

Mother assured the conference that they are both prepared to make the necessary changes for Terry and that the situation will never be allowed to revert back to how it was.

Probation/Alcohol Report

Mother is subject to a community rehabilitation order for threatening behaviour towards another adult while drunk. Part of the order specified that she should address her alcohol misuse. The probation officer reported that mother's attendance and cooperation is good. She views the incident by mother as a one-off that will not be repeated. She commented that mother's mood is often low but that she did not feel there were any outstanding alcohol issues.

Views of grandmother

Grandmother explained that Terry was doing very well but clearly misses his mother. She does not see why Terry cannot return to his parents and feels unable to continue his care in the long term, as it is causing animosity between herself and her daughter. She is aware that the couple have difficulties and that there have been violent rows, but she feels this has shocked the couple into tackling their problems.

Health visitor report

The health visitor stated that Terry is progressing within expectations. He was admitted to hospital for an eye infection, but this has now cleared. He is up to date with all his immunisations. Terry's height and weight are fine and he eats well. There have been some difficulties in contacting parents at home, but when Terry has been observed with his parents he seems relaxed and shows them affection. The health visitor has let the parents know about SureStart activities and the parents are keen to start some activities with Terry.

Police

Apart from the response to the anonymous referral, there have been two other calls to the family home. The mother made one of the calls, stating that her husband was beating her up. When the Police arrived at the home the situation was calm and mother had no visible injuries. Police have reliable information from an informant that there is drug dealing at the address.

Summary of information

Social Services and Police express concerns about the parents' drug use and lifestyle that according to police information includes drug dealing from the home.

Mother has raised issues of domestic violence in respect of her husband. However both parents at the conference have made a commitment to address these difficulties and not allow the situation to deteriorate to that level again.

Mother is low in mood and it is unclear whether or not she is suffering from depression.

Grandmother, although wary of animosity with her daughter, has been supportive in caring for Terry.

Terry has appeared fine. Observations made by the health visitor indicate he is attached and comfortable with both parents. His physical and cognitive development is fine. However, it should be noted he is a young child who is currently separated from his parents and there has been no contact. Consideration should be given to this fact and the balance between the concerns expressed by agencies and parents, and his need to be with his parents.

1. Consider the above information and again draw up the main issues in relation to the child, parenting capacity and environment.

2. Decide if, given the current circumstances, the child is at continuing risk of significant harm and why.

Working together in core groups

Once an initial conference has agreed a child protection plan, the meeting will agree a core group and a review conference date that should be set within three months of the initial conference.

Core group

The core group is a group of key professionals identified at conference, together with relevant family members, who are responsible for developing the child protection plan into practical application. As an Early Years Practitioner, and someone who is likely to have frequent contact with the child subject to conference, you will usually be appointed a member of the core group.

> *The core group is responsible for developing the child protection plan as a detailed working tool, and implementing it, within the outline plan agreed at the initial child protection conference.*
>
> Department of Health 1999: p.57

The group will address the outline child protection plan agreed at conference and add detail about what needs to be done, why, by whom and when.

Aims of the child protection plan

The aims of the child protection plan are shown on the next page.

The following is an example of how a child protection plan might appear.

Jessop Family

Action	Why	By whom	Point for review
Regular visits fortnightly to monitor the well-being of Mol	To check on safety and welfare, provide support and note positives in care	Key worker	At next initial conference. Regular feed backs to core group – how visits have gone and if Mol has been available to be seen
Advice and guidance to be offered to Jay re routine boundaries	Help Jay settle Mol into her care and establish a carer's role	Lynn Smith the family support worker with Jay	Appointments will be weekly and will be reviewed in a month's time at the next core group meeting. Updates will be provided verbally to Jay as work takes place.

			Progress will be reviewed on Jay's ability to receive advice and put parenting guidance into practice consistently
Jay to make an appointment with Burford school to discuss Mol	To enrol Mol in school	Jay	Mol to be in school by next core group meeting on 25 May
To complete core assessment	To check family has all support needed and provide a better picture of the care of Mol	Social Services to complete with family and other agencies.	Social Services to have gathered all information from family by next core group meeting and have begun to seek information from professionals.
Written agreement about work and family contact	To ensure Mol's safety from sexual harm	Key worker will complete with family.	Draft agreement has been drawn up at this core group meeting. Adherence to the agreement will be reviewed at core group meeting in May

Date of next core group meeting: 25 May 04

Circulation of notes to:

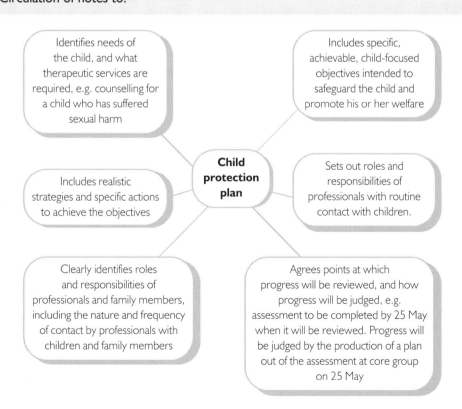

Identifies needs of the child, and what therapeutic services are required, e.g. counselling for a child who has suffered sexual harm

Includes specific, achievable, child-focused objectives intended to safeguard the child and promote his or her welfare

Includes realistic strategies and specific actions to achieve the objectives

Child protection plan

Sets out roles and responsibilities of professionals with routine contact with children.

Clearly identifies roles and responsibilities of professionals and family members, including the nature and frequency of contact by professionals with children and family members

Agrees points at which progress will be reviewed, and how progress will be judged, e.g. assessment to be completed by 25 May when it will be reviewed. Progress will be judged by the production of a plan out of the assessment at core group on 25 May

Aims of a child protection plan   *Source: Department of Health 1999: p.54*

The written agreement

One of the recommendations of government guidance regarding child protection, and an indication of good practice, is to draw up a written agreement with the family to fulfil the child protection plan.

Below is an example of what a written agreement may look like. There are many different formats, but essentially it should contain the elements of who is doing what to carry out the child protection plan, what the consequences are if the agreement is broken and when/how the agreement will be reviewed.

Written Agreement between Jay and Greymoor Social Services

Aim:
To ensure the safe care of Mol.

Jay agrees to:
- work in partnership with Social Services and other professionals involved in Mol's life
- undertake parenting work with the family support service
- ensure that Mol is enrolled in school and attends every day
- ensure that Mol's medical checks and immunisations are up to date
- not allow contact between Mol and stepfather without prior consultation and agreement of Social Services.

Social Services agree to:
- work in partnership with Jay and involve her in making any plans/decisions regarding Mol
- ensure family support is made available to Jay
- keep Jay informed of any information they receive regarding her lifestyle
- visit Mol and Jay on a regular basis to check how the family are progressing.

Health Services agree to:
- help Jay with checks and immunisations for Mol
- provide regular checks on Mol's health.

Education Services agree to:
- help Jay enrol Mol in a local infants school.

If the agreement is broken:
- Social Services will seek advice about a further child protection response, and will consult the Legal Department for guidance
- Jay can make use of the ACPC complaints procedure and consult her own legal advisor, if required
- The agreement will be reviewed in three months' time at a core group meeting to take into account any changing circumstances

Signed: .... Carer

Signed: .... Agency

Date: ....

The agreement should contain suggestions from the family and professionals and both will sign to agree it.

Membership of the core group

Members of the core group should comprise the key worker (social worker for the child), child (if appropriate) and family members, professionals or foster carers, who will have direct contact with the family, e.g. health visitor, teacher, nursery worker, GP, probation officer, and midwife. Although the key worker takes the lead role in the core group process, all members of the core group are jointly responsible for the formulation and implementation of the child protection plan, amending the plan as necessary and monitoring progress against agreed objectives.

Opportunities for working in partnership with families

The core group can be a very effective forum for engaging families in work to reduce significant harm to their children. It is a smaller group and families may feel they can participate more easily than in a conference. Child protection plans should be formulated with parents and children; both should be encouraged to identify actions that might contribute to the child's welfare. Responsibilities for actions will be given to family members as well as professionals. Child protection plans will be a reflection of the views of parents and children (when age appropriate) as well as the views of professionals.

Securing family involvement in plans

Working Together to Safeguard Children (Department of Health 1999) outlines a number of actions that should be undertaken by the group to ensure the engagement of families in plans.

> The plan should be constructed with the family in their first language and they should receive a written copy in their first language. If family members' preferences are not accepted about how best to safeguard the child, the reasons for this should be explained. Families should be told about their right to complain and make representations, and how to do so.
>
> Department of Health 1999: p.59

Without the partnership of the family, child protection plans will fail, so it is important that professionals ensure they work with the family. This does not imply agreement with the family when their suggestions might place a child at risk, but it does involve listening to parents' suggestions with an open mind, and involving them fully in the process of agreeing actions.

Importance of core groups

The core group is a small group that can be a key element in progressing work within a family. Core groups incorporate the principles of working together and are the forum in which child protection is carried out.

They are a vital part of the child protection process and, as such, professionals need to be committed to attendance and participation.

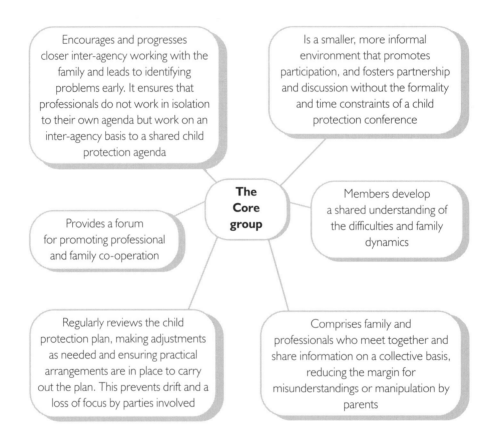

Encourages and progresses closer inter-agency working with the family and leads to identifying problems early. It ensures that professionals do not work in isolation to their own agenda but work on an inter-agency basis to a shared child protection agenda

Is a smaller, more informal environment that promotes participation, and fosters partnership and discussion without the formality and time constraints of a child protection conference

Provides a forum for promoting professional and family co-operation

The Core group

Members develop a shared understanding of the difficulties and family dynamics

Regularly reviews the child protection plan, making adjustments as needed and ensuring practical arrangements are in place to carry out the plan. This prevents drift and a loss of focus by parties involved

Comprises family and professionals who meet together and share information on a collective basis, reducing the margin for misunderstandings or manipulation by parents

Elements of a core group

Core groups are the means by which the plan is put into effect. The groups report information and progress back to the review child protection conference for consideration of whether the child remains at risk of significant harm and requires continued child protection registration, or whether the name can be removed.

TIPS FOR PARTICIPATION IN CORE GROUPS

1. They are important meetings and you should aim to attend them all.

2. Bring with you updates about information from your work with the family. These can be as detailed as you like, as the group is about addressing the specifics.

3. Bring with you any problems regarding your work with the family to encourage the group to help you to reach a resolution.

4. Be prepared to address the whole plan in the group and offer suggestions about all the work to be carried out if required. Remember this is about working together to ensure the plan is carried out.

5. Plans can be refined, if required, by changing circumstances, e.g. a new adult may move into the household and need to be included in the assessments taking place.

6. Feel free to offer a venue if it is more convenient for family and professionals.

7. If there is a significant change in circumstances that affects the plan, you can suggest that the key worker consults with the chair of the conference to see if a review conference is required.

REFLECT ON YOUR PRACTICE

◆ Key people are invited and able to attend. (The first date is usually set at the end of the initial child protection conference when key people are present.)

◆ Arrangements should be made to ensure parental/child attendance, i.e. childcare should be offered, and transport provided to the venue.

◆ The chairperson, who is usually the key worker, should make clear the purpose and aims of the meeting.

◆ The group should be able to share information in an open and honest way.

◆ Tasks are agreed in relation to the plan. Each is recorded with who will carry it out and when it should be completed by, together with when and how it will be reviewed.

◆ Minutes should be made of the meeting, together with a written record of the child protection plan.

◆ The process for resolution of professional disagreement will be outlined in the Area Child Protection Committee procedures. However, parents and carers should also be aware of the right to complain.

◆ A timetable of core group meeting dates with venues should be set out at the first meeting.

Child protection review conferences

Throughout the period that the child's name is on the child protection register there will be a number of review child protection conferences. The timescale is shown below:

The initial child protection conference should take place within 15 days of a strategy meeting regarding the S47 inquiry into significant harm. If the child's name is placed on the child protection register at the initial conference a review conference date will be set for 3 months from the initial conference. Thereafter, the review conferences will take place at six-monthly intervals, until the conference members decide that the child is no longer at risk of significant harm and the child's name can be removed from the child protection register.

Purpose of the review conference

The review conference requires as much commitment and preparation as an initial conference. Its purpose is to review the progress of the child protection plan and any new information and decide if the child is at continuing risk of significant harm and requires continued child protection. It promotes continuity if the same professionals can attend throughout so that they have an overview of the case. If you attended the initial conference, then it should be you that attends the reviews. To send another professional in your place leads to difficulties because he/she will not have been party to the initial concerns at the initial conference or have the information from core group participation.

The review conference should:

- Review the safety, health and development of the child against intended outcomes set out in the Child Protection Plan.
- Ensure that the child continues to be adequately safeguarded.
- Consider whether the Child Protection Plan should continue in place or be changed.

It is important that the relevant professionals attend a review conference, as each review should consider the de-registration of the child. If there is an absence of information, or key professionals, the decision about whether or not to deregister a child will be taken on an unsound basis. This may result in a child being kept on the child protection register needlessly or in a child becoming de-registered without the child protection umbrella that might be required to keep him/her safe. Each review conference will always address the question of whether or not, given the information, the child is at continuing risk of significant harm and requires child protection registration.

Quoracy

Area Child Protection Committees will usually give guidance regarding the nature and number of professionals that are required to make the conference quorate to make a decision. It is often the same requirement for an initial conference as it is for a review conference, usually three separate agencies or professional groups who have had direct contact with the child.

Criteria for de-registration

A child's name may be removed from the register if:

- It is judged that the child is no longer at continuing risk of significant harm requiring safeguarding by means of a child protection plan (e.g. the risk of harm has been reduced by action taken through the child protection plan; the child and family's circumstances have changed; or reassessment of the child and family indicates that a child protection plan is not necessary).
- The child and family have moved permanently to another local authority area. In such cases, the receiving local authority should convene a child protection conference within 15 working days of being notified of the move, only after which event may deregistration take place in respect of the original authority's child protection register.
- The child has reached 18 years of age, has died or has permanently left the UK.

When a child's name is removed from the child protection register notification should be sent to all those agencies that were invited to the initial conference.

A child whose name is removed from the child protection register may still require additional support services and deregistration should never lead to the automatic withdrawal of help.

This activity is designed to make you think about what needs to be considered when making a de-registration decision at a conference. Although when in a conference situation you will have greater information, it helps if you have thought about the kinds of scenarios you might be dealing with.

Scenario 1	A mother with three children under the age of ten, who are on the child protection register under the category of physical harm. The children's names were placed on the child protection register because the youngest child sustained an injury when he was trying to protect his mother from his father. Since the initial child protection conference and child protection registration, Mother has left her husband, with the support of the domestic violence services. She has instigated divorce proceedings and will only allow her children to see their father under the supervision of grandparents.
Scenario 2	Cory is an eight-year-old child, whose name was placed on the child protection register under the category of emotional harm, as a result of concerns about her mother's mental health and the impact this had on her parenting. Cory had displayed aggressive and bizarre behaviour both in school and with the neighbour's children. Mother had been unresponsive and would not undertake any work with professionals.
	Review conference information indicates that the daughter has now settled at school and her aggressive behaviour has ceased. She is making plans and appears to be a focused child. Assessment of mother shows her not to have any enduring mental health problems and that her health is stable at present. Mother is continuing to undertake counselling on a voluntary basis and is happy to work with Health and Social Services for support into the future. The core assessment recommended at conference has not been completed.

➡

Scenario 3	A mother has moved to your area with her children, who were placed on the previous authority's child protection register with concerns about the violence and drug misuse of the mother's partner. The children's names automatically transfer onto the new authority's child protection register, but a child protection conference is required to ascertain if the children continue to be at risk of significant harm given the changed circumstances. Mother herself was also known to have misused alcohol, and as a result there were issues of neglect with the children. Social Services have completed an initial assessment of mother and children in the new accommodation. Although it is cramped, the children appear to be well cared for and are attending nursery and school. Mother has sought help for her alcohol misuse and receives regular monitoring and support via the alcohol advisory service.
Scenario 4	A father is currently being investigated for viewing child pornography via the Internet and is awaiting Police scrutiny of his computer. He is living outside the home with his parents. Mother has a baby and young toddler living with her and wants her husband to return home, as soon as possible. She is undecided about his use of the Internet. However, she is clear that she will work with Social Services and will not allow her husband to return to the home or have unsupervised contact until the results of the police investigation are known.
Scenario 5	Jonathan is a young child who has suffered physical harm at home from over chastisement by his mother. Mother stated that she lost her temper with him several times as she found his behaviour difficult to manage. The local authority accommodated Jonathan on a voluntary basis and he currently lives with foster carers, while difficulties in family relationships are addressed. Jonathan has contact with his mother once a week, unsupervised, as mother now states that she does not have a problem with his behaviour in the short time that she sees him. Jonathan was originally placed on the child protection register because of a risk of physical harm.

Scenario 6	Maryam's name was placed on the child protection register at risk of sexual harm from her father. Allegations were made about her father sexually harming an older child from a previous marriage. The investigation was unsubstantiated and father was not prosecuted. A child protection conference held in respect of Maryam placed her name on the child protection register, following concerns about sexual harm pending a risk assessment of father. Her mother and father are now separated and her father's whereabouts are unknown. The risk assessment has not been completed, but mother is adamant that her husband will not return.
Scenario 7	Jake was placed on the child protection register because of concerns about neglect. As a young baby he never reached the appropriate growth for his age, frequently suffered minor illnesses and appeared grossly under-stimulated. Since the last child protection conference Jake has been removed from his parents' care. He is now subject to a care order and the plan is one of adoption.

1. Consider the above scenarios.
2. Based on the initial information given here, would you de-register in the circumstances?

CASE STUDY:

RUTH

Think about the information provided below both at the initial and review conference.

Ruth Morrel was placed on the child protection register two years ago, originally under the category of sexual harm because her father had been prosecuted for sexual assault of an older child in another family. Ruth's mother has learning difficulties. She separated from Ruth's father and has not allowed contact. However, at review conferences, professionals have become increasingly alarmed at the care provided for Ruth and the category of registration was changed to neglect to reflect those concerns. The concerns included a poor home environment, as the house is often messy and cluttered; there is usually little evidence of food in the house, but Mrs Morrel appears to provide tea for Ruth. The family have a dog and do not always clear up after it. The house has one bedroom and mother has had several partners staying over. Ruth slept on the sofa, which meant that she could not sleep until her mother went to bed and this could be very late. Ruth was often found asleep at school. There also appeared to be a lack of supervision and Ruth had been seen wandering in the village alone. Mrs Morrel has difficulty controlling her daughter and often just responds to her requests. There is no evidence of boundaries or routine in the household. Ruth herself is showing signs of having learning difficulties and requires a great deal of input with work at home to progress at school, which is not provided by Mrs Morrel. In addition, Mrs Morrel is never at home when a support service arrives to work with both Ruth and herself.

The original plan for Ruth was as follows:	
A core assessment	To be completed by Social Services with the family and other professionals involved. The assessment was intended to establish the strengths and weaknesses of the family to target support.
A family support service	To be provided to mother to help her establish parenting skills with Ruth. The work would include helping mother understand what children need, e.g. health, diet and also to advise and guide in putting parenting advice into practice.
Social Services support	To be provided to mother to find larger accommodation
A written agreement	Not allowing contact between Ruth and her father without prior consultation with Social Services.
Support learning service	To work with mother and Ruth at school.
Review	Sleeping arrangements in the home.
Mother's current partner	To be included in the assessment.

Review conference information

Social Services Report

Mrs Morrel has been unable to attend conference because she has had to attend a medical appointment. Mrs Morrel is pregnant with her second child.

The house is in an improved condition compared to two years ago when it was in a very poor state. The home is now clean and tidy and Ruth uses the bedroom while Mrs Morrel sleeps in the living room on the sofa. Mrs Morrel appears well in herself and feels she is progressing with Ruth. Mrs Morrel does now have a relationship with a man called Brian, although she has not supplied his last name to Social Services to check. Mrs Morrel states that Brian has no contact with Ruth and only visits the home when Ruth is out.

School information

Ruth is a sickly child who seems to pick up illnesses. Ruth has suffered from ongoing head lice, which has been brought to Mrs Morrel's attention several times and has also been addressed by the school nurse.

➡

Ruth is often not in school on time and Mrs Morrel is frequently late in collecting her to take her home.

Ruth is subject to a Statement of Special Educational Needs and requires a lot of school support; she is making very slow academic progress. Mother now goes into school to work with Ruth and learn the activities she needs to do with her at home.

Ruth's teacher has informed the head teacher that Ruth often looks tired and lacks energy. Staff believe that Ruth now has her own bedroom.

Education Welfare Report

Education Welfare reported they had no involvement with Ruth and she appeared to be attending school regularly.

School nurse

The school nurse stated that she had been monitoring Ruth's growth and she is slightly underweight for her height and growth. She agreed that Ruth presents as a pale sickly child. The nurse has given Mrs Morrel extensive advice about how to manage head lice over a long period of time, but this does not seem to have had the desired effect. The nurse has even taken Mrs Morrel to the GP to request medication to treat the lice, but they seem to return.

Police

The police have no new information since the previous conference.

1. Consider the reasons why Ruth's name was placed on the register.
2. Examine the information at the review conference.
3. Are there any areas about which you would like more information?
4. Would you recommend Ruth's name be removed from the child protection register?
5. If not, what work would you like to see carried out with the family?

Dual registration

Most child protection conferences will need to consider the appropriateness of continued child protection registration when there is a care order or interim care order in place.

There are occasions during a period of child protection registration when circumstances alter significantly and legal action has been initiated because the risk of harm has significantly increased and it may no longer be safe to leave the child in the home. If a child is subject to an interim care order or care order then the conference may wish to consider de-registration to avoid a situation of dual registration.

A care order or interim care order provides the local authority with shared parental responsibility. Either legal order will also include a care plan that has been agreed in the court arena. The care plan will decide where a child lives and what, if any, work needs to be carried out with the family. As such, the plan will ensure that the child is not placed at continuing risk of significant harm. As a looked-after child, under the auspices of shared parental responsibility with the local authority, regular inter-agency reviews are carried out to monitor and plan for the best interests of the child.

In such circumstances, the conference should seriously consider why it would feel that the child is at continuing risk of significant harm, given the court agreement to a plan, and whether the child protection plan will not just duplicate the looked-after arrangements involving the same professionals.

It may often be appropriate to remove the child's name from the child protection register to avoid dual registration and involving the family in a similar process twice. The chair of the child protection conference will guide you as a professional in this matter, but it is helpful if you have an awareness of the issue to be considered. You can ask questions of the chair if you need to check the situation further in relation to a particular child you work with.

Summary

- An outline of a child protection plan is formulated when a child protection conference has made a decision to place a child's name on the child protection register.

- Once an initial conference has agreed a child protection plan the meeting will agree a core group and a review conference date that should be set within three months of the initial conference.

- Members of the core group should comprise the key worker (social worker for the child), child (if appropriate) and family members, professionals or foster carers, who will have direct contact with the family, e.g. health visitor, teacher, nursery worker, GP, probation, and midwife.

- The core group will address the outline child protection plan agreed at conference and add detail about what needs to be done, why, by whom and when.

- One of the recommendations of government guidance regarding child protection and an indication of good practice is to draw up a written agreement with the family to fulfil the child protection plan.

- Both parents and children should be encouraged to identify actions that might contribute to the child's welfare when formulating the child protection plan. Responsibilities for actions are given to family members as well as professionals.

- If the child's name is placed on the child protection register at the initial conference a review conference date is set for 3 months from the initial conference. Thereafter, the review conferences will take place at six-monthly intervals, until the conference members decide the child is no longer at risk of significant harm.

◆ The purpose of the review conference is to review the progress of the child protection plan and any new information and decide if the child is at continuing risk of significant harm and requires continued child protection

◆ A child's name may be removed from the register if it is judged that the child is no longer at continuing risk of significant harm requiring safeguarding by means of a child protection plan.

CHECKPOINT

1. What is a core group?
2. Who might be the key members of a core group?
3. What is the timescale for review conferences?
4. What is the criteria for de-registration?
5. What information might be required for a review conference?
6. What is dual registration?
7. What areas should be covered in a written agreement?
8. What are the advantages of core groups?
9. What are should be agreed at core groups?
10. What are three good practice tips for core groups?

Chapter 8

Lessons from Inquiries

> At his trial, Manning said that Kouao would strike Victoria on a daily basis with a shoe, a coat hanger and a wooden cooking spoon and would strike her on her toes with a hammer. Victoria's blood was found on Manning's football boots. Manning admitted that at times he would hit Victoria with a bicycle chain. Chillingly, he said, 'You could beat her and she wouldn't cry… she could take the beatings and the pain like anything'.
>
> Victoria spent much of her last days, in the winter of 1999–2000, living and sleeping in a bath in an unheated bathroom, bound hand and foot inside a bin bag, lying in her own urine and faeces. It is not surprising then that towards the end of her short life, Victoria was stooped like an old lady and could walk only with great difficulty.
>
> © Crown copyright

The extracts above are from 'The Victoria Climbie Inquiry' (Department of Health & Home Office 2003), one of the most recent inquiries into child death and one that has affected the structure and organisation of services to protect children in the community. The most lasting tribute to the memory of Victoria would be if her suffering and death resulted in an improvement in the quality of the management and leadership in these key services.

This chapter consolidates both what has been learnt from inquiries into child deaths and findings from research that can inform our learning in relation to thinking about and identifying when we should be worried about something that we have seen or have concerns about, at any stage in working with a family.

A brief outline of the details of the major inquiries in child protection is given and there is a discussion of the common problems encountered by those involved with the individual cases when things have gone wrong.

By the end of this chapter you should be familiar with the common features of inquiries and failings of the child protection system. Good practice suggestions aimed at strengthening inter-agency working, and supporting children in their community, should help you in your work.

Background

Several children die each year at the hands of their parents, but not all child deaths appear in the public press.

There are calls for major changes largely when there has been public interest in specific tragic cases. These are cases where the family has generally been known to a number of agencies. Few people have not heard of Maria Colwell, Jasmine Beckford or Kimberley Carlile. These cases have brought about major changes in the way that child protection services are organised and delivered.

The enquiries into the deaths of these children brought about a number of major changes in social work.

The death of Maria Colwell caused the government to bring about a number of major changes, including a new piece of legislation, the Children Act 1975, which strengthened the position of foster families.

The Cleveland inquiry resulted in the implementation of the Children Act 1989, strengthening requirements on Social Services to work in partnership with families.

The recent publication of the inquiry into the death of Victoria Climbie is likely to bring about major changes in the way that information is shared between agencies and in the way that child protection services are organised and managed.

Some major inquiries

1973: Maria Colwell, aged 7 years

Maria died after being beaten and starved by her stepfather, William Kepple. Maria's aunt and uncle had fostered her because of neglect by her mother. Five years later, Maria's mother decided that Maria should return to live with her and she was supported by Social Services. Maria's aunt and uncle wished to continue looking after her. Fifteen months after returning home, Maria was killed.

Neighbours and school had reported physical abuse and neglect of all the children. Maria was seen less often and her school noticed that she was losing weight. All agencies involved in the case were criticised.

1984: Jasmine Beckford, aged 4 years

Jasmine was starved and battered to death by her stepfather, Maurice Beckford. Jasmine had been in the care of Social Services for two-and-a- half years and was then returned to the care of her mother. Health and Social Services then monitored the care of Jasmine for two years, although she was seen by a social worker only once in 10 months. Jasmine was not seen regularly at nursery and stopped attending ten months before she was killed.

1984: Tyra Henry, aged 21 months

Tyra was assaulted and bitten by her father, Andrew Neil, and was left abandoned outside a hospital. Tyra was still on a Care Order to the local authority at the time of her death. Tyra had been placed on a Care Order because Andrew Neil had seriously assaulted her brother when he was four-months-old, causing him to be blind and mentally handicapped. Andrew Neil was violent to both Claudette, Tyra's mother, and to Tyra.

1984 Heidi Koseda, aged 10 years

Heidi Koseda was locked in a room and was starved to death. Her body was found in a cupboard. Her stepfather, Nicholas Price, was found guilty of murder and her mother, Rosemary, was found guilty of manslaughter and detained in a high security psychiatric hospital.

An inquiry into her death in 1986 identified that a complaint of child abuse by a neighbour had not been responded to by Social Services. The neighbour had reported that she had not seen Heidi and that her brother was bruised.

1986: Kimberley Carlile, aged 4 years

Kimberley was beaten to death with a belt, scalded with water and burned with cigarettes in 15 places by her stepfather, Nigel Hall. He was found guilty of murder and her mother was found guilty of assault and cruelty.

The children had previously been in the care of Social Services, but Pauline Carlile had decided that she wanted them to live with her new partner, Nigel Hall, and herself. The local authority that had been looking after the children, Wirral, asked Greenwich Social Services to monitor the children's care, but this did not happen. Nigel Hall obstructed Social Services and health workers when they tried to visit. The only time that the children were seen was when Nigel Hall brought the children to the Social Services office, instead of allowing a visit to the home. Kimberley was not seen alive again after this visit.

1987: Doreen Mason, aged 16 months

Doreen died after her mother and boyfriend bruised, burnt and broke her leg and then did not take her for treatment. Christine Mason and Roy Aston were convicted of manslaughter and cruelty.

1992: Leanne White, aged 3 years.

Leanne was beaten to death by her stepfather, Colin Sleate. Leanne had 107 external injuries and died of internal bleeding. Her stepfather was found guilty of murder and her mother of manslaughter.

Social Services had failed to respond adequately to reports of concerns by her grandmother and neighbours.

1994: Rikki Neave, aged 6 years

Rikki was strangled by an anorak zip. His body was found in a wood. His mother, Ruth, admitted cruelty. Rikki had been on the 'at risk' register and his mother had repeatedly asked social workers to take Rikki into care.

2000: Victoria Climbie, aged 8 years

Victoria died from hypothermia following months of severe abuse and neglect. She had suffered 128 injuries. Victoria had come to Britain to live with her aunt in order to improve her life chances. Her aunt and her boyfriend were both found guilty of murder.

Victoria had been presented with injuries at hospital on a number of occasions, but no action had been taken to protect her. On one occasion, there was concern about a non-accidental injury, but this was later diagnosed as a skin condition and Victoria was discharged to her aunt's care.

2000: Lauren Wright, aged 6 years

Lauren was killed by her stepmother, Tracey Wright, after being punched or kicked by her, causing internal injuries. The pathologist commented that Lauren had injuries 'like those of a road traffic victim'.

Lauren's name was on the Child Protection Register, but there was a delay in informing Social Services when the family moved. Neighbours had reported concerns to Social Services, but they had failed to respond in time.

2002: Ainlee Labonte, aged 2 years

Ainlee was starved and tortured by her parents, Leanne and Dennis. She had 64 scars and bruises on her body and weighed 9.5 kilogrammes, which was about half the normal weight for a child of that age. Workers were afraid to visit the family.

Learning from inquiries

What do we know about these children and their backgrounds that might help to prevent deaths in the future?

Each time that there is a child death, or an incident of serious injury to a child, and abuse or neglect are known, or suspected, to be a factor in the death, each agency holds an inquiry. The purpose of this inquiry is not to attribute blame to particular individuals or agencies, but to learn about what went wrong and to make recommendations about how future tragedies might be avoided in the future. This inquiry is called a case review.

> *Where a child dies, and abuse or neglect are known or suspected to be a factor in the death, local agencies should consider immediately whether there are other children at risk of harm who need safeguarding (e.g. siblings or other children in an institution in which abuse is alleged.) Thereafter, agencies should consider whether there are any lessons to be learned from the tragedy about the ways in which they work together to safeguard children.*

Department of Health 1999: p.87

The Department of Health advises Area Child Protection Committees always to hold a case review in the following circumstances:

♦ Where a child dies and abuse or neglect are known or suspected to be a factor in the death.

In addition the ACPC should also consider a review:

♦ in cases of both child death and where a child 'sustains a potentially life-threatening injury or serious and permanent impairment of health and development'

♦ where a child has been subject to particularly serious sexual abuse and the case gives rise to concerns about inter-agency working to protect children.

The purpose of carrying out a case review is to consider the factors shown in the diagram below:

Purpose of a case review

What has been learnt?

In the inquiry reports into child death, there has been a focus on what went wrong and what changes we can make in practice to reduce the risk of the same thing happening again.

Until recent years, little or no attention had been paid to try and identify common features in relation to the children themselves and their families, in order to discover whether lessons could be learnt from this, to inform practice in the future.

Research studies

Reder, Duncan and Grey carried out the first major study into child deaths and published a book about this, entitled *Beyond Blame* (1993).

Prior to this, a number of authors had considered individual child deaths in some detail, or had studied the backgrounds of those involved (Greenland, 1987), but this was the first time that a study into the key features of child deaths had been carried out. The authors reviewed thirty-five inquiry reports, beginning with Graham Bagnall in 1973 and finishing with Doreen Aston in 1989.

Reder and Duncan (1999) considered both the children and their family context. A number of their findings are outlined below.

The children

Gender

Of the thirty-five deaths, nineteen were boys and sixteen were girls.

In a subsequent study, boys accounted for twenty-six deaths and twenty-four deaths were attributed to girls, with the gender of one child not recorded.

Age

In the first study, six of the children (18 per cent) were below the age of one and sixteen (47 per cent) were under two years. All of the children were aged nine years or under, with most (91 per cent) younger than six years. In the second study, 47 per cent were under one year and 78.4 per cent under two years.

Position in the family

Sixty-six per cent were the youngest or only child in the household. This is illustrated in the graph below.

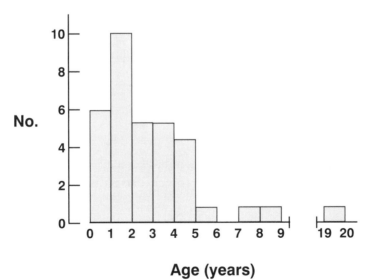

Age of the fatally abused children (known for 34 children)   Source: *Reder and Duncan, 1999*

Types of abuse

Physical harm

The majority of children in child abuse inquiries had been physically abused for some time before their death. A number of children had received treatment in hospital for their injuries. This is a pattern that has continued from the earlier inquiries, when Kimberley Carlile's broken leg was concealed, until the Victoria Climbie enquiry. Many children had also suffered neglect, including malnutrition, along with physical injury. Again, this is a pattern that continues, and was evident in both Ainlee Labonte's case and Victoria Climbie's. Victoria had arrived at hospital on two occasions, prior to the final one, with physical injuries. Whilst in hospital, one nurse noticed what she thought was a belt buckle mark on Victoria's shoulder and another nurse also observed bite marks.

Neglect

Neglect is often combined with physical abuse, but in some cases is the main form of abuse. In those cases, studies suggest that the parents and carers do not recognise or are not able to put their children's needs before their own.

In the Charlene Salt case, her parents were often in bed when professionals called and Charlene was left dirty and hungry. The parents spent money given to them to buy things for Charlene on a new car.

The Gates children were often left alone in the house without food and had infected scabies and nits. As babies, their mother tried to feed them crisps, cola and sour milk. All of them had been admitted to hospital following various accidents, including swallowing rat poison and their mother's pills. Lucy died when an electric fire fell on her while her mother was out.

A number of children were locked or shut away, as if they did not exist. These children had no contact with the outside world or even with the rest of the family living in the house.

Heidi Koseda began to be neglected when her mother moved in with Nicholas Price, and Heidi was seen only rarely after that. It is suggested that Heidi was shut away from the time that her mother became pregnant.

Likewise, in the Malcolm Page case, Malcolm's mother was about one month pregnant at the time of Malcolm's death. Malcolm died from malnutrition and hypothermia.

It is likely that during the most part of the last four months of her life, Victoria slept in the bath and in the latter part of this period, spent time during the day there, including being given meals on a piece of plastic.

The carers

Gender

In the *Beyond Blame* study (Reder, Duncan & Gray 1993) 54 per cent of the caretakers causing death were male and 46 per cent were female.

In the *Lost Innocents* study (Reder & Duncan 1999) based on deaths in the year to 1994, 57 per cent of the caretakers causing death were female and 43 per cent were male.

Age

Most of the caretakers (71 per cent) were aged between 20 and 29 at the time of the child's death in the *Beyond Blame* study and 53 per cent were in their twenties in the *Lost Innocents* study.

Relationship to child

It was mostly a child's birth parent who was responsible for killing him/her, with step-parents being responsible for a minority of deaths.

Family relationships

Parents who have difficulties in parenting their children sometimes have these problems because of their own experience of parenting. There are a number of ways that parenting might be affected:

◆ Where the carer has been so harmed by the way that they have been looked after that they are not able to put their child's needs first. For example, the mother of Rosie in Chapter 3, who was heard to tell her that she would have to wait for her dinner, as her mummy was hungry and needed to have her dinner first.

◆ The parent may have left home at an early age, hoping that a new partner will meet their needs. They may feel that a baby will provide them with the love and attention that their own parent didn't provide and may continue to have more babies, in an attempt to find this. (Maria Colwell's mother had ten children). In fact, having a baby means that the relationship will change, as the baby will have its own needs to be met, which may mean that it is not possible to put the parent's own needs or the needs of a partner first. This then causes further problems, especially where both parents have had previous difficulties.

THINK ABOUT IT

Most relationships are affected by the birth of a baby, as there is another person in the family, whose needs have to be met. In the case of a baby, he or she is dependent on its parents and carers for all of its needs, as the baby is unable to care for itself. This requires parents to know what the child's needs are and to provide for them on a regular and consistent basis.

Think about a baby's needs for care. What are they?

How might these needs affect a couple's lifestyle and relationship?

What happens when one partner does not want to change his/her lifestyle, or be involved in the baby's care?

REFLECT ON YOUR PRACTICE

When you are working with a family about which you have some concerns:

◆ What do you know about the couple's history/relationship?

◆ What is their current lifestyle?

◆ Are the couple planning any changes?

◆ Have they thought about how a child might cause some changes?

Unplanned/unwanted pregnancy

In a number of cases of child death in the *Lost Innocents* study (Reder and Duncan, 1999), the mothers concerned had been unsure about having or had not wanted their children. An indication of this may have been that they did not keep regular antenatal appointments (evidenced in the Doreen Aston, Shirley Woodcock inquiries). Failure to keep antenatal appointments occurred in 55 per cent of the cases in the *Lost Innocents* study. Other mothers discharged themselves from hospital, leaving their children behind. The mothers of three children in the *Beyond Blame* study (Reder, Duncan & Gray 1993) discharged themselves from hospital, against medical advice.

There is no evidence from these studies, but it is recognised elsewhere that concealed pregnancies are another factor in child deaths.

In the death of baby G, the mother, who had previously had difficulties related to her own experience of parenting, concealed her pregnancy and gave birth at home. No one, except the mother, was aware of the baby's existence. The mother concealed the child within the home and eventually placed it out of sight, where she ceased to feed or care for it.

REFLECT ON YOUR PRACTICE

◆ Is the mother preparing for pregnancy?

◆ Is she attending antenatal classes and health appointments? Is her partner also attending?

◆ Have the parents/mother made any lifestyle changes in planning for the baby's birth, e.g. looking for a new house, budgeting/saving, arranging a bedroom?

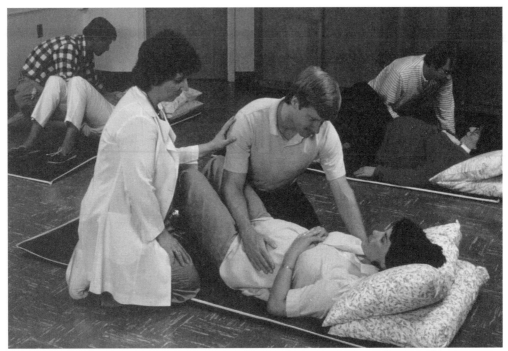

Regular attendance at antenatal classes is an indicator of parents preparing for parenthood

Crises in relationships

Children can be particularly at risk in times of difficulties and crises in their parents' relationship, especially when there is a chance that the relationship may finish and one parent may be left alone with the child.

For example, the mother of child A left her child and partner after several incidents of domestic violence. On the last occasion, the mother left her child in the care of his father, who subsequently shook the child on two separate occasions, causing serious brain damage to the child on the second occasion. Hester and Pearson (1998) in a study of child abuse cases in which domestic violence was an issue, included an example of a father holding a six-week-old baby over a first floor balcony in order to prevent the child's mother from leaving him, after she had been physically assaulted by him.

Use of drugs/alcohol

It is not possible to say that the use of drugs or alcohol per se are a factor in child deaths, since there will also be other factors that have been contributory, such as the parent's life experiences. Some parents with personal difficulties use drugs as a means of coping with the stresses of everyday life, or of blotting out uncomfortable feelings. In the *Lost Innocents* study, drug and alcohol use were a feature in seven deaths. Two children died as a result of ingesting drugs. In five of the seven cases, the children died as a result of a violent assault.

(Reder and Duncan 1999: p.52)

Violence

Violence between the partners was a feature in at least a half of the cases in Reder and Duncan's study into child deaths.

Domestic violence was a feature in the deaths of Maria Colwell, Sukina Hammond and Toni Dales, but at the time, the relevance of this information was not really recognised. It was only in the 1990s that research identified the links between domestic violence and child abuse. Previously, domestic violence was very much a 'hidden' problem.

There is considerable evidence from child protection studies that identifies a causal link between child abuse and domestic violence.

Cleaver and Freeman found, in a study of S47 inquiries, that almost 50 per cent of the cases involved in their study of 30 families involved domestic violence (Department of Health 1995).

Farmer and Owen found that 52 per cent of a sample of 44 cases involved domestic violence (Department of Health 1995).

Violence was such a concern in the family of Ainlee Labonte that workers were afraid to visit.

THINK ABOUT IT

If adults are afraid to visit a house because of fear of violence, what do you think it feels like to be a child in that family? Children will also be fearful of violence, as well as suffering actual violence.

In a study by NCH Action for Children (Abrahams 1994), at least 27 per cent of children, whose mothers were victims of domestic violence, reported violence towards themselves. A survey of children calling Childline who rang up about domestic violence reported that 38 per cent had also been physically abused (Epstein and Keep 1995).

In the cases of Sukina Hammond and Toni Dales, neither child was specifically asked about their experiences at home. Both had expressed fears about their fathers to social workers, hospital staff and nursery staff, but their fears were ignored, rather than explored.

REFLECT ON YOUR PRACTICE

- ◆ It is important that we talk to and listen to children and adults when we have concerns about domestic violence and abuse.
- ◆ If questions are not asked, then problems remain hidden. It is not easy for victims to ask directly for help.
- ◆ Do ask children about domestic violence, where there is an opportunity.
- ◆ It should not be assumed that someone else will do this, or that the child will want to talk to someone else.

Warnings

These occur when families make comments or give signs that there are serious problems and a child may be in danger. For example, when a mother with a history of mental health difficulties says on more than one occasion that she does not want the child, or makes threats to harm it. Such remarks should be taken seriously and reported to Social Services. Rikki Neave's mother had frequently asked for him to be taken into care.

Closure

'Closure' is a term used to describe when families withdraw from contact with involved agencies, for example by moving away, or not allowing anyone into the house. This happened in the case of Kimberley Carlile.

Management of individual cases (agency context)

Response to reports of child concern/child abuse

A recurring feature of child abuse inquiries is how the initial inquiry is received and responded to. Inquiries emphasise the need for both a response to inquiries and one that is timely. There have been examples of failures to respond to referrals.

For example, a telephone call to the NSPCC from a neighbour of the Price/Koseda family, expressing concerns about possible ill treatment to Heidi and her brother was not responded to.

In the case of Victoria Climbie, a referral was made to Social Services by a distant relative, Esther Ackah. Esther gave details of a child called 'Anna'. She said that she was worried about the unfit accommodation that the child was living in; the child was having problems with incontinence; she had a scar on her face, which her mother said was due to a fall from an escalator; and she had concerns for Anna's well-being. Mrs Ackah said that she believed Victoria's life was in danger due to her living conditions and that she wanted Social Services to make an urgent visit. The member of staff in the call centre took the details and passed these on to the child protection team.

No one picked up the referral in the team that afternoon and the next sighting of the referral was three weeks' later.

Mrs Ackah had called again a few days later to ask if anyone had visited, and was reassured that something would have been done, but her second call was not passed on to the Social Services team.

REFLECT ON YOUR PRACTICE

Follow up all referrals made to Social Services in writing and, if not contacted, write again or ask your manager or local contact to make enquiries about progress.

Seeing the child

Inquiries emphasise that children must be seen. The Kimberley Carlile inquiry describes that toward the end of a visit, the team leader was permitted to peep through the small glass panel at the top of the door into one of the children's bedrooms.

In the Heidi Koseda inquiry, there was a failure to see all the children, even when executing a legal order. The room in which Heidi was lying dead was not entered because it was considered to have been treated with chemicals.

It is also important that children are seen in their home surroundings and not presented in an office, as was the case with Kimberley Carlile.

Talking to and listening to children

This was discussed at length in the Cleveland inquiry, which emphasises that children should be seen and spoken to.

It is a serious concern that in some instances, where there are issues of child protection, some children may still not be seen and spoken to.

In the Climbie case, when Victoria was admitted to hospital and there were serious concerns about her injuries, she was taken into police protection, without being spoken to. Indeed, a S47 inquiry was never started, and Victoria was never interviewed, as part of this inquiry. When Victoria was subsequently seen, a translator was not involved, as Social Services accepted her carer's view that she spoke English.

Persistence

On occasions, there are difficulties in gaining access to children, for various reasons. However, it is important that social workers persist in their intention to see children and in checking out the explanations given, rather than seeing what they want to believe.

Two workers in the Hall/Carlile case were told that the children were in bed and could not be seen.

Assessment

In a study of inquiry reports, published in 1991, it is identified that 'the need for assessment is considered in government guidelines, and established in professional practice, as an essential of moving from receipt of referral or investigation to treatment. Yet assessment is consistently missing from the practice of the cases described in the inquiries.' (Department of Health 1991: p.78).

'In the Shirley Woodcock inquiry, Shirley was part of a family that was well-known to the local authority. It should have been possible to establish a clear approach to the social work service to be offered to the family. Instead, the response appears to have been unfocused and unplanned. If focused assistance, based on a proper assessment, had been provided from early stages of the case, evidence might have emerged which would have provided the basis of legal intervention at an earlier stage.' (Department of Health 1991: p.78)

The Cleveland inquiry also recommended that there should be a full assessment of the family.

REFLECT ON YOUR PRACTICE

The Department of Health has outlined the role of other agencies in assisting with assessments.

'Everyone should...contribute to the initial or core assessments and undertake specialist assessments, if requested, of the child or family members.'

Confidentiality

In 1991, it was noted that 'the issue of confidentiality remains problematic for clients and professionals.' (Department of health 1991: p.100)

In the Christopher Pinder inquiry, it was noted that 'there are, however, situations in childcare where the concept of confidentiality becomes a barrier to communication and may place the child unnecessarily at risk'.

Sadly, this is noted as an ongoing difficulty, following the introduction of the Data Protection Act, with professionals being confused about information sharing.

The Climbie inquiry recommends that:

The government should issue guidance on the Data Protection Act 1998, The Human Rights Act, and common law rules on confidentiality. The government should issue guidance as and when these impact on the sharing of information between professional groups in circumstances where there are concerns about the welfare of children and families.

Department of Health & Home Office 2003: Recommendation 16

REFLECT ON YOUR PRACTICE

Recent guidance states that it is best to seek consent to making a referral, but you should not do this if you think this would be contrary to a child's welfare. For example, if the information is needed urgently the delay in obtaining consent may not be justified. Seeking consent may prejudice a police investigation or may increase the risk of harm to a child.

Record keeping

Good record keeping is seen as essential to good practice in casework. The case records are the evidence of all contact and work done with a family.

In respect of school records, the Beckford inquiry noted a lack of any centralised system of recording information about child abuse registration or statutory orders in schools. An issue of how much information should be passed on when a child changes schools was also identified.

Inter-agency working

Some of the recurring themes identified from difficulties encountered in inter-agency working are discussed below.

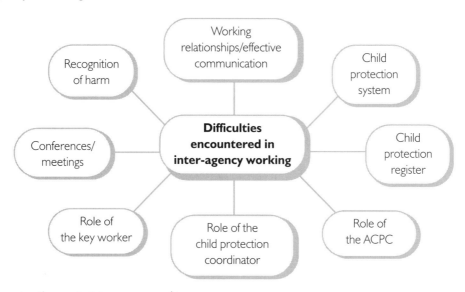

Recurring themes in inter-agency working

The table on page 214 illustrates the range of workers involved in 19 case reviews of child deaths.

As can be seen, day nursery staff were involved in 54 per cent of the cases and teachers were involved in 54 per cent of cases.

In most cases, there were at least five professionals involved with the children. One would like to think that this could be an effective, community-based support network, with all professionals working together to provide care and safety for the children. Often this is the case, but sometimes things go wrong.

	CLV	'A'	DA	JB	JC	KC	RC	RF	LG	CH	TH	EJH	LJ	HK	KMcG	CP	JP	CS	SW
Workers & others involved																			
Social Worker	X	X	X	X	X	X	X	X	X	X	X	X	X	X	X	X	X	X	X
Police	X	X	X					X	X		X		X	X	X		X		
Police Surgeon	X													X					
NSPCC	X								X					X					
Child Abuse Consultant Co-ordinator					X	X			X					X					
GP	X	X		X	X	X	X		X				X		X	X	X		X
Health Visitor		X	X	X	X	X	X	X	X	X	X		X	X	X	X	X	X	X
Paediatrician	X	X		X	X			X	X						X				X
Psychiatrist	X								X										
Accident & Emergency Dept				X	X		X	X	X				X		X		X	X	X
Nurse	X		X		X									X			X		
School Nurse						X			X										
Midwife			X						X	X				X			X		
Day Nursery Staff			X	X	X				X	X							X	X	
Teacher		X		X		X			X	X	X		X						
Childminder									X										
Education Welfare Officer/ Social Worker	X				X		X		X	X	X			X					
Psychologist	X	X							X										
Probation Officer								X			X		X				X		
Housing Welfare Officer											X								
Homeless Persons Officer/ Unit											X		X						X
Social Security Officer									X										
Home Help/Family Aide									X									X	
Independent S.W./Guardian			X												X	X	X		
Court Welfare Officer						X													
Magistrate	X			X														X	
Family	X		X				X				X		X	X	X				
Foster Parents	X	X		X		X			X			X	X		X		X	X	
Neighbours									X					X	X				

The range of workers involved in 19 case reviews of child deaths

Source: Department of Health: A study of inquiries © Crown copyright

Inter-agency communication

'Once upon a time there was a little chicken called Chicken Licken. One day an acorn fell from a tree and hit Chicken Licken on the head.

Chicken Licken thought that the sky was falling down ...so he ran off to tell the king.

On the way he met Henny Penny and told her that the sky was falling in and that they must go and tell the king. So they rushed off together ...

On the way they met ...Cocky Locky ... and ... Ducky Lucky ... and ... Drakey Lakey ... and ... Goosey Loosey ... and Turkey Lurkey ... and they all hurried on to tell the king that the sky was falling down.

Then they met Foxy Loxy. 'Oh! Foxy Loxy!' said Chicken Licken. 'The sky is falling down and we are on our way to tell the king.'

'I know where to find the king,' said Foxy Loxy. 'You had better all follow me.'

Foxy Loxy led them straight into his den, where his wife and their little foxes were waiting for their dinners ...

So Chicken Licken never found the king to tell him that thought the sky was falling down.

Source: *Dangerous families*, by Dale, Davies, Morrison & Waters (1987), p42: Routledge

The above tale illustrates the most common feature of child death reviews, with information not being passed on to new workers or agencies, the core of the information being lost, or information not being shared amongst the involved workers.

The main problems have occurred in the following areas:

- crucial information is not passed on/shared /information not known
- 'not hearing', re-interpreting, or ignoring the message
- professional relationships/hierarchy
- role confusion
- workers absent/not available.

Information not passed on or shared/information not known

Examples of cases in which information was not passed on or shared are given overleaf:

Extract from the Inquiry into the death of Kimberley Carlile, 1987	'The report of the inquiry into the circumstances surrounding the death of Jasmine Beckford in December 1985 showed clearly that no system of exchanging information among the relevant agencies existed' (London Borough of Greenwich 1987)
Extract from the Inquiry into the death of Victoria Climbie, 2000	'Victoria was known to no less than two further housing authorities, four social services departments, two child protection teams of the Metropolitan Police Service, a specialist centre managed by the NSPCC, and she was admitted to two different hospitals because of suspected deliberate harm. The dreadful reality was that these services knew little or nothing more about Victoria at the end of the process than they did when she was first referred to Ealing Social Services by the Homeless Person's Unit in April 1999.' (Department of Health and Home Office 2003)

The two statements above illustrate the continuing problem of agencies not passing on or sharing information. Time and again, crucial information is either not passed on, or not acted on when it is received.

In the case of Lauren Wright, Social Services passed information on to Norfolk Social Services about the care of Lauren, but this was not acted upon.

In the case of Victoria Climbie, the concern reported by Mrs Akah was never pursued as a child protection matter, and the social workers were unclear about why they were visiting.

When Victoria was admitted to hospital with suspected non-accidental injuries, there was a delay in starting the inquiry and neither a S47 inquiry nor a S17 inquiry was ever completed. There was no assessment to put information together.

It was a serious oversight that there appears to have been no contact made with Education Services about Victoria. When social workers had contact with Ms Kouao, they did not ask where Victoria was attending school. Victoria was not enrolled in any school when she died, at the age of eight years and three months. A number of recommendations have been made in the Report of the Inquiry into the death of Victoria Climbie to address these problems.

They are set out in the table which follows.

Recommendations made in the Report of the Inquiry into the death of Victoria Climbie include:	
Recommendation 12	Front-line staff in each of the agencies that regularly come into contact with children must ensure that in each new contact basic information about the child is recorded. This includes the child's name, address, age, the name of the child's primary care giver, the child's GP, and the name of the child's school, if the child is of school age. Gaps in this information should be passed on to the relevant local authority in accordance with local arrangements.
Recommendation 24	Where, during the course of an assessment, Social Services establish that a child of school age is not attending school, they must alert the education authorities and satisfy themselves, that in the interim, the child is subject to adequate day care arrangements.

© Crown copyright

REFLECT ON YOUR PRACTICE

Members of the community and those providing day care for children should pass this information on to the local authority, to ensure that the child's needs are not overlooked.

In some cases, even when children are known to be on child protection registers, crucial information is not shared. For example, in the case review of PM (see page 224), it was noted that concerns noted by the hospital and the children's school were not shared with Social Services after PM's discharge from hospital.

Not hearing, re-interpreting or ignoring information

In some cases, social workers have been convinced that their plan for a family has been the correct one and have pursued this doggedly, seemingly ignoring or not paying attention to information from, or the views of, other agencies.

In the case of Lucie Gates, the social worker was sure that Lucie's mother could meet her needs and didn't take account of the many reports of concern from other agencies. These included, in the latter stages of Lucie's life: two-year check showing that she was underweight and under-stimulated; the mother hitting Lucie's sister in front of a teacher; hospital concerns about the number of reported accidents; and a volunteer worker finding Lucie alone in the flat.

In the case of Victoria Climbie, the social workers visiting Victoria Climbie at home were not sure why they were visiting.

In the case of PM, reports of physical injuries were reported to Social Services on two occasions, shortly before PM's name was removed from the Child Protection Register. On one occasion, the school reported bruising on the chin and a bite mark on the cheek. The consultant paediatrician said that the marks on PM's chin were inappropriate and needed further investigation.

When Victoria Climbie was admitted to hospital for the second time with a serious scald to her face, a strategy meeting was held and the case was allocated to a social worker. It was subsequently decided that Victoria should return to Kouao's care. A S47 inquiry was not carried out.

Role confusion/work allocated to a person who is not aware of it

This happens when someone thinks that someone else has the responsibility to do something, or has done something. It also means not taking any action, including not knowing that a task has been assigned.

In the case of Jasmine Beckford, a recommendation of a child protection conference was that the mother should be encouraged to attend a clinic monthly and that the health visitor should visit fortnightly.

A health visitor was not present at the meeting and the information was not passed on.

GOOD PRACTICE GUIDE

◆ For any child that Social Services are involved with, there will be a written support plan.

◆ A copy should be sent to all those involved in the plan.

◆ Check if you have copies of plans for families that your agency are involved with.

Professional relationships/ hierarchy of roles

In some cases, workers who see themselves as less important than other people think that their views are less important than those of someone whom they see as being more 'important' in their organisation, or in the community, e.g. a teaching assistant in a classroom, compared to a head teacher, or compared to a hospital paediatrician. This may result in the views of one professional dominating, with others not feeling confident to express their views or to challenge the opinions of others. Often, those who see themselves as less important have the most information about a child. Others may see a child only once or twice.

For example, in the first Jasmine Beckford child protection conference, the health visitor did not feel able to express her opinion that Jasmine was failing to thrive.

More recently, Social Services in the Victoria Climbie case did not challenge the medical opinion of the second doctor who saw Victoria at hospital and diagnosed scabies, when the first doctor had diagnosed non-accidental injury.

THINK ABOUT IT

◆ How easy do you find it to challenge the views of others, when you think they are wrong? Does the presence of someone that you see as more important affect what you feel able to say?

◆ What makes it easier for you to express your views? Would accompanying your manager, or someone more senior to a meeting help, or could you ask someone more senior to express your concerns if you don't feel they are being given enough consideration?

◆ Would some training help you? Your ACPC may run a child protection or child protection conference training course where this is addressed.

ACTIVITY

Find out about the training that your local ACPC offers. Is there a list in your work place, or do you have a contact who could advise you? If you are unsure, you may contact the ACPC directly.

Agencies not working together effectively

This happens when there is a split in views between the agencies or workers in a case, and these are not addressed or resolved. An example of this is when the social worker in the case feels there are serious child protection concerns about illness in a child being fabricated, whilst the GP thinks that this is only a minor problem of the mother being over-anxious. Both workers then become 'stuck' in this position, to the detriment of the child.

An example of this occurred in the Jasmine Beckford case, when foster carers complained about the condition of the children on their return from weekend visits to their mother, and Social Services did not follow these concerns up.

In the case of PM, when the paediatrician expressed a view in writing that he was concerned that the child's name had been removed from the register, no action was taken, although the conference could have been re-convened.

Child protection conferences

Child protection conferences have been seen as central to the management of inter-agency child protection case management. These are generally recognised to be an effective means of agencies coming together with families and exchanging information, which is then formulated into a child protection or family support plan.

Child protection registration is seen as an effective means of protecting children and, indeed, it is significant in studies of child deaths, that where a child protection conference hasn't been held, 'their absence usually signals a failure in the network's functioning' (Reder & Duncan 1999: p. 67). In fourteen of the thirty-five cases that Reder and Duncan reviewed, fourteen conferences had been held (40 per cent).

In the case of Victoria Climbie, a S47 inquiry was never completed and, therefore, there was no decision made about the need for a child protection conference and an inter-agency plan.

However, it is recommended in the Climbie inquiry that the child protection register should be replaced.

One of the difficulties at child protection conferences is the perceived 'hierarchy' of decision-making, as discussed above.

Another issue is that of attendance at the conference. Decision-making can only be influenced by those attending, or represented at the meeting.

It is crucial that professionals attending conference are aware of previous concerns, as well as having a current involvement.

The Doreen Aston inquiry recommended that not only should written information be provided to a conference, but also there should be a written case history, to be up-dated for each meeting (a **chronology**).

THINK ABOUT IT

- Have you attended a child protection conference?
- How did you feel when you attended?
- Did anyone prepare you for the event before you attended?
- Did you take a report with you?
- Were you confident about the conference decision and plan?
- Did you contribute to the Child Protection Plan?

If you have not attended a conference, ask your line manager or link worker if it might be possible for you to attend a meeting as an observer.

The keyworker/implementation and review of plans

The Beckford inquiry detailed the role of the key worker in notifying all agencies of their position as key worker and how to contact them, to disseminate information promptly and seek information from other agencies.

The key worker also has a role in ensuring core group meetings take place on a regular basis to review the child protection plan. These meetings are essential in exchanging information and to ensure that plans progress.

In the case of Tyra Henry, the conference minutes indicated that many of the previous conference recommendations had not been carried out and were being carried ahead to the next conference.

THINK ABOUT IT

◆ Where change isn't happening, should we carry on doing the same thing? For example, if the repair to your car repeatedly failed and you returned to the garage each time, only for the mechanics to carry out the same repair, would you be satisfied? Would you talk to a representative at your garage about it?

◆ In a case where the plan is not being implemented, or not working, it is important that someone identifies this.

Working with diversity

None of the studies of child deaths identifies the racial identity of those children. More recently, both Ainlee and Victoria Climbie were black.

In the Victoria Climbie inquiry (Department of Health & Home Office 2003), one of the ways in which race may influence the case involving a child was identified by Rattna Dutt, Director, Race Equality Unit:

> 'There is some evidence to suggest that one of the consequences of an exclusive focus on 'culture' in work with black children and families is that it leaves black and ethnic minority children in potentially dangerous situations, because the assessment has failed to address a child's fundamental care and protection needs.'

It is stated in the inquiry report that whilst it is not suggested that the ill-treatment of Victoria was 'neither condoned nor deliberately ignored', it may be that assumptions made about Victoria and her situation diverted caring people from noting and acting upon signs of neglect or ill-treatment.

Examples of such assumptions included the following:

◆ Victoria 'standing to attention' before Manning and Kouoa. The social worker concluded that this type of relationship was one that can be seen in many African-Caribbean families. Victoria's parents, however, said that she was not required to stand in this way when she was at home with them.

◆ Medical practitioners noticing marks on Victoria's body considered that children who have grown up in Africa might have more marks on their body than children brought up in Europe. This assumption, whether it is valid or not, may prevent a full assessment of those marks being made.

How can we work together more effectively?

The recommendations of the Climbie inquiry that relate to the structure of child protection services are outlined below. In addition, a number of suggestions, based on practice experience, are also made.

The most important point is that to ensure the safety of children in our community we all have a responsibility. None of us would wish to say after the event of a child death that we knew something was wrong, but had not acted on our concerns.

It is not enough to say that you have been keeping notes, ready for when someone asks for them. Everyone has a responsibility and concerns should be acted on if there is a commitment to improve the quality of the lives of children in the community. If there is a concern that your identity may be recognised by the child's carer, make this known.

Making a referral of concerns

When a referral is made, give as many details as possible and give your own contact details. If you wish, you may ask for it to be noted on your referral that you would like someone to contact you for further details.

Follow the referral up in writing, giving as much information as possible.

If no one contacts you to let you know the outcome of your referral, ring again and put your concerns in writing.

If you work for an agency, speak to the child protection specialist in your establishment or agency, who can follow this up.

If they still have concerns about the response of Social Services, they may contact the agency's child protection coordinator who will liaise at a more senior level.

Keeping track of children

The mobility of children and families makes keeping track of children more difficult.

It is proposed in the Climbie inquiry that all practitioners who come across a child for the first time should 'as a matter of routine, make sure they obtain basic information'. This would include:

◆ The name of the child

◆ Age

◆ Address

◆ Relationship to the primary care giver

◆ Who the parent is

◆ Whether they are registered with a GP and if so, who

◆ If he or she is of school age, whether or not they are enrolled at and attending school.

Assessments

Role in supporting assessments:

- Provide information requested for an assessment as soon as possible and if possible, provide detailed information with your referral
- Make suggestions about support needed
- Attend any planning/multi-agency support meetings and contribute to plans
- Ensure that you receive a copy of the family support plan when the assessment is complete.

Attend meetings

It is crucial that all those who are actively involved with a family, or who have information about them, should attend meetings when asked.

- If you are invited to a meeting, try to attend. If you are unable to attend, find out if someone else can attend in your place.
- A written report should be sent, with a chronology of key events. If it is felt strongly by anyone that the meeting should not take place without their being present, then the chair should be contacted, to request that the date be changed.

Child protection conferences/multi-agency meetings

To be effective:

- all those attending conference should arrive prepared with information and a report, together with a willingness to contribute their views to the meeting. Participants should be prepared to comment on and contribute ideas to plans being made at the meeting
- where plans do not seem to be progressing, participants should both identify and talk about this
- participants should always receive a copy of a detailed child protection plan
- if meetings are not taking place, contact the key worker and request one, and if this proves unsuccessful, write to the team manager or ask your specialist worker to become involved.

Differences of opinion

Where there are differences of views, it is always best to try to talk about and resolve these locally. Talk to your child protection coordinator/Early Years partnership for advice.

Where it is felt that differences cannot be resolved locally, they should be brought to the attention of the agency's child protection specialist or local authority's child protection co-ordinator. Some issues may be referred to the ACPC for resolution.

GOOD PRACTICE GUIDE

It is useful to establish and maintain good local working relationships. This can be done by meeting with local groups or groups of agency staff on a regular basis. This gives the opportunity to talk about any issues informally and to discuss views with others.

Training

Good practice is dependent on being well-informed and aware of changes in practice. To be most effective in child protection, training should be multi-agency.

Most ACPCs now offer basic child protection training to both statutory and voluntary groups.

It is important that you should:

◆ attend all level one training courses organised by your local ACPC. Contact the ACPC, or your local link worker, for a list of training offered by the ACPC. Ask for a copy of the training diary

◆ up-date your knowledge from time to time.

CASE STUDY:

Peter

The extract below is from a Part 8 Review, This is a report in which all the information from each agency is put together in a chronology, showing the information and actions from each. This information is an accurate record of all action and involvement with the family.

Peter was four-years-old when he died.

Family structure		
Mother	Rita	age 26 years
Brother	Tom	age 9 years
Brother	Billy	age 8 years
Brother	Tony	age 3 years

Extract from a Part 8 Review		
Date	Agency	Details
13/12/02	Education	Older brothers Billy and Tom are reported missing from home. Police attended and found the children. This occurred after a domestic dispute between mother and her partner.
14/12/02	Education	Tom came to school with a bruise on right cheek, right ear, skull and behind ear. Child protection coordinator informed Social Services.
14/12/02	Social Services	Hand-written child protection recording from school, signed by nursery nurse. Hand-written child protection recording from school, signed by child protection coordinator, indicating a conversation between herself and police constable. Bruises to Tom's right cheek and ear. Older brothers went missing yesterday and were found by a police constable at 6.15. Police constable believes mother is living with partner in poor conditions.
14/12/02	Education	Child protection coordinator talked to police constable about older brothers, who went missing yesterday and were found by him. PC was to inform Social Services.
18/12/02	GP	Peter seen by GP with superficial bruises to the L. parietal region, no head injury symptoms, pupils equal and reacting to light.
20/12/02	Education	Mother self-refers to educational psychologist, as she says the boys are getting her down. Mother sounding very depressed, saying that she's never regretted having the boys, but is beginning to feel like that now. Tom reported to be crying all day and slashed the sofa today.
22/12/02	Social Services	Note on referral to close case.
4/1/03	GP	Tom seen by GP. Treatment for infection.
17/1/03	Education	Letter offering appointment to elder brother Tom and family for educational psychologist.

➡

23/1/03	Social Services	Letter to Social Services from the Guardian ad litem, wishing to make a referral on all three brothers at the request of the children's grandmother, who has concerns for their welfare, based on the children's mother telling her that she was addicted to heroin and that around 12/1/03 she had attempted suicide.
24/1/03	GP	Prescription for salbutamol and amoxycillin for Peter.
30/1/03	Social Services	Re-referral by Guardian ad litem. Case allocated to social worker for assessment.
1/2/03	Education	Billy turned up at school half-an-hour late with very bad untreated burn on left hand. He told the teacher that he did it at home on the fire. Mother still in bed, so didn't know about it. School bandaged hand.
2/2/03	Education	Mother seen by teacher. Mother had a go at Billy and made him cry. Bandage had been removed but mother had taken no other action. School re-bandaged hand.
5/2/03	Education	Mother seen by teacher on another matter. She said that she had not done anything about the burn, but would take her son to the doctor's that evening. Burn has scabbed over, but looked sore and inflamed.
6/2/03	Education	Billy told teacher that he had put some cream on himself, but was not taken to the doctor's.
Feb 03	Education	School talked about brother receiving an eye test.
8/2/03	GP	Peter's chest clear since treatment.
9/2/03	NHS Trust	
12/2/03	Education	Teacher recorded that Tom said that he could not sit down because his bottom hurt. He said that he had fallen out of bed. There was a bruise on the right upper thigh observed by teachers.
22/2/03	GP	Peter seen for conjunctivitis and head cold.

➡

29/2/03	Social Services	Initial visit made by social work assistant. Mother is in bed ill. Mother admits addiction to valium; she is seeing a drugs counsellor. There is scarring to her wrists and she describes going berserk during blackouts. States that she has an eating disorder and weighs under 7 stone. Has rent arrears, and is looking for new home. Partner has been opiate user and has been in prison. He is due to appear in court charged with assault. Says she feels physically and emotionally unstable. Another male, aged thirty, is also living in the house. Advice given.

1. Where might concerns/risks have been picked up or addressed at an early stage?
2. What action should have been taken, by whom and at what point?
3. When should a child protection referral have been made and by whom?
4. What might have prevented information being 'lost' or not seeming to be acted upon?

THINK ABOUT IT

Consider the position of the child in the above case study if he had a disability, involving poor communication skills.

Children with disability are vulnerable due to possibly having limited communication skills and being cared for by a number of people. What are your views on how they can be effectively safeguarded?

Assessments and regular reviews of support plans are one way that concerns can be shared and support addressed.

Summary

◆ Part 8 inquiries are a review of practice in cases of child death, intended to identify what lessons, if any, can be learned.

◆ Most children are killed by a natural birth parent. The highest 'risk' group is children under two years of age.

◆ Effective communication is crucial in protecting children. When difficulties are identified, they should be raised with the specialist worker within the agency, who can liaise on their behalf.

◆ All those involved in working with a family should be clear about their role and the role of others. They should be clear about their role in assessment and support. Written plans should be clear about the roles of each party involved.

◆ Everyone involved in safeguarding children should be aware of and work to local ACPC Procedures, including knowing how and when to make a referral.

◆ Where someone is not confident in acting to safeguard a child, he/she should seek support from someone else. Likewise, if there are concerns about information being acted on, or progress of a case.

◆ Involvement in assessments and attendance at reviews and support meetings is a responsibility for all those involved with a family

◆ Wherever possible, individuals should seek ACPC Training. Local Early Years Partnership Coordinators, SureStart Coordinators and school head teachers should have copies of the Area Child Protection Committee's Training Diary, in which all dates and joining instructions are published.

CHECKPOINT

1. What is the purpose of a case review?
2. How should anyone ensure that a referral to Social Services has been received and acted upon?
3. What is your role in assisting Social Services with assessments?
4. Does your place of work/do you keep written records of your contact with children? Are you informed where a child that you are working closely with is on the child protection register?
5. Are all child protection concerns shared promptly with Social Services in your place of work?
6. What actions should be taken where you are aware or it is brought to your knowledge that a child is not attending school?
7. What should be brought to a child protection conference?
8. What should all of those attending a child protection conference receive after the meeting?
9. Where there are concerns about the progress of a plan, how should these be raised?
10. Who holds responsibility for safeguarding children?

Chapter 9

Format for a Statement to Court

If you are asked to write a statement for a criminal court hearing the Police will provide guidance on how to do so. However, the guidance set out below will be useful if, for example, a local authority has made an application for a legal order in respect of a child you have contact with and you are asked for a statement for civil proceedings.

You will not be expected to provide as much detail, or cover the same areas, as the social worker involved with the family. If you are a key social worker working with the child then the local authority legal department will supply you with a format.

Front sheet

The front sheet of the statement should contain the following information:

◆ the name of the Court dealing with the case

◆ case number

◆ child's name and date of birth

◆ the name of the author, professional address and telephone number

◆ the date and number of the statement (in case it is one of a series).

Setting your statement out

The body of your statement should conform to the following guidance, unless your legal advisor advises differently:

◆ each paragraph should be numbered

◆ line spacing should be one-and-a-half lines

◆ sub-headings should be dictated by your content, but it does help to include them, as it makes the information more readable and easier to reference if a Judge or Magistrate needs to be directed to a particular part of your statement under discussion.

Example extract of statement to demonstrate format

1. Information Parenting Capacity

1.1. Mrs Green brings Lucy to school in plenty of time for the start bell at 9 o'clock and is always prompt when collecting her. There is clearly a loving relationship between the two and Lucy has no reticence in going to her mother. If mother cannot collect Lucy she always contacts the school with the name of the adult who will be collecting her daughter.

1.2. Lucy appears to do her homework and mother informs the class teacher when she has been able to help with the schoolwork at home. Mother has a good relationship with school staff and seems to respond to their guidance and help.

1.3. There have been concerns about Lucy's physical presentation. She often appears in dirty clothes and does have a smell of urine about her on occasion. This is the source of some derogatory comments from her peers. Lucy has also suffered from head lice for several months, despite mother's assurances that she has tried to treat Lucy for them.

Content

When thinking of what to include in the content of your statement you should consider the following:

Introduction

The Court will want to know your professional role and qualifications. They will also want to know the nature of your involvement with the family, e.g. child attends nursery, foster carer for child, family support worker. You could also state how long you have known the child/family. This information should be at the start of your statement.

Chronology

It is then helpful to put in a chronology of any significant events, e.g. when child started nursery, if child raised an issue of harm to you, if you became aware of changes in the family structure, etc. If you do not have any significant events, or only one or two, you can miss out the chronology and move straight on to the body of the statement. However, if you do have a series of significant events it is helpful if you can put them in a chronology as illustrated below:

➡

18 June 1999	Lucy registered at Little Legs nursery.
25 August 1999	Lucy removed from nursery by mother.
10 October 1999	Lucy re-registered at nursery by grandmother, who is helping to care for Lucy.
12 December 1999	Nursery informed Lucy had returned to care of mother and new partner. Staff observed a decline in Lucy's physical presentation and the onset of head lice.

Body of the statement

The areas that you will be expected to address are the same as those highlighted in the *Framework for Assessment* and the child protection conference format. Once you are familiar with this format it will be a useful way for you to organise information in reports in all childcare settings.

The child

Your starting point should be information about the child. The Court will want to know any information you can contribute to the following areas:

- physical well-being of the child
- emotional well-being
- development, including cognitive, physical and social
- relationships the child has with staff and parents.

The parents

The Court will want to hear about any observations you make about the parent/child relationship and the parent's care of the child, together with the parent's relationship and work with yourself.

Information you may be able to supply includes the following:

- whether or not the child is brought to nursery school on time
- if the child has been collected on time consistently
- the interaction between the child and parent, e.g. parent is cold towards the child or parent is always angry when they arrive. Or it may be that the parent appears to have a very loving happy interaction with the child, which you have observed.
- the parent may have made negative comments to you about the child, or the parent may have been more candid with you about the difficulties the family may be having.

The environment

You may be aware of particular support networks available to a family, e.g. grandmother may collect the child from your service sometimes. You may also be aware of stresses on the family, e.g. housing, financial. This information should also be included in your statement.

At the end of your statement you may provide a conclusion with your professional view of your concerns if you have any and why you have them. Or your view may be that in your professional opinion there are no concerns. Again, you would need to support this view from factual information within your statement.

The difference between fact and opinion

You will need to make clear distinction between facts and opinion in your statement. You will also need to be accurate about events and occurrences that you have actually observed, the facts of a situation, information that people have passed onto you and your opinion on matters.

The table below gives an example of two descriptions of the same event

Example A	Mrs Smith telephoned the office to say that her neighbours Mr and Mrs Campbell were fighting and that she could hear objects being thrown around. She stated that two young children were screaming in the home and she understood that the children's names were on the child protection register. When I arrived at the home Mr Campbell let me into the house. The children appeared upset and the parents had obviously been fighting.
Example B	Mrs Smith telephoned the office to say that her neighbours, Mr and Mrs Campbell, were fighting and that she could hear objects being thrown around. She stated that two young children were screaming in the home and she understood the children's names were on the child protection register. When I arrived Mr Campbell answered the door. Mrs Campbell appeared to have been crying. Her face was red, her cheeks were tear stained and she continued to wring her handkerchief anxiously in her hands. The children were red-faced and their cheeks were also tear-stained. They cuddled their mother and were wary when their father approached them. Two coffee cups were broken in the fireplace and Mr Campbell seemed still to be angry when he stated that they had had a disagreement. I concluded that the neighbour had been correct and the couple had been fighting to the point of causing distress to the children.

Example B provides a more factual informed basis of a professional view for consideration by the court.

Remember that your statement should be balanced and include the strengths of the family as well as any weaknesses.

Once you have completed your statement, it is always useful to take time to review what you have said and to check the information you have given. It is also important that you show the information to someone else for an independent view. This may be a line manager or the legal office that requested the statement. Either way your statement will need to be completed in plenty of time so that alterations can be made if necessary.

Outline procedure for agencies working with children

Below is an example of a procedure for agencies working with children. You may like to build on this for your own service if you do not have an agreed process at present.

Agency ethos

Underneath this heading you may like to outline the agency's commitment to child protection and what this commitment involves.

◆ Staff share responsibility to safeguard children.

◆ Staff will be provided with training to safeguard children.

◆ Agency adheres to local Area Child Protection Procedures and Guidelines.

◆ A complaints system is present for children and families.

◆ Staff will make sure any concerns about harm to children are dealt with appropriately in accordance with guidance.

Guidance on child abuse

This is the provision of brief guidance about the forms that abuse can take and how it can involve a series of one-off incidents, that constitute a picture of significant harm over time, or a one-off incident that reaches a serious level on its own. This can contribute to staff identifying harm and enabling them to avoid harm to children.

How harm may come to the notice of the agency

It is helpful to highlight for staff the ways in which they may encounter allegations, or instances, of harm in their practice within the particular agency's activities.

◆ A child may disclose harm to a member of staff.

◆ A member of staff may witness harm to a child either by a family or a colleague.

◆ A member of staff may have allegations made against them.

◆ A member of staff may observe behaviour or physical injuries to a child that may be attributable to abuse.

If staff are made aware of the variety of ways they may encounter harm, it can help them to be alert to it if it happens.

Response to concern

All guidance should:

◆ provide information about steps to take if there is a concern about significant harm

◆ be clear about who in the organisation is the dedicated person to inform of child protection concerns, how to contact that person and what information they will need

◆ advise in what situations it would not be appropriate to inform parents and carers

◆ explain whether or not a child requires a medical and what action to take if s/he does

◆ detail where to record what has happened for agency information.

Response to disclosure of harm

There should be brief guidance about what to do if a child is making a **disclosure of harm**. This should include listening to the child without interruption, not asking the child leading questions (for example, did your father do this?), giving reassurance to the child and recording what the child has said in writing.

Child protection representative

All agency guidance about child protection procedure for the organisation should specify who the **child protection representative** is in that agency and how to contact the individual. Guidance should also be given about whom to contact if the allegation is about the child protection representative.

Achieving Best Evidence Guidance

Achieving Best Evidence in Criminal Proceedings (Home Office 2001) is a published government document that provides guidance to Police and partner agencies during an inquiry about how to ensure vulnerable and intimidated witnesses, both adults and children, give best evidence in proceedings.

It had already been agreed in the 1991 Criminal Justice Act that child witnesses in cases about sexual or violent abuse could give their evidence via video-recorded statement. The investigation involves an initial assessment, as outlined in Chapter 4. However, it will involve gathering information from professionals involved with the family. The inquiries themselves will include all children in the family, not only the child that is the subject of initial concerns.

Best Evidence

Unless you are a Social Worker or police officer trained in interviewing children for criminal evidence, you will not be involved in the direct interview of a child.

However, it is useful for you to understand the process so that you can fully empathise with the child whose experience it is, and because you may at some point in the future have a role as a supporter in an interview. A supporter is someone whom a child trusts and may be needed in an interview, when an assessment has been completed about the ability of the child to answer questions, and the conclusion is that a supporter would help the child in interview.

During a S47 inquiry, consideration will be given to whether or not a criminal act has taken place. If there is a suspicion it has, Police and Social services will plan a video-recorded statement from the young person/child.

The video interview

The video interview will take place away from a police station in a specially built building fit for this purpose. It will include a video suite that on the exterior is anonymous and secure from the public. Inside, the facilities will be as comfortable as possible and will include a video room with soft furnishings and lighting, a control room next door, with video link and controls on picture and sound. The building will also have refreshment and bathing facilities.

There is no minimum age limit for interview, and in many instances children as young as 4 have given statements on video about harm they have suffered.

Achieving Best Evidence in Criminal Proceedings (Home Office 2001) does provide guidance for Police and Social Services when interviewing very young children.

Factors to consider when interviewing very young children

The following factors should be taken into account when interviewing very young children:

- venue
- adequate time in interview to build up a relationship
- time for appropriate toys, colouring tools to settle a child in
- seeking specialist advice or bringing in an interviewer with specialist skills
- it may require interviewers to seek social support from an independent adult known to the child.

Pre-assessment interview

Prior to interview Police/Social Services will complete a pre-assessment interview.

This interview will cover the following areas:

- child's ability/willingness to talk within a formal interview
- explanation to a child about interview
- child's competency to interview

◆ child's race, gender, cultural and ethnic background

◆ any special requirements, disability, language difficulties.

Police and Social Services may conclude that it would be helpful for the child to have a supporter in interview besides the family. If you have a particularly close relationship with a child you may be identified as such a supporter.

If you are going to be a supporter you will be included in the planning stage of the interview and will be able to establish your role.

Role of the supporter

The supporter is there to provide reassurance and to offer comfort in times of distress during the recorded interview of the child for criminal evidence purposes. It may seem obvious that the supporter should be a parent or carer. Often this is the case; however, research has indicated that sometimes children find the presence of the parent in the room an additional source of stress.

The video interview forms the child's evidence in chief in Court and, as such, there remain strict guidelines about how the interview proceeds. It is important that the supporter is not seen to offer the child inducements to talk, e.g. toys or rewards. There are several important rules to follow as a supporter to a child:

◆ The supporter will be instructed not to participate in the interview.

◆ The supporter should not be a person involved as a witness in the case. It should not be the person the child disclosed to for instance.

◆ The child should be given the opportunity to choose the supporter.

◆ The supporter will be identified at the beginning of the interview.

◆ The supporter will need to be included in a video shot.

◆ *Achieving Best Evidence in Criminal Proceedings* advises that the supporter should sit outside of the child's vision, perhaps behind the child.

Process of interview

Rapport

The first stage of any interview is known as the rapport stage.

This involves the interviewer establishing a relationship with the child, helping him/her to feel comfortable and settle into his/her surroundings. This may involve discussion about a hobby or interest but will only be about non-threatening subjects. For younger children, this stage may include playing with toys and moving around the room. At the end of the rapport stage, the interviewer will talk with the child about understanding the importance of telling the truth.

Free narrative

At the second stage the interview will move into free narrative stage, when the child will be asked to give in his/her own words the account of what has happened.

Questioning

The child will then be asked questions, both open and specific, about events.

Closure

When all possible facts and information have been established the interview will draw to a close. The interviewer will let the child know what will happen next, check if they wish to ask questions and will return to neutral non-threatening topics.

Following the interview, Police/Social Services consider whether there is a need for a medical examination of the child, depending on what the child has said in interview. Police will proceed with criminal actions that might include interview of the alleged perpetrator. Social Services will take steps to address any outstanding issues of child protection or child in need of support. These actions might involve therapeutic help for the child, or helping a protective parent take steps to ask a perpetrator to leave the home.

The video interview is sealed on tape and stored in a secure place. It will form part of the file of information that the Police will eventually send to the Crown Prosecution Service. The Service will consider whether or not the case will proceed to a prosecution in court.

Structure of a core assessment report

The structure of a core assessment report might look like the example, which makes suggestions about information to be included. A similar format is being used in some areas for agencies to provide information for multi-agency meetings and child protection conferences.

CORE ASSESSMENT REPORT

Name of child _____

Date of birth _____   Sex _____

Ethnicity and first language _____

Disability _____

Address _____

Family Details _____

_____

Your name _____

Agency _____

Your role in assessment _____

Reason for assessment _____

_____

Who has been involved and consulted in the assessment _____

_____

Child's Developmental Needs

Detail observations in this section, including strengths and weaknesses.

Remember to address any specific needs, including those arising from disability and race and culture.

Summary

Give a summary of the child's developmental needs and the extent to which they are met or unmet and the parent's and carer's ability to meet needs.

Parental capacity

This section should detail observations and information collected from others in the course of the assessment.

Summary

In this section, there should be a summary of details given in the above section, which relates to any parental factors that may affect the care of the children in the family and on family and environmental factors

Family and Environmental Factors

This section should detail observations and information

Summary:

In this section there should be a summary, which relates to the details in the above section.

Analysis

This section draws together all the information gathered in the assessment process, to arrive at a conclusion.

Pro-forma of information required when making a referral

Family details
Name of Child
Date of birth
Address
Telephone number
Names of Parents/carers and relationship to child
Ethnicity
Gender
First language
Disability

Other involved adults

School
GP
Agencies known to be involved with the family

Your involvement

Name
Place of work
Role with the family

Concerns

Reason for making a referral now
Background/previous concerns
Evidence of concern(what has been seen/heard)
Is the information from someone else?
Who?
Is this a serious incident that requires immediate action (e.g. where a child has an injury)
Who is the risk of harm from, if known?
Risk of harm to other children

Consent

Have you informed parents that you are making a referral and sought their consent?

References and further reading

Abrahams, C. (1994) *The Hidden Victims: Children and Domestic Violence* (London: NCH Action for Children)

Bell, M. (1999) *Child Protection: Families and the Conference Process* (Aldershot: Ashgate)

Birchall, E. and Hallett, C. (1995) *Working Together in Child Protection* (London: HMSO)

Boateng, P. (2003) in 'Every Child Matters' (London: HMSO)

Calder, M. C. (1996) Inter-agency Arrangements for Post-registration Practice (Report to Salford ACPC)

Calder, M. and Barratt, M. (1997) 'Inter-agency Perspectives on Core Group Practice', *Children and Society*, **11**

Cleaver, H. and Freeman, P. (1995) *Parental Perspectives in Cases of Suspected Child Abuse* (London: HMSO)

Cleaver, H., Unell, I., Aldgate, J. (1999) *Children's Needs-Parenting Capacity: The impact of parental mental illness, problem alcohol and drug use, and domestic violence on children's development* (London: HMSO)

Cox, A.D. (1988) 'Maternal depression and impact on children's development', '*Archives of Disease in Childhood*', **63**, p.90–95

Cox, A. and Walker, S. (2002) *The HOME Inventory* (Brighton: Pavilion Publishing)

Dale, P., Davies, M., Morrison, T. and Waters, J. (1986) *Dangerous Families: Assessment and Treatment of Child Abuse* (London: Routledge)

Department of Health (1989a) 'The Children Act 1989 Guidance and Regulations, Volume 2, Family Support, Day Care and Educational Provision for Young Children'. (London: HMSO)

Department of Health (1989b) 'An Introduction to The Children Act 1989' (London: HMSO)

Department of Health (1991) 'Child Abuse A Study of Inquiry Reports 1980–1989' (London: HMSO)

Department of Health (1997) 'Child Protection: Messages from Research' (London: HMSO)

Department of Health (1999) 'Working Together to Safeguard Children' (London: HMSO)

Department of Health, Department for Education and Employment, Home Office (2000) 'Framework for the Assessment of Children in Need and their Families' (London: HMSO)

Department of Health (2003a) 'What to do if You're Worried a Child is Being Abused' (London, Department of Health)

Department of Health (2003b) 'What to Do If You're Worried a Child is Being Abused: Summary' (London: HMSO)

Department of Health & Home Office (2003) 'The Victoria Climbie Inquiry: Report of an Inquiry by Lord Laming' (London: HMSO)

Epstein, C. and Keep, G. (1995) 'What Children tell Childline about Domestic Violence', in A.Saunders with C.Epstein, G.Keep and T.Debonair. *It Hurts me Too: Children's Experiences of Domestic Violence and Refuge* (Life Bristol: WAFE/Childline/NISW)

Family Rights Group, (1991) *The Children Act 1989: Working in Partnership with Families*, Reader (London: HMSO)

Greenland, C.C. (1987) *Preventing CAN Deaths: An International Study of Deaths due to Child Abuse and Neglect* (London: Tavistock)

Hester, M. and Pearson, C., (1998) *From Periphery to Centre: Domestic Violence in Work with Abused Children* (Bristol: Policy Press)

Hallett, C., (1995) *Inter-Agency Co-ordination in Child Protection.* (London: HMSO)

Home Office (2001) 'Achieving Best Evidence in Criminal Proceedings' (London: HMSO)

Lonsdale, G. (1991) 'A Study of Parental Participation at Initial Child Protection Case Conferences'. (Wiltshire Social Services Department)

Macdonald, G. and Roberts, H. (1995) *What Works in the Early Years?* (Essex: Barnardo's)

McGloin, P. and Turnbull, A. (1986) 'Parent Participation in Child Abuse Review conferences'. (A Research Report: London Borough of Greenwhich)

Murphy, M. (1995) *Working Together in Child Protection* (Aldershot: Arena)

NSPCC, University of Sheffield (2000) 'The Children's World: Assessing Children in Need'. Training and Development Pack. (London: NSPCC)

Plotnifkoff, J. and Woolfson, R. (1996) *Reporting to Court Under the Children Act* (London: HMSO)

Reder, P., Duncan, S. and Gray, M. (1993) *Beyond Blame: Child Abuse Tragedies Revisited* (London: Routledge)

Reder, P. and Lucey, C. (1995) *Assessment of Parenting: Psychiatric and Psychological Contributions* (London: Routledge)

Reder, P. and Duncan, S. (1999) *Lost Innocents: A Follow-Up Study of Fatal Child Abuse* (London: Routledge)

Thorburn, J. Shemmings, D. and Lewis, A. (1993) 'A Study of Client Participation in Child Protection Work, Report to Department of Health' (Social Work Development Unit: University of East Anglia, Norwich)

Treasury Office (2003) 'Every Child Matters' (London: HMSO)

White R., Carr P., and Lowe N., (1990) *A Guide To The Children Act 1989* (London: Butterworth & Co)

Websites

http://www.open.gov.uk/doh/quality.htm

https://www.the-stationery-office.co.uk/doh/worktog/worktog.htm

Appendix 1: EVERY CHILD MATTERS

On September 2003 the government produced a Green Paper for consultation entitled *Every Child Matters*. The paper was a response to the inquiry headed by Lord Laming into the death of a child – Victoria Climbie.

Victoria died of neglect and physical harm at the hands of a carer, known as her aunt, and her carer's partner . Victoria was from the Ivory Coast in Africa and her parents had allowed her to leave for Britain in the hope of a better quality of life and education. Sadly for Victoria her journey ended in tragedy. (HMSO: 2003)

The Green Paper *Every Child Matters* seeks to make changes to improve the child protection system in the light of the recommendations by Lord Laming. Professionals working with children will need to be aware of government proposals which in the future may mean changes in the way we approach and deal with issues of children's safety and welfare.

The paper focuses on four main areas:

◆ Supporting parents/carers

◆ Early intervention and effective prevention

◆ Accountability and integration locally, regionally and nationally

◆ Workforce reform.

Supporting parents and carers

The government proposes the creation of a Parenting Fund of £25 million and are seeking consultation on the provision of improved support via advice and information to parents through health, education and social services, and the provision of specialist support to parents who need extra help and compulsory action by Parenting Orders, if all other intervention fails. As an Early Years Practitioner you may find that your role is enhanced to provide advice and assistance to vulnerable families, if you do not already do so.

Early intervention and effective protection

As already discussed within the text of this book one of the keys to safeguarding children is to identify difficulties early in order to offer help and prevent their escalation into problems of a more serious nature. The Green Paper proposes to enhance this activity by several means:

1. **Improving information sharing.**
   To develop systems that ensure relevant information is shared between professionals on all children and ensure that the local authority has a list of children in their area that identifies the services a child has had contact with and the detail of current professional involvement. As an Early Years Practitioner you may be required to share information regarding the input you provide for children.

2. **Common framework assessment**
   Every local authority will be required to nominate a lead person to ensure information is collected and shared across services for children. Early Years services will be expected to participate in the common assessment.

3. **Lead professional**
   Children known to more than one agency will have a single named professional to lead their case.

4. **On-the-spot service delivery**
   Professionals will be encouraged to work in multi-disciplinary teams based around schools or children's centres.

Accountability and integration – locally, regionally and nationally

To achieve greater accountability and integration the government proposes:

- to create a Director of Children's Services accountable for local authority education and children's social services
- to create a lead council member for children
- to bring together services for children under children's trusts to create multi-agency delivery of services
- to create local Safeguarding Children Boards as a replacement for Area Child Protection Committees. Safeguarding Children Boards may take on the current responsibilities of Area Child Protection Committees under *Working Together* (1999) and have additional regard to commissioning independent reviews and looking at unexpected child deaths to consider any public health issues. Like the ACPC, the Boards will have multi-agency membership and will have a pooled budget to consider service spending to safeguard children
- the government has already created a Minister for Children, Young People and Families to co-ordinate policies across government.

Workforce reform

The government would like to consider a strategy to improve the skills and effectiveness of the children's workforce developed in partnership with local employers and staff. This will have implications for all professionals working with children. More detailed information regarding the government proposals can be found in the full document *Every Child Matters* (HMSO: London: 2003).

This paper is the beginning of a process of change for children's services to meet the needs of children and families. All professionals working with children will find it helpful to continue to update themselves regarding developments and this can be achieved by access to the Department of Health website, where new plans and changes can be found documented.

Appendix 2: Child Protection in Scotland

Background

Scotland has a devolved government and its own legislature to which particular areas of policy and government are attributed. As such, elections to Scotland's Parliament are separate from elections to the Westminster and European Parliaments and so an administration can be elected in Scotland which is of a different political hue to that in power at Westminster. At the time of publication the national administration in Scotland is a coalition of parties, whereas at Westminster one party has majority control.

Among the issues that affect children and which fall under the legislative control of the Scottish Parliament and administration are: health, education, justice (law and order) and social services.

The protection of children and young people is therefore, in Scotland, a matter for the Scottish Parliament. Even before the establishment of the Scottish Parliament, Scotland enjoyed a distinct legal/judicial system and distinct structures for the delivery of children's services.

The Children's Hearing system

One example of this distinction in legal systems and children's services structures is the existence in Scotland of the *Children's Hearing system.* This system exists in civil law and provides a legal 'tribunal' where both child welfare and juvenile offending cases are heard. The system has been in place since 1967 and has always held to the overarching philosophy that the welfare of the child is central to all decisions concerning them.

The system is administered by legal officers known as Children's Reporters, who are employed by a national agency (*the Scottish Children's Reporters Administration*). They are therefore independent of the Local Authorities and distinct from the criminal justice system (although there is close liaison between these two systems of justice). Referral is made to the Children's Reporter by agencies and members of the public where they consider that a child may be in need of compulsory measures of supervision. The Reporter may require the authorities to provide information regarding children referred to them. On the basis of this they then consider this information by testing it against criteria set out in law (Section 52 of the Children (Scotland) Act 1995). These criteria are known as 'Grounds of Referral to a Children's Hearing'. Where the information available suggests that Grounds of Referrral are met, the Children's Reporter may call a *Children's Hearing*. It is the job of this Hearing to hear evidence; discuss the circumstances with the child, their parents and representatives, and with the relevant agencies; and conclude whether the child does require compulsory measures of supervision or not. There are a number of disposals available to a Hearing including issuing a *Supervision Requirement* which is a compulsory order enforced by the Local Authority. Supervision requirements can mean that the child is removed from home but often these are carried out without this being necessary.

Children's Hearings are made up of panels of three lay individuals recruited from the general public. They are trained and resourced to make legal decisions and the Children's Reporter provides legal advice and backup as necessary.

Evidence is evaluated on *the balance of probabilities.*

Children's Hearings do not convict individuals. Where children commit serious offences, or where they are so young as to require a judicial ruling on proof (in relation to Grounds of Referral for example), they are referred to the *Sheriff Court* for a decision. Sheriffs do so with due regard to the advice of Children's Hearings. The Sheriffs and their Courts provide the administration of justice in a range of cases in both the criminal and civil systems.

The Children's Reporter and the Procurator Fiscal (the legal officer responsible for the investigation and prosecution of crime) maintain close liaison, particularly in relation to juvenile offenders and adult prosecutions in cases involving offences against children.

In Scotland, where children above the age of criminal responsibility (8 years of age) commit very serious offences, these may be heard in the High Court of Justiciary.

The Children (Scotland) Act 1995

The primary child welfare and protection legislation in Scotland is contained in the *Children (Scotland) Act 1995*. This legislation was enacted by the UK Government prior to the creation of the Scottish Parliament. The Children Act 1989 has very few areas of application in Scotland and largely applies only in England and Wales. Any decisions concerning child protection in Scotland are made using the provisions of the Children (Scotland) Act 1995.

The Children (Scotland) Act 1995 contains some similarities to its English/Welsh counterpart. It states, for example, that *the paramount consideration is the welfare of the child* in decisions being made in respect of them.

The Act also gives particular duties and powers to the Children's Reporters, the Children's Hearings, the Sheriff Courts, the local authorities and other public agencies. In child protection, these include measures aimed at ensuring that children who are at risk of *significant harm* are made safe.

These measures include:

Child Assessment Orders (Section 55). This Order is granted by a Sheriff (if judged to be necessary through consideration of the evidence) on application by a local authority. The Order allows an assessment of the child's health or development to be undertaken if the local authority has reasonable cause to suspect that the child is suffering or is likely to suffer significant harm. Furthermore the Sheriff has to be satisfied that an assessment would be unlikely to be carried out (or carried out satisfactorily) unless an order is granted. Conditions can be attached to the Order as necessary. This is *not* an emergency order.

Child Protection Orders (Section 57). This *is* an emergency order. This Order is granted by a Sheriff (if judged to be necessary through consideration of the evidence) on application by *any person*. The local authority has additional provision to apply if they are undertaking enquiries concerning possible significant harm to a child but these enquiries are frustrated because access to the child is unreasonably denied. The granting of a CPO effectively authorises the removal of the child to a place of safety. Once granted, notice of this has to be made by the Local Authority to the Children's Reporter who will consider framing Grounds of Referral to a Children's Hearing while the CPO is continued. This process takes place within set (short) timescales. Ultimately, if a CPO is not allowed to lapse it can be superceded by the issuing of a Supervision Requirement by a Children's Hearing if Grounds of Referral have been established.

A Police Officer may remove a child to a place of safety (Section 65 (1)) for 24 hours in immediate emergencies. This allows further enquiry to take place and application for other measures to be made if necessary.

Exclusion Orders (Section 76) allows the local authority to apply to the Sheriff to exclude a named person from a household if they believe that a child is likely to suffer significant harm. It would also have to be shown that it would better safeguard the welfare of the child than removing them from the family home. This is *not* an emergency order.

Other legislation

There is much other legislative provision affecting the protection of children and young people in Scotland. This includes: particular sex offender legislation; the Criminal Justice Act 2003 (amending the laws on physical punishment of children); and the Protection of Children Act 2004 (making provision for an index of adults unsuitable to work with children).

Government Guidance

In Scotland, the Guidance issued by central government in respect of protecting children is called *Child Protection – A Shared Responsibility*. The document *Working Together* is not applied in Scotland. The Scottish Guidance is quite different to *Working Together*. For example, in Scotland there is no Part 8 Review system or equivalent.

Following an independent inquiry into the death of a child in Dumfries and Galloway in 2000/2001, the Scottish Executive undertook a national Audit and Review of the child protection system. This Audit/Review reported to the First Minister and to the Minister for Education and Children in 2002 in a document called *It's Everyone's Job to Make Sure I'm All Right*. The recommendations of this report led the First Minister, with the approval of the Scottish Executive and of Parliament, to initiate a National Child Protection Reform Programme. This programme is ongoing at the time of publication. The Reform Programme has so far set out to reform not only the child protection system but also the child welfare system in which it operates. It is doing so in a number of ways: including the publication of a Children's Charter for Scotland; the issuing of National Standards for child protection; the creation of an inter-agency inspection system; and review of the function of Child Protection Committees.

At this stage it is not clear what the end result of the Reform Programme will look like, but the child protection system and its constituent agencies have been given a three-year timescale within which necessary change must be demonstrated. In the meantime, other independent inquiries following the deaths of children have taken place in Scotland and Lord Laming's report in England has also been published. These reports and their recommendations may also have a significant impact on the process of reform in Scotland. It is likely therefore that the face of the child protection system in Scotland will look quite different over the next few years, with different guidance underpinning it.

Other guidance has also been issued by the Scottish Executive in respect of particular groups of children at risk. These include children and young people living with drug abusing parents (*Getting Our Priorities Right*); young runaways (*Vulnerable Children*) and children and young people abused through prostitution (*Vulnerable Children*).

Local Guidance

As in the other countries in the UK, single agencies issue their own internal guidance for staff working with children. Additionally, Child Protection Committees issue inter-agency guidelines within their own areas.

Framework for assessment

There is no national framework for assessment in Scotland for assessment of either children's needs or risks to children.

It is not clear at the time of publication whether this might emerge from the National Reform Programme or not.

Particular areas or agencies may have adopted frameworks for assessment which are implemented by them. They may also have developed (or imported) tools to undertake assessments. Individual practitioners likewise may also utilise particular frameworks and tools for themselves in the conduct of their work. It remains to be seen how robust these might be at satisfactorily assessing the particular vulnerabilities of children or the risks that they face in their lives.

It is likely that, in that absence of a national agreed framework for assessing risk, some authorities and practitioners will be using the Department of Health's *Framework for the Assessment of Children in Need and their Families* which is currently applied in England and Wales.

Child Protection Committees

As part of the National Reform Programme, the functions of Child Protection Committees in Scotland are being reviewed. Currently, there is no certain consistency of either how CPCs function or how they look, although there is general guidance issued from the Scottish Executive regarding this.

Some CPCs have appointed their own officials, such as Child Protection Co-ordinators, Development Officers and Inter-agency Training Co-ordinators. Some have not. In some areas, local authority social work departments have Child Protection Co-ordinators who oversee their own activities and performance in this field.

As CPCs are not directly funded or resourced, the implementation of inter-agency training for example is difficult to undertake consistently, but this is generally seen as one area of responsibility that falls to the Child Protection Committee to undertake.

Referrals and Child Protection Case Conferences

The norm in Scotland for processing referrals concerning possible abuse or neglect is that the referring agency or individual contacts either the local authority social work department Children and Families Service or the local Family/Child Protection Unit in the Police. These two agencies share information about the child/situation with a view to jointly determining how and what response needs to be made and when. This initial discussion and ongoing planning normally also involves the relevant Community Child Health Specialist (Paediatrician).

Information and accountability in this process is shared between the statutory agencies.

There are several possible decisions that might be made jointly in respect of a referral. These include a request for further information from the referrer; no further action; a single agency inquiry; or a joint investigation which may involve joint paediatric/forensic medical examinations and Joint Investigative Interviews.

It would normally be the case that where inquiries/investigations have been carried out a *Child Protection Case Conference* would be convened. This multi-agency event would consider risks to the child, whether the child required to be registered on the local Child Protection Register, whether the child required onward referral to specialist services and the formulation of a *Child Protection Plan* as necessary. The arrangements for Child Protection Case Conferences differ across Scotland, although their core functions are likely to be the same wherever they are held.

Martin Henry
Child Protection Co-ordinator
(Edinburgh and Lothian)